State as a Giant with Feet of Clay

Jan Kysela (ed.)

State as a Giant with Feet of Clay

PL ACADEMIC RESEARCH

Bibliographic Information published by the Deutsche Nationalbibliothek
The Deutsche Nationalbibliothek lists this publication in the Deutsche Nationalbibliografie; detailed bibliographic data is available in the internet at http://dnb.d-nb.de.

Library of Congress Cataloging-in-Publication Data
State as a giant with feet of clay / Jan Kysela (ed.).
p. cm.
Includes bibliographical references and index.
ISBN 978-3-631-65375-3
1. State, The. 2. International law. 3. Law—Political aspects.
4. Sociological jurisprudence. I. Kysela, Jan, editor.
KZ4002.S73 2014
320.1—dc23

2014035574

The monograph was written within the scope of the grant project of the Czech Science Foundation (GACR) No. P408/12/1255 "The Key Concepts of Constitutional Theory in the Age of Changes of Paradigms".

ISBN 978-3-631-65375-3 (Print)
E-ISBN 978-3-653-04593-2 (E-Book)
DOI 10.3726/978-3-653-04593-2

PL Academic Research is an Imprint of Peter Lang GmbH.

Peter Lang – Frankfurt am Main · Bern · Bruxelles · New York · Oxford · Warszawa · Wien

This publication has been peer reviewed.

www.peterlang.com

Jan Kysela is an Associate Professor at the Law Faculty of Charles University in Prague, Czech Republic, and the head of its Department of Political Science and Sociology. He also works as a constitutional expert in the Senate of the Parliament of the Czech Republic. He specializes primarily in constitutional theory, parliamentarism, bicameralism and theory of law-making.

Jana Ondřejková is a Senior Lecturer at the Department of Political Science and Sociology at the Law Faculty of the Charles University in Prague. She earned her Ph.D. in Jurisprudence and focuses on issues of EU law and constitutional law.

Pavel Ondřejek is a Senior Lecturer at the Department of Legal Theory and Legal Doctrines, Law Faculty of the Charles University in Prague. He also works at the International Relations and EU Department of the Ministry of the Interior of the Czech Republic. In his research he concentrates on the theory of human rights and theoretical aspects of international law.

Jan Grinc is a Lecturer at the Law Faculty of Charles University in Prague, the Department of Constitutional Law. He specializes in the role of national parliaments in the European Union and topics related to European integration in general.

Jan Broz is a final-year student of the Law Faculty of Charles University in Prague. He has completed his bachelor's degree in Political Science and Public Administration.

Michal Urban is a Senior Lecturer at the Law Faculty of Charles University in Prague. As a member of the Department of Political Science and Sociology, he specializes in sociology of law, professional legal ethics and legal literacy.

We wish to thank both reviewers of the book, Petr Pithart and Jan Komárek.
We wish to thank Tereza Krupová, Tomáš Havel and Tomáš Friedel, who have commented on the text and helped us to prepare the book manuscript for print.

Table of Contents

Jan Kysela

Outline of the field of research

The image of a giant with feet of clay seems to be an apt metaphor for contemporary states, and even more so for European states. Such states tend to be greater in terms of the scope of government and its work, rather than necessarily in terms of their area or population. Since they are great, they are also costly, however often not very strong, and hence limited in various respects. Clay feet are susceptible to excessive humidity on the one hand and excessive aridity on the other – that is to say, they may often prove to provide insufficient support for the body of the giant. A recumbent giant without the ability to move is a powerless giant. And a powerless state is a useless state. One alternative to a weak giant or failed state - a phenomenon more often found in Africa - is the effective state-giant of *T. Hobbes*, a bloated version of which was exemplified by the totalitarian systems of the 20th century. An alternative of another kind is the liberal state, also effective, however small or lean; and possibly also the dreamt up state of the conservatives, based on the principle of subsidiarity, acting only as a complement to civil society.

Our fundamental thesis is that the states in which we live are great, however weak. This is not necessarily a very original idea. We will, nevertheless, attempt to summarise the causes and symptoms.

I. Contemporary scepticism about modern state

The 2013 volume of the prestigious Czech legal journal "Právník" opened with a study by *P. Holländer*, a leading legal philosopher and constitutionalist, and at that time also vice president of the Constitutional Court of the Czech Republic. The study was significantly titled "Soumrak moderního státu" [The twilight of the modern state] and relied primarily on German literature.[1] During 2013 a

1 This is not to say that German literature is a monolith, however it is traditionally thorough when it comes to dealing with the topic of the state. Holländer's "twilight" relates to references to a "metaphysical correlate" limiting the power of the majority (natural law bans), disagreements in the justification of human rights (what rights, based on what), the "outsourcing" of state, deconstruction of the legal order in the form of its fragmentation as well as the loss of ordering principles, vagueness of responsibility, constitutional pluralism with conflict of various instances of courts claiming to have

number of younger authors responded to this study, either sharing the diagnosis of a "twilight," but, unlike *Holländer* (who recently reached his sixties) welcoming the diagnosis, or else rejecting the image portrayed of the modern state as something that never existed. The authors referred primarily to articles in English and French that concerned government rather than the state, with government often being prefaced by adjectives such as "post-sovereign" or "post-national." The state is associated with repression (by power), and the divide between "us" and "them." In contrast, preference is given to a somewhat indefinite process involving everybody (inclusiveness) and hearing everybody out (responsiveness). The procedural concept is close to deliberative theory, which has far-reaching political as well as legal implications.

Can we draw any conclusions on that basis? Is there a generational gap ("the good times are gone" versus "joyful jurisprudence in a post-national society" - which was the subtitle of one of the related articles[2])? Does German literature contemplate the importance of the state differently? Should there be an attempt to differentiate between descriptive writing (something is happening) and normative writing (it is good / bad that something is happening)? Such an attempt only makes sense however if we don't believe that a description is also a kind of construction of reality. And when it comes to the end of a period having perceptible substance, the subsequent period is then defined by those of its features that differ from those of the past period (various "post").

It is not unusual for those raising doubts about the contemporary state to refer back to the Middle Ages, when it was possible to observe many features that are occurring once more. This applies to the personality of law (among other things, multiculturalism), overlapping of jurisdictions (constitutional pluralism), weakening of the state as only one of many social bonds as opposed to the state as hegemonic leader of the domain of the political (pluralistic perspective), and so on.[3]

N. MacCormick sees a similarity between "then" and "now" when comparing contentions between the jurisdiction of the pope and the emperor, and the

---

the final word in a dispute or weakening of the relationship between an individual and the state.

2 Přibáň, Jiří: *Ranní červánky globálního konstitucionalismu: O „radostné" právní vědě v postnacionální společnosti.* [*Early Morning Red Twilight Sky of Global Constitutionalism: On "Joyful" Jurisprudence in a Post-national Society*] Právník, vol. 2013, no. 2.

3 On the "new Middle Ages" also see Beck, Ulrich: *Co je to globalizace? Omyly a odpovědi.* [*What is Globalisation? Misconceptions and Replies*] Brno: Centrum pro demokracii a kulturu, 2007, p. 131.

European Communities and their Member States, respectively. Conflicts between particular co-existing orders provoke the question which of the orders will prevail; and that question is relevant from the point of view of those subject to the rules.[4] Similarly, in view of the European reality, with supranational structures and various mediators of power, influence and interests, *W. Reinhard* feels that the modern state has ended and that it will survive only as one of a number of competing entities. He speaks literally of the "new Middle Ages," which differ from the real Middle Ages in terms of an absence of common concepts of value, but not by plurality of mediating instances.[5] *H. Huber* focuses more on intra-state similarities with medieval corporativism in the contemporary polyarchy (the rule of many) created by pluralism.[6]

By contrast, *D. Grimm* emphasises differences between the present and the Middle Ages: in the Middle Ages there was a single system of public authority claiming divine consecration, whereas contemporary states are like a sea with islands of "international public authority." *Grimm* is of the opinion that analogies with the Middle Ages have nothing to offer to understanding of the present.[7] However, at the end of another work of his he also agrees to the use of a medieval analogy, in relation to the international community which *Grimm* views as a number of independent holders of scattered authority.[8]

It is not important to discuss to what extent the loosening of state is similar to the Middle Ages, or whether it is a novelty. The importance of thinking about the Middle Ages consists primarily in the fact that this reminds us of the period before modern state emerged. This demonstrates that the modern state is just one type of political organisation of society. Before the modern state there was polis, empire, or a personalised organisation of public authority prevailing during most of the Middle Ages. Certainly, something new may also emerge to follow

---

4 MacCormick, Neil: *Questioning Sovereignty: Law, State, and Nation in the European Commonwealth*. Oxford: Oxford University Press, 1999, pp. 8-9 and 20-21.

5 Reinhard, Wolfgang: *Geschichte des modernen Staates*. München: C. H. Beck, 2007, p. 123.

6 Cf. Belling, Vojtěch: *Legitimita moci v postmoderní době. Proč potřebuje Evropská unie členské státy?* [*Legitimacy of Power in a Postmodern Period. Why the European Union Needs its Member States?*] Brno: Masarykova univerzita, 2009, p. 124.

7 Grimm, Dieter: *Souveränität. Herkunft und Zukunft eines Schlüsselbegriffs*. Berlin University Press, 2009, pp. 105-106.

8 Grimm, Dieter: *The Achievement of Constitutionalism and its Prospects in a Changed World*. In: Dobner, Petra, Loughlin, Martin (eds.): *The Twilight of Constitutionalism?* Oxford: Oxford University Press, 2012, p. 18.

the modern state. On that note, the above-mentioned study by *P. Holländer* started with an extensive quotation from the "The Concept of the Political" by *C. Schmitt*, focusing on the end of the time of states. This may be understood both as an adumbration of the idea of "Grossraum" (a large space) developed by *C. Schmitt* from the end of the 1930s, and a vision of European integration transcending nation states.[9]

Schmitt's perception of a "departure" from states was not wholly unique. In 1920, *A. D. Lindsay* stated: *"The first thing to be said about this doctrine of the independent sovereign state is that political facts have obviously outrun it."*[10] He meant that the development of the international community brought into question the (post-Westphalian) sovereignty of states, both through a series of conferences resulting in the Hague Conventions on the laws of war before the First World War, and the creation of a Permanent Court of International Justice within the League of Nations. Even two decades before *Lindsay, G. Jellinek* pointed out differences between the sovereign states of the 16th to 18th century which assumed only short-term obligations and a rather long-term limitation of laws and administration in his times. However, because *Jellinek* was aware of the fact that absolutely unlimited state authority is incompatible with historical experience, he did not assume that the limitation of the state by treaties results in the reduction of state sovereignty.[11]

---

9 The trend of antiquating national states appears on a regular basis. It differs, of course, in motives, manners and results. "Grossraum" represents a parcelling of the world among several powers – hegemonic leaders.

10 Skinner, Quentin: *O státě.* [*About State*] Praha: Oikoymenh, 2012, p. 97.

11 Jellinek, Georg: *Všeobecná státověda.* [*General Theory of State*] Praha: Jan Laichter, 1906, pp. 786-787. Similarly concerning membership in a grouping of states or assuming international obligations as manifestation of sovereign authority: Filip, Jan, Svatoň, Jan: *Státověda.* [*Theory of State*] Praha: Wolters Kluwer, 5th edition, 2011, pp. 42-43. The same is noted by the Constitutional Court of the Czech Republic in the first so-called Lisbon judgment (Pl. ÚS 19/08), when dealing with an objection concerning conflict of the Lisbon Treaty with the sovereignty of the Czech Republic – the capacity of the state to limit oneself is a manifestation rather than a denial of sovereignty. Cf. point 100. It is necessary to add, however, that from the point of view of legal sovereignty this is not to be a permanent, or unlimited, limitation. From this point of view the regulation of the right of states to terminate their membership in the European Union has a declaratory character, so the important aspect of the regulation consists in the parameters of the process of terminating membership. Such regulation, however, should not be applied in the following manner: as you can terminate membership and you are not terminating it, you therefore submit to anything.

The continuing importance of the state is stressed in the contemporary Czech writing of *V. Belling*, another author with extensive knowledge of German literature.[12] Such importance is due to thinking of the legitimacy of public authority as being related to the existence of a political nation with a certain level of homogeneity. In such an entity it is possible to conceive of a general will, general reason or general interest - categories that are associated with *T. Hobbes*, *J.-J. Rousseau* and *E. Burke*, but also *C. Schmitt* and *H. Heller*. Reference to generality indicates the inclusion of the interests of minorities and individuals who were not in favour of a specific decision, who however form part of "us." In the absence of homogeneity, a feeling of cohesion, equality or uniformity, reaching a majority decision seems difficult in terms of capacity to require dissenters to be loyal and to submit to the decision. This is the point of comments that cite the absence of a European "demos" as a limit on majority decision-making by the bodies of the European Union.

This does not mean that "the people" or "the nation" must necessarily be a natural entity, or an entity defined by blood. It is accepted that nations are social constructs, products of imagination (*B. Anderson*).[13] Imagination in this case does not indicate a mere fabrication, but rather it means self-awareness associated with symbols, myths, and fate. This therefore does not exclude the existence of a European "demos" as a modular concept, that is a concept of non-exclusive (telescopic) identity involving the local – regional – national – European identity. It is assumed, however, that, in terms of self-identification among the majority of citizens of the European Union states, the European identity is not very strong, and differs in individual states. If we do not necessarily require in advance a feeling of solidarity, we may of course construct the people through law, or by constitution. This is how the difference between political unity and pre-political multitude (*multitudo*) is viewed by some political philosophers.[14] It reflects, to a certain extent, development in the United States (US), where American identity as a dominant identity grew gradually once the institutional framework was created. In the 1860s, Lord Chancellor *Northington* perceived the people as being construed by law,[15] and *Aristotle* also referred to the artificiality of the people.

12 Cf. primarily Belling, 2009.

13 Anderson, Benedict: *Představy společenství. Úvahy o původu a šíření nacionalismu.* [*Imagined Communities: Reflections on the Origin and Spread of Nationalism*] Praha: Karolinum, 2008.

14 Michelman, Frank, J., Ferrara, Alessandro: *Polemika o ústavě.* [*Polemic about the Constitution*] Praha: Filosofia, 2006, p. 66.

15 McIlwain, Charles Howard: *Constitutionalism: Ancient and Modern.* Indianapolis: Liberty Fund, 2007. To a considerable extent this is a variation of the dispute

Opinions based on the homogeneity of the people may be compared with *H. Kelsen* and his sceptical attitude toward homogeneity of the people as well as toward the general will: they are only fictions; there is only the multitude (*multitudo*). *Kelsen* explains the legitimacy of majority rule through the easiest changes: it is sufficient to reach the agreement of one half plus one member of the decision-making body.[16] This assumes, however, a positive attitude toward the change, rather than toward preservation of the *status quo*.

We are of the opinion that the state is not a necessary arrangement, but that it quite clearly dominates the contemporary world as a form of political organisation of people. After all, there are still nations or national groups that seek to form their own state as a means of realising their needs and interests. Clearly they do not consider the state to be something abandoned on the scrap yard of history. However, not all states are the same. Differences among states show how the modern state changes.[17] The metaphor of networks both in the international environment and within states plays a role in this process.

II. Networks, legal polycentrism, constitutional pluralism

In relation to law, the concept of networks appears in theories of legal polycentrism and constitutional pluralism. It is an attempt to depict a shift in perception of the structure of legal order where either the focal point is lost (basic norm), or the concept of this focal point changes. The focal point is no longer the top of the pyramid (even though this also has always been only a simplified analogy for reality) from which all the lower levels of legal order derive their basis. Significant components of the legal order no longer originate on the territory of the state, therefore their existence (validity) is not derived from this focal point. On the other hand, we could speak about maintaining the focal point of the legal order when we associate with the focal point the effect, rather than the creation, of legal rules formed outside the territory of the state (incorporation of international treaties, integrative authorisation for accession to the European Union, or possibly provisions dealing with the effects of European law). Law

---

concerning the relation between the king (rex) and the law (lex) which started in medieval England and continued until James I: does the law derive from the king, or does the king derive from the law?

16 E.g. Kelsen, Hans: *O podstatě a hodnotě demokracie*. [*On the Essence and Value of Democracy*] Praha: Orbis, 1933.

17 "*It is generally observed that we are living in a period of erosion of statehood,*" says D. Grimm, 2012, p. 13.

could in such a case be "a command of the sovereign," even though the sovereign creates this law only to a limited extent. The sovereign however determines what the law is, irrespective of its origin.

What is new about the described phenomenon is not the existence of legal systems outside of the territories of individual states (see the ancient roots of international law, and before that conflicts among imperial, Roman, and canon law and the law of territorial states), but the intensity of operation of these legal systems, or their reflection in constitution-making decisions and judicial decisions of the constitutional courts. As a result, the hierarchical model is at the least complemented, and even perhaps put under pressure, by networks, or network relations.[18] Instead of superior law clearly prevailing over inferior law (*lex superior derogat legi inferiori*) it is necessary to "translate" between the networks, also because, among other things, it is impossible to determine what is superior and what is inferior, because the perspectives differ. Illustrative of this (despite the fact that it does not directly deal with mixed or shared governments or overlapping legal orders) is a quotation from *B. Latour,* who said "*Our ship is the concept of translation or a network. A network that is more flexible than the concept of system, more historical than the concept of structure, more empirical than the concept of complexity. It is the Ariadne's thread of mixed histories.*"[19]

Along the same lines, the European Court of Justice claims the supremacy of European law over the legal orders of Member States, including their constitutions. The constitutional courts of Member States on the other hand declare their constitutions to be supreme, and allow the possibility to examinc European acts as acts *ultra vires* in relation to the delegation of powers.[20] Czech legal theorist

18 More generally on "flattening" of the world, where hierarchies of authorities, values, organisations and so on are replaced by "flat" networks (see for example antiglobalisation or terrorist networks having no clear leaders) cf. Friedman, Thomas L.: *Svět je plochý. Stručné dějiny jednadvacátého století.* [*The World is Flat: A Brief History of the Twenty-first Century*] Praha: Academia, 2007. For a critical view of the massive abandonment of hierarchies cf. Fukuyama, Francis: *Velký rozvrat. Lidská přirozenost a rekonstrukce společenského řádu.* [*The Great Disruption: Human Nature and the Reconstruction of Social Order*] Praha: Academia, 2006. Fukuyama says: "*One way or the other, people have nothing against hierarchies in general, but they hate those in which they are at the bottom*" (pp. 239-240). Hierarchies are an expression of human longing for recognition.

19 Burke, Peter: *Společnost a vědění. Od Gutenberga k Diderotovi.* [*A Social History of Knowledge: From Gutenberg to Diderot*] Praha: Karolinum, 2007, p. 243.

20 The Czech Constitutional Court transformed the threat into reality in the case of the so-called Slovak pensions, where the court explicitly refused to follow the opinion of the European Court of Justice.

and constitutionalist *J. Wintr* says: *"In European law it is the European Court of Justice who has the last word, in national law it is the constitutional court. As none of these legal systems may be clearly superior over the other (unless the EU becomes a state), a possible conflict of opinions between the European Court of Justice and the constitutional court of a Member State would be legally irresolvable and would have to be bridged politically."*[21] Moreover international law considers other legal systems to be mere *questiones facti*.[22] From the point of view of normativists, for whom the state coalesces with legal order, the order that prevails at the end would correspond to the state.

Polycentrism is associated with constitutional pluralism through the attention paid to the issue of the centre, focal point, or origin of the legal order in mutually incompatible perspectives. Constitutional pluralism is a model that explains European integration on a basis that is different to the more or less well-established idea of a federal state (classical constitutionalism). Constitutional pluralism also rejects any determination of "superior" law and tries to operationalise competitive claims of individual legal systems (and constitutional jurisdictions) in such a manner that there are no stalemates. It prefers dialogue among stakeholders over the last word of authority based on "force" - which is considered not to be necessary for maintaining order in law by "pluralists." However, constitutional pluralism does not exist in a single variant, and is not exclusively associated with the European Union,[23] as illustrated for example by the European Court of Human Rights case *"Bosphorus Airways" v. Ireland* (application no. 45036/98). This case shows how international law reacts to the coexistence of national and (particularly) European law, with the last word in this case being claimed by the Strasbourg court.

---

21 Wintr, Jan: *Principy českého ústavního práva*. [*Principles of Czech Constitutional Law*] Plzeň: Aleš Čeněk, 2nd ed., 2013, p. 191.

22 Article 46 of the Vienna Convention on the Law of Treaties represents an exception that proves the rule: *"1. A State may not invoke the fact that its consent to be bound by a treaty has been expressed in violation of a provision of its internal law regarding competence to conclude treaties as invalidating its consent unless that violation was manifest and concerned a rule of its internal law of fundamental importance. 2. A violation is manifest if it would be objectively evident to any State conducting itself in the matter in accordance with normal practice and in good faith."*

23 Avbelj, Matej, Komárek, Jan (eds.): *Constitutional Pluralism in the European Union and Beyond*. Oxford and Portland, Oregon: Hart Publishing, 2012. A concentrated introduction to this topic can be found in the edited record of a seminar at the European University Institute called "*Four Visions of Constitutional Pluralism.*" Eds: Avbelj, Matej, Komárek, Jan, EUI Working Papers, Law 2008/21.

This proves that it is open to dispute whether constitutional pluralism is a term that is more descriptive or normative. *J. Baquero Cruz* takes a critical approach and in his quoted anthology on visions of constitutional pluralism he states that pluralism is a work that adds a postmodern flavour to constitutionalism, where postmodernism is associated with both a fluid and fragmentary nature. In his opinion pluralism may realistically reflect the changing reality, however he considers this to pose a risk.[24] Perhaps he feels that assigning a label means legitimising of the status, conflicting with an ideal that corresponds with the project of modernism, with the conviction of the possibility to form and control the world (on the same topic see also *N. Walker*, who states, in the same anthology that the world in which we live has changed – instead of exclusivity there is an overlap of "networks"). From this point of view constitutional pluralism would be a kind of self-fulfilling prophecy, rather than a descriptive "plurality."

D. Halberstam builds upon the more or less well-established concept of constitutional pluralism (the idea of competing claims for constitutional authority within a single system of government) with his own concept of constitutional heterarchy, a non-hierarchical order.[25] The European Union and US are, according to *Halberstam*, similar in terms of an absence of hierarchy among legal systems and rules on the one hand (the EU), and an absence of hierarchy among institutions interpreting the constitution on the other hand (interpretation of pluralism in the US): a final legal authority is missing in both systems, but in spite of that there is discernible order. This order however does not arise from the unilateral assertion of a superior, it arises from mutual accommodation with the aim of enforcing three fundamental values of constitutionalism. These are: "voice," or the right to be heard (represented), expertise, and rights (or protection of rights). These values cannot be unequivocally conferred on individual state powers (or rather the bodies endowed with such powers – the president, Congress, the Supreme Court) – each of these powers relies on the above-mentioned values in various situational combinations, each of them wants to be the final arbiter, and each of them succeeds as such from time to time. The supreme authority therefore oscillates and it is not possible to determine in advance whose opinion will prevail, even though in "ordinary" matters the judicial interpretation will prevail.

---

24 Avbelj, Komárek (eds.), 2008, p. 7.

25 Halberstam, Daniel: *Constitutional Heterarchy: the Centrality of Conflict in the European Union and the United States*. University of Michigan Law School. Public Law and Legal Theory Working Paper Series, Working Paper No. 111, June 2008.

The above-described cases illustrate the limited predictability of who will make decisions and how - a kind of "liquidity." Liquidity is a property of water, and, as a famous historian of religions *M. Eliade* pertinently pointed out, in many myths the depths of water symbolise chaos (the deluge being a retreat into shapelessness), whereas the establishment of "solid forms" is associated with the act of Creation, or the victory of order.[26] In the complex reality of the contemporary world, the creation of order seems to shift to the level of specific decisions made by a decision-maker who is acknowledged by the relevant audience, or community, as the final decision-maker in a given case. After all, decision as a dividing line between "non-order" and order is found in the work of many authors, both in relation to the micro level of judge-made decisions and the macro level of sovereign-made decisions.

III. Growth of modern state

The creation of modern statehood is a process of eliminating competition among centres of power. Restriction, or elimination (in the case of England), applied to the direct influence of the pope and the catholic church, and to an even greater extent other churches were placed under the supervision of the state, even though churches still influenced the state to a considerable extent. The autonomy of the aristocracy was undermined, and nobles were increasingly bound to service in court, the administration or the army. The nobility lost the status of administrative unit no later than in the 19th century. The organs of the estates were suppressed by bureaucracy. An individual was subordinated to state authority through territorialisation: the individual's legal status had a territorial rather than a personal basis. After all, affiliation to a territory under the Peace of Augsburg was not for the purpose of deciding only about the law but also about the religion, whereby a public element is mixed with the private element and the profane is mixed with the transcendental.

An impressive description of the above development is provided by *A. de Tocqueville,* who explains how the old regime contributed to the work of the Revolution.[27] Centralisation and etatisation destroyed intermediary structures that restricted the immediate reach of state authority and to a certain extent also individuals (typically the guilds). Nevertheless, intermediary structures represented

---

26 Eliade, Mircea: *Mýtus o věčném návratu.* [*The Myth of the Eternal Return*] Praha: Oikoymenh, 2nd ed. 2009, p. 55.

27 Tocqueville, Alexis de: *Starý režim a revoluce.* [*The Old Regime and the Revolution*] Praha: Academia, 2003.

to a point a shelter offering protection against the state authority: after they were destroyed there was no intermediary between the state and an (atomised) individual. The negative impact became pronounced during the Revolution, with its ambitions to interfere with individuals' lives which considerably exceeded the ambitions of the kings.

A similar account may be found in the work of a great historian of the French Revolution, *F. Furet*: "*The Revolution in the end resulted in an atomised society of isolated individuals united on a political level by the general will proclaiming what was common to them. In reality though, they were very quickly subordinated to administrative dictatorship which was the only way to stop anarchy, which is an inseparable companion of such radical individualism.*"[28] To strengthen the impact of this account *Furet* quotes a speech by *P. P. Royer-Collard* in the Parliament in 1822: "*Where there is nothing but individuals, all matters not directly related to individuals become public matters, state matters.*"[29]

If the state takes control of the public space, then all non-private expectations are directed toward the state, rather than also toward the churches, municipalities, guilds or estates. Who will take care of the weak? Who will take care of everybody, if we do not expect anything from the family or from ourselves? It may be something close to a self-fulfilling prophecy: the state crushes its competitors, thus focusing on itself various expectations which further drive the state to strengthen its functions. It proceeds from the function of maintaining order, toward ensuring material welfare (prosperity) in the form of a welfare state (various types of insurance and social care institutions). In this respect it differs from the church, which was concerned primarily with eternal welfare. Nevertheless its continuity from the church is reflected in the concept of pastoral power (*M. Foucault*). The state authority gains the character of an educator, reflected in its care for the education and welfare of each individual. Pastoral power considerably exceeds the mere safeguarding of order or safety; elements of pastoral power are present in every modern state.[30]

Tocqueville noted a democratic pressure toward conformity, which results in growing government control over individuals also in the form of "soft" invisible power. Democracy is the rule of the majority, which gives rise to considerations

---

28 Furet, Francois: *Francouzská revoluce. Díl 2. Ukončit revoluci. Od Ludvíka XVIII. po Julese Ferryho (1815 – 1880)*. [*Revolutionary France. Part II. End the Revolution. From Louis XVIII to Jules Ferry (1815 – 1880)*] Praha: Argo, 2007, p. 50.

29 Furet, 2007, p. 51.

30 Šejvl, Michal: *Stát jako nositel sekularizace?* [*State as the Vehicle of Secularisation*] Právník, vol. 2013, no. 10, p. 981 et seq.

of what exactly should be subject to decisions of the majority: should the majority decide also about taste, or good and evil, for example? For *Foucault* there is a clear relation to the pastoral role of the state, which wishes to be the arbiter of human happiness.[31] This gives rise to, inter alia, biopolitics concerned with the health and life, or mere non-political life (*zóé*), of people to an unprecedented level, such that it breaks one of the traditional limitations of politics and public authority. Intimate questions engaging issues such as eugenics or euthanasia, which used to be deemed beyond the reach of public authority because they pertained to God or nature, are now subject to decisions by the majority.[32] Wherever there is an interest of the state, or a political interest, there is also the law.[33] After overthrowing the duality of state and society common in the 19th century, public authority dropped another limitation and penetrated deeper into the private sphere. Public authority then started to be halted by the commencement of human rights, reversing the achieved status: instead of automatic decisions of the majority controlling political authority over everything, the majority decisions were questioned with reference to their human-rights aspects.

There may be various manifestations of welfare, such as putting food on the table or ensuring different types of equality. If "*protego ergo obligo*" applies in the case of *Hobbes,* it is important to know what an individual is protected against and hence what they are bound to obey. The issue consists in the fact that a state providing comprehensive protection also has considerable potential to become a state of comprehensive oppression.

In 1941 *F. D. Roosevelt* derived the concept of four freedoms, which were later incorporated into the United Nations Universal Declaration of Human Rights. In addition to civil and political freedom there was also freedom from fear and from want. There is a difference between the state securing an individual against crime, and the state making sure that the individual has enough to eat. The state may also protect the individual against injured feelings, a frequent subject of many anti-discrimination cases. Some anti-discrimination cases are based on a tacit assumption that majority attitudes and preferences are repressive, and so

---

31 Loughlin, Martin: *Sword and Scales. An Examination of the Relationship between Law and Politics*. Oxford and Portland, Oregon: Hart Publishing, 2000, pp. 29-30.

32 Agamben, Giorgio: *Homo sacer*. Praha: Oikoymenh, 2012, p. 11 et seq., p. 119 et seq. For a book dealing with the topic see Foucault, Michel: *Zrození biopolitiky*. [*The Birth of Biopolitics*] Brno: Centrum pro demokracii a kulturu, 2009.

33 Filip, Jan: *Biojurisprudence – nový pohled na právo nebo jen nový směr právní vědy?* [*Biojurisprudence – a New Perspective on Law, or Merely a New Trend in Jurisprudence?*] Časopis pro právní vědu a praxi, vol. 2009, no. 2.

the identity associated with such attitudes and preferences is reported into privacy, whereas the attitudes and preferences of various minorities penetrate into the public space. The state is therefore expected to make sure that the bearers of majority identities do not behave in a manner that may be perceived prejudicial to those carrying minority identities. In doing so, the state might not pay sufficient attention to equality before the law and to negative freedom as a demarcation of the space of one's own self-determination, as if these were matters of course, requiring no attention. History shows though that this is not the case. In the past a different type of emphasis was placed upon comparing people: in the past equality had primarily social parameters, while now differences in physical handicap or cultural identity are compensated in the name of equality in dignity. But this mode of achieving equality is based on conscious differentiation: because XY is different, he needs to be compensated. And differentiation divides, rather than unites society (this of course depends on the degree).

The key value attached to human dignity forms the basis of the dignitaristic concept of human rights which can be associated with the German Basic Law and its spiritual background. This concept is different from the English (perhaps liberal or perhaps libertarian) concept of negative liberty.[34] The importance of human dignity is unquestionable and essential. It would become precarious if it were used as a tool of judicial policy: repealing laws, or enforcing the adoption of laws with a certain content because only that content is compatible with human dignity - which of course is not very well specified by positive law. Then the whole catalogue of human rights would be useless – everything would be derived from this single value.

The role of state covers various new challenges, such as technological development, environmental issues, and international terrorism (see below). In order to cope with such challenges the state needs money, and so, as opposed to the state having originally been funded from the monarch's domain, there was introduced a growing number of one-off tax levies and "donations" (taxes were approved by estates upon the request of the monarch and church congregations made voluntary and sometimes involuntary donations), and later regular payments were introduced in the form of customs duties, direct and indirect taxes, which further increased in the 20th century. At the same time, it turned out that

34 M. Rosenfeld and A. Sajó take notice of the difference in relation to the freedom of speech, however these are more general concepts. See Rosenfeld, Michel, Sajó, András: *Spreading Liberal Constitutionalism: an Inquiry into the Fate of Free Speech Rights in New Democracies*. In: Choudhry, Sujit (ed.): *Migration of Constitutional Ideas*. Cambridge: Cambridge University Press, 2006.

the nature of the above challenges rules out any successful resolution thereof by a single state. This then stimulated interstate cooperation, which on the one hand increases the capacity of the state to reach a resolution, but on the other hand restricts the state's room for manoeuvre as an autonomous actor.

IV. Factors limiting a state's power

Limits to a state's power are manifested in various ways. Such limits restrict the state in what it can realistically do, and possibly in what the state may do if it wishes to be considered legitimate. In other situations, limits may bind a state in the form of orders, something that the state must do or else be subject to various types of sanctions. In our opinion, it is possible to distinguish two large groups of such limits, external and internal. Human rights particularly act as a limit across all public powers. It is becoming more common for states to be positively bound to adopt measures required by one right or another. This is no longer up to the discretion of the state but is based on an imperative often derived from a loose interpretation of the text of human rights provisions. The limiting effect is clear in relation to states internally as well as externally: human rights represent a limit to state power and a title for external interest in the exercise of state power on the territory of the state as well as outside the territory.

IV.1 External limits

IV.1.1 Plurality of states

A natural external limit to the power of the state is the existence of other states. A state exercises public power on its territory, while mutual relations between states have long been deemed to have a natural status, free from any regulatory authority. This is why, in the relations between states, a dyadic model for the solution of disputes was applied, with the two parties either reaching a consensus or declaring war.[35] Also, any claim of sovereignty as the supreme and final authority relates to specific territory, which fails to take into consideration the pre-modern sovereignties (supremacies) that were claimed by popes and emperors in Middle Ages in relation to *Imperium Christianum.*

---

35 We are talking about modern states which generally did not acknowledge the arbitral authority of the pope, such as in the year 1494, when the world was divided between Portugal and emerging Spain. This does not mean however that the pope could not decide disputes as an arbiter based on the initiative of the parties. One example of such a decision is a border dispute between Chile and Argentina in the 1970s.

The necessary collisions with other states had different impacts on the various involved parties depending on their power, i.e. depending not only on the size of the territory and the population, but also on their wealth, capacity of the army, loyalty of citizens, and so on. Life in the shadow of a great power certainly did not restrict the sovereignty of a small state in the legal sense of the word; however it may have limited its elbow room (cf. the phenomenon of Finlandization in the 20th century).

IV.1.2 International law

These limits of an almost physical nature started in the 20th century to be added to by other limits, primarily from the world of social constructs. There was a growing number of international treaties focusing on an ever expanding range of issues (besides political issues, also trade issues, rules of war, transport and so on). Over time the effect of international treaties became more intense as a result of states including general incorporation clauses in their constitutions, based on which treaties became not only an integral part of the body of laws, but also gained precedence over domestic law in terms of their application. The constitution-maker thus limited the law-maker. At the same time, international mechanisms for enforcing obligations under the treaties were developed in the form of supervisory committees and arbitration panels, as well as tribunals and courts.

The sphere of international customs gave rise to the category of rules referred to as *jus cogens*, which are independent of individual states' willingness to adhere to them. The perception of the subjects of international law also started to change when, in addition to state and international organisations, individual persons also started to become beneficiaries of international law. Both these phenomena are related to the establishment of human rights as positivised natural rights. Such rights even entitle the overriding of the principle of sovereign equality of states and their territorial integrity in the form of so-called humanitarian intervention: a state does not need to wage war yet may be perceived as violating the international order if the state for example commits genocide. A legitimate institutional support for humanitarian intervention may be provided by the United Nations.

Despite the above, international law focuses primarily on states. The international environment is however also populated by other actors that are not subject to state regulation (companies, groups of people and individuals) which is why the phenomenon of unregulated social power, which will be discussed briefly, is growing stronger.

IV.1.3 European law and European integration

In addition to international law, Europe gave birth to European law, which has a contractual basis. For the states involved the project of European integration represents a more pronounced limit than the rules and institutions of international law. This is due to the wide range of issues dealt with, its well-developed structure of institutions comparable with state institutions, as well as the effect of European law. In this respect it is possible to regard the European Union as a distinct public power operating on the territory of the Member States. Certainly it is not possible to say that it is a power independent of the states, however in relation to any individual state it is an external power. It is the states that founded the European Union, who decide about its contractual basis (which from the point of view of effect is close to the constitution of a state), and who participate in the operation of the institutions of the European Union. It is also true that the European Union may have interests that are not a vector sum of the interests of its Member States. Within the EU the states have unequal weight and influence and are confronted with pro-integration judgments of the European Court of Justice: to put it simply the Member States are "the masters of the treaties" however they are not necessarily the masters of the Union itself. In addition, to be the master of the text of a treaty is not the same as being the master of the meaning of the text, a rule known from analyses of the relation between law-makers and judicial power.

International law as well as European integration has an important impact on the sovereignty of states, a classical concept associated with the modern state since the very beginning. Sovereignty will be covered in at least three chapters and we will return to it in the conclusion. It is useful to note in this context that internationalisation and Europeanisation has a different effect on different states. The current situation therefore cannot be described using a single scheme. *G. Sörensen* describes three types of state: modern states, post-colonial, and post-modern states.[36] The first type claims control over the use of force, has centralised systems of government with a key role assigned to legal rules; it relies on national identity and on a relatively self-sufficient economy. The second type suffers from weak institutions, and so features rather personal government and clientelism; state officials and personnel often focus primarily on seeking rent and such a state often does not control its entire territory; furthermore, in such a state tribal or religious identity is more important than nation; and the economy

36 Sörensen, Georg: *Stát a mezinárodní vztahy.* [*Changes in Statehood: The Transformation of International Relations*] Praha: Portál, 2005, p. 91 et seq.

is underdeveloped, often focused only on mining raw materials, or growing a single key crop (coffee, cocoa beans, cotton). Finally, the third type of state relates to our European present time, and so reflects supranational integration, multi-level governance with suprastate and substate elements, the complementing of national identity with reference to the European "we", and highly interrelated economies.[37] All of the above types, however, exist simultaneously, a fact that some Western thinkers may tend to forget.

In any case in Europe we are most markedly confronted with the fact of multitier government, in which the state somewhat fades away. This makes it considerably more difficult to identify where the power and the related responsibility lie; however it enables organized interests to multiply the channels of their influence. This may be of benefit for specific organized interests and their supporters; however, it may not necessarily be beneficial to the general (public) interest.

Government at the "supra-European" level misses an identifiable entity, therefore the nature of the processes is emphasised rather than a person or body's decision-making. It is described as a polycentric network involving not only states and international organisations, but also multinational corporations, as well as individuals - who some describe as cosmopolitans, and others describe as the global elite. The scattered nature of its authority brings back reflections of empire, however it is a delocalised empire without a main nation or clear centre - yet nevertheless ruling and dividing. In confrontation with the empire, states still seem more democratic (*M. Albrow, A. Negri, P. Carrozza, D. Zolo* and others).[38]

It therefore depends on point of view. For some, states are repressive and restricting and they desire liberating flat networks of interactions and negotiations

---

37 The last type is referred to by N. MacCormick as post-sovereign states: sovereignty does not pertain to them, nor it does to the European Union. See MacCormick, 1999. The contemporary Czech literature also offers a contrary opinion, in which (tiered) sovereignty pertains to both Member States and to the European Union. See Hamuľák, Ondrej: *Integrující se Evropa a suverenita České republiky.* [*Integrating Europe and Czech Sovereignty*] Olomouc: Acta Iuridica Olomoucensia, 2013. For an overview of various positions taken in the dispute of the (non)existence of sovereignty, refer to Walker, Neil (ed.): *Sovereignty in Transition.* Oxford – Portland: Hart Publishing, 2006.

38 Cf. e.g. Carrozza, Paolo: *Constitutionalism's Post-Modern Opening.* In: Loughlin, Martin, Walker, Neil (eds.): The Paradox of Constitutionalism. Constitutional Power and Constitutional Form. Oxford: Oxford University Press, 2007, Barša, Pavel: *Síla a rozum. Spor realismu s idealismem v moderním politickém myšlení.* [*Strength and Sense: A Controversy between Realism and Idealism in Modern Political Thought*] Praha: Filosofia, 2007, or Belling, 2009.

on everything. For others, networks are spun by a spider – in the case of the empire, as a veil over its own power, so it is better to focus on states.

It is certainly possible to look at the phenomena of internationalisation and Europeanisation as not only a limitation of states, but also as an augmentation of their power potential. However, this would not imply an augmentation of the power of all the states as such but would rather apply only to some states. A change of international law makes it possible to associate interests with values, so exerting pressure on a state XY does not necessarily have to be perceived as the implementation of policy of a great power, but may be perceived as the enforcement of values acknowledged by the international community. The "international community" in this context does not necessarily mean all states. *Marsilius of Padua* in the 14th century considered people to be the source of authority in this world, and at the same time considered the people to be "*pars valentior*" - the more valuable part of the populace, or the notables. "*Pars valentior*" definitely exists also in the international community: Botswana does not usually set the pace.

This applies similarly to the European Union, which may serve as a veil for the intentions of states that would be the movers of the EU or possibly tip the balance of the scales. Each Member State may co-decide on developments in other states, which would otherwise not be possible. It remains unclear what the ratio is between this cross-border "power" and the reduced power for states to decide about theirselves.[39] A Member State cannot do anything in the field of exclusive competences of the European Union, and in other fields the Member State is bound to refrain from legislative activity where the European Union regulates an area through a regulation, and to engage in legislative activity in the case of transposing directives.

IV.1.4 Globalisation

International law and European integration are, at least in part, dependent on states. However, they do not have a significant influence on globalisation. According to *U. Beck*, globalisation represents an escape of politics from the framework

39 If the introductory chapter were to be more ambitious it would go into more detail about what (who) is a state: an abstract concept, government officials and personnel, or organised interests from a specific territory? A state as a legal entity may be weakened, but its banking sector however may grow stronger than ever as a result of the free movement of capital. Similarly the interests of certain states may be supported by its citizens working for European institutions and so on. We would have to think about the continuation of state policy using other means.

of the nation state.[40] States are unable to prevent the movement of polluted air over the border nor the movement of capital.[41] Their currencies may become victims of financial speculators. Multinational corporations with an income higher than the income of many states have an advantage in negotiating investments because they can go elsewhere. This does not apply only to developing countries who are particularly willing to give up social and environmental regulation. They simply do not have a "counterweight to the power."[42] In the case of any indication of resistance the mobile capital moves elsewhere in order to avoid a clash with "otherness", i.e. with other preferences or values.[43] Free trade and freedom to conduct business are certainly desirable, but it remains questionable whether they represent distinct values at the top of an imaginary hierarchy. The emphasis placed on them was in the past often associated with an expectation that some cultural and perhaps also moral limits would be observed (i.e. that some things are just not done). The weakening of such corrections resulted in states putting in place regulation, however the large economic players are able to avoid such regulation.[44] The effort to curb large corporations' possible lack of sensitivity to the environment or local population is not motivated by states; it is rather based on the public propagating the concept of social responsibility. Globalisation processes at the same time involve the universal message of human rights, which may be presented by those in a critical frame of mind as the cultural imperialism of the West. Global issues contribute to the debate on global response – and so global governance and possibly also global democracy are under debate (*D. Held*).

IV.2 Internal limits

IV.2.1 Disappearance of the raison d'état

The national interest, or *raison d'état*, are concepts associated in the history of political thinking with the early phase of the existence of modern states.[45]

40 Beck, 2007, p. 9.

41 The ability to control the border is an indicator of one of the types of sovereignty identified by S. Krasner. Cf. Krasner, Stephen D.: *Sovereignty. Organized Hypocrisy*. Princeton: Princeton University Press, 1999.

42 Beck, 2007, pp. 9-10.

43 Bauman, Zygmunt: *Globalizace. Důsledky pro člověka*. [*Globalization: The Human Consequences*] Praha: Mladá fronta, 1999, p. 19.

44 It is generally stated that hypertrophy of legal regulation is associated to the fall of other normative systems, or fragmentation of societies which leads to fragmentation of value systems.

45 For more details on the topic see Sadurski, Wojciech: *Reason of State and Public Reason*. Ratio Juris, vol. 2014, no. 1. Of various conceptions, the one in which national

These concepts are sometimes related to *Machiavelli* and his contemporaries, or regarded as a reflection of circumstances during the French Wars of Religion, when the state in the conflict of religions seemed to be in a neutral stance. In any case, identification of the national interest was vested in the political authorities. A nice illustration of this is Lock's concept of the prerogative, as the duke's authorisation to act without law and even in contravention of the law in extreme cases when it was necessary to protect the general interest. This is reflected in current institutes of constitutional (national) emergency and crisis management of the state in the form of a so-called constitutional dictatorship (*C. Rossiter*) or the dictatorship of commissioners (*C. Schmitt*).

There remains the question whether we actually believe in the existence of the national interest. Is the state a distinct person, with a specific national interest? Similarly, we could ask whether there is anything akin to a public interest that would be different from the interests of individuals. Sometimes also the existence of society as supra-individual fiction is contested. If only individuals are real, then why talk about the general, public or national interest?

This is not only about contemporary debates tinged with neoliberal rhetoric, but also about classical topics associated with the American and French revolutions and strongly resonating in German thinking of the 19th and 20th centuries. It is a conflict between a critique of the particularism of political parties and various formulas for remedy such as the search for a general estate (bureaucracy), the state represented by a monarch versus society overarched by parliament, the general will stemming from the people, or the creation of a Union in order to prevent any particular interest from prevailing. Differing points of view have become clear also in an evaluation of parliaments since the rise of mass political parties toward the end of 19th century: is the goal to search for truth and justice, or is it just a defence of various interests on the principle of exchange?

At present the idea of searching for a general interest has weakened, be it because of political parties or bureaucracy. The contributing factor behind this weakening is an economic approach to politics which emphasizes the implementation of own interests by political actors and sometimes mere rent-seeking by individuals or groups of individuals. The ethos of life-long civil service is crushed by managerialism and other elements imported from the world of business. There are observed and medialised manifestations of corruption that undermine service to the general interest. Sometimes it even seems that corruption

---

interest is identical with general welfare is declared to be meaningful. However this assumes thinking within the categories of homogeneity or the general will.

is discussed so frequently that it is omnipresent, even though such an impression is not supported by everyday experience. This increases the distance between citizens and politicians, between citizens and the state. The state is often perceived not as a civilising facility, but is rather seen as an estranged and often incomprehensible "general treasury." Politicians are not usually considered to be the best of us, but rather they are perceived as "them." This is particularly true in the post-communist space, where politics has been discredited over a long period due to the fact that it was "stolen" by communist parties. This however stands completely in contrast with the understanding of political career as a respected path toward public recognition, as presented in texts concerning the formation of the United States of America, as well as those illustrating the golden era of British parliamentarism in the second third of the 19th century.[46] The numbers of members of political parties (not only in this part of Europe) are falling, and political parties now work less directly with the public. They are more focused on attracting voters using marketing methods, funded by sponsors or state money

46 Unfortunately the reputation of politics in the Czech Republic was damaged also by the case of former Prime Minister P. Nečas. Nečas was a conservative politician, a practising Catholic with the reputation of "Mr. Righteous." In spring 2013 he was forced to resign from his office as prime minister of the government when it turned out that the manager of his office was not only his lover, but that she had abused her authority. According to police investigations she was, among other things, actively involved in forming a network of influence that occupied key positions in state administration. She proceeded in agreement with persons who are known in the Czech Republic as "godfathers" or "political entrepreneurs." It is in their interest for their controversial - to say the least, if not illegal - activities not to undergo examination and for them to have free access to public contracts. For this reason they need cover from politicians, prosecuting attorneys, and the police. The persons forming part of this network of course were not aiming to serve the state, but rather each other. The prime minister not only did not prevent it, but to a certain extent he even assisted it, in an effort to maintain his intimate relationship. Nečas' party suffered a crushing defeat in the following parliamentary elections. All traditional political parties were "punished" through losing votes to new movements with strong leaders who self-funded their own political movements. It is interesting that a few years ago the Czech Republic saw another case where a (clientelist) network of influence was formed, with its centre at Pilsen Law School. Policemen, officials, politicians and even persons later criminally convicted studied at the law school under very non-standard conditions. There was concern that this was not just a case of corruption but rather the formation of relations among persons inter-related by unfair interests and prepared to help each other. Such networks are capable of breaking the state as a mechanism of service for the general interest.

(which is received for votes): the political parties use state money to fund campaigns, in return for which they participate on decision-making on the state, and again receive more state money. The fundamental defect consists of the fact that there is a growing number of citizens who do not believe that this share in decision-making about the state serves the general benefit. This adds complexity to the role of political parties as the main channels of political participation, as well as the legitimacy of the political system. It creates room for a search for alternatives (see Chapter Five).

IV.2.2 Human rights

When there are doubts about the national interest and those who interpret the national interest, the rights and interests of individuals are enforced as legitimate. Human rights in general serve as a reason for the existence of the (liberal) state and as the main limit to its authority. It is somewhat open to question whether human rights are an expression of the will of the majority at a certain point in time, which is "frozen," and so the majority cannot dispose of them in the future either relatively - in the case of the requirement of a qualified majority - or absolutely, if the rights are inalienable. In such a case they have the effect of legal taboo – legislative interventions are inadmissible from a legal point of view, so they do not occur. Nevertheless, such entrenchment weakens the body that has legislative power; it however does not weaken the courts, which may in fact modify the scope of the right by way of interpretation.[47]

Human rights have a clear vertical effect as a limit on all branches of state authority. Their horizontal effect may be slightly ambivalent. Countries such as Canada, Great Britain or South Africa have been reserved in their application of human rights between private parties. This can be attributed to the above-mentioned emphasis on human freedom rather than dignity. At least in Great Britain, the horizontal effect started to gain in importance under the influence of the European Convention on Human Rights.[48] A typical demonstration of horizontal effect is a prohibition of discrimination where the prohibited grounds for discriminating against people are determined by the state. So there is a restriction of people's freedom to behave in a discriminatory manner, which may

47 Schwartzberg, Melissa: *Democracy and Legal Change*. Cambridge – New York: Cambridge University Press, 2009.

48 Moran, Mayo: *Inimical to constitutional values: complex migrations of constitutional rights*. In: Choudhry (ed.), 2006, p. 236 et seq. The case of Campbell, decided by the House of Lords in 2004, is considered to be a ground-breaking case.

include sometimes unexpected conduct. It is questionable though whether this increases the authority of the state. There is probably a state interest at stake, but rather other people are prevented from behaving in a certain way. The state's authority is increased only in a pastoral sense, whereby the state interferes in relationships that were previously ignored. Depending on what kinds of behaviour the state curtails, questions may be raised as to its neutrality toward different ethnical concepts.

Human rights are often viewed as an unquestioned good for everybody: individuals as well as the community. On the other hand, public goods such as public safety, order, morals, and so on, are, unlike human rights, sometimes suspected of obscuring a particular interest. One such example is where a group wishes to enforce its idea of morals at the expense of others. Yet, human rights themselves may be perceived as particularistic: certain interpretations suit specific individuals or groups of individuals, and do not necessarily suit the majority or possibly society.

It seems that in the US the relationship between human rights and public goods developed differently after September 11. There is a role played by reference to state emergency or national emergency, including its theoretical construction in the work of *C. Schmitt*.[49] Explorations of differentiation in criminal procedure depending on the type of offender by *M. Shapiro* are more specific in nature: ordinary procedure for ordinary danger, as opposed to special procedure for highly organized groups, terrorists and so on, i.e. enemies of the society.[50] It is therefore possible that Europe is different thanks to its relative safety and affluence. In the case of mass immigration or drought it may be demonstrated how contextually dependent our legal institutes and high level of protection of rights are.

IV.2.3 Strengthening the judicial branch at the expense of political branches

Quite apart from the persuasiveness of the existence of a national or public interest, let us now have a brief look at the issue of competence to reveal it. We

49 Cf. e.g. Sarat, Austin (ed.): *Sovereignty, Emergency, Legality*. Cambridge University Press, 2010.

50 Shapiro, Martin: *Courts in Authoritarian Regimes*. In: Ginsburg, Tom, Moustafa, Tamir (eds.): Rule by Law. The Politics of Courts in Authoritarian Regimes. Cambridge – New York: Cambridge University Press, 2008. In Europe we tend to be rather sensitive to this adjustment of procedure according to the type of offender, as it is reminiscent of the classification of offenders by race or class.

discussed above prerogative, which in French and German theory transformed into learning about acts of government, one feature of which was, among other things, the exclusion of judicial review.[51] During the course of the 20th century however the number of excluded issues decreased.[52] This resulted in a shift, where the agenda, which had formerly been reserved for political branches, now included the courts, which are not really the state: after all, they decide on disputes between the state and individuals.[53]

This shift is visible in the "new tripartite dynamics of division of power," as enumerated by *K. Loewenstein*.[54] The three functions include firstly a determination of policies - i.e. making fundamental decisions about the political system such as the economy, relations between employees and employers, creating alliances and so on (*policy determination* in the form of constitution, laws and international agreements). The second function is the execution of fundamental decisions through implementing statutes and mainly acts of application of the law (*policy execution*); and the third function is *policy control*, resulting in responsible government.

The fundamental decisions are made by parliament and the government, and possibly also by the head of state or constitutional court, in conjunction with citizens voting in elections and referendums. It is a view of government as a creative

---

51 The model for dividing issues regulated by law and other issues was probably found in H. de Bracton's differentiation between "gubernacula" and "jurisdictia" in the 13th century. Cf. Kantorowicz, Ernst Hartwig: *The King's two bodies*. Princeton: Princeton University Press, 1997.

52 For example, in Great Britain the acts of prerogative were declared by the House of Lords as being subject to judicial review in 1985 in the case of Council of Civil Service Union v. Minister for the Civil Service, [1985] A. C. 374.

53 In addition to the increased involvement of courts in the resolution of political issues, the number of disputes between private persons is also growing. "*To many Americans, it appears that issues that used to be settled with a handshake are now fought out in court*," says F. Fukuyama. The same conclusion regarding the European situation is drawn in various texts by the above-cited P. Holländer. Fukuyama however does not condemn the phenomenon automatically because various actions for damages fulfil a regulatory function, replacing reliance on the central authority of the state. Cf. Fukuyama, 2006, pp. 36-37. Very interesting insight into these issues is offered by Slovak legal theorist and failed presidential candidate R. Procházka. He shows a difference between American and Slovak mentality, in that the former tend to look after themselves, whereas the latter expect the state to look after them. See Procházka, Radoslav: *Mak proti Gatsbymu. Osud, vina a zodpovednosť za škodu.* [*Mak versus Gatsby: Fate, Fault and Liability for Damage*] Trnava: Edition Ryba, 2009.

54 Loewenstein, Karl: *Verfassungslehre*. 2nd ed., Tübingen: Mohr, 1969, p. 40 et seq.

process through which the state and its substance are determined and realized; not only the execution of predetermined legal rules, or a technical administration.[55] The executive branch dominates the execution of decisions, however this function is also fulfilled by parliaments and courts. Policy control may be a shared, divided authority (mutual control by concurrence – lawmaking, confirmation of appointment, countersignature and so on), or control on the basis of the discretion of the holder of the relevant competence (vote of no confidence in the government, dissolution of parliament, veto, judicial control of laws). Mutual control involves all branches and again the voters must be included among the branches. The idea of a wide sharing of authority also underpins the thinking of Swiss lawyer *B. Ehrenzeller,* who states that management of the state (government) is undivided (*Staatsleitung zur gesamten Hand*), but has however multiple participants who cannot do without each other: government and parliament, and to a lesser extent the courts.[56]

The involvement of courts in the execution of political power revived interest in mixed constitution and mixed government, and by extension also thinking on various types of democracy and the scope of questions that should (must) be decided directly by a body with democratic legitimacy.[57] As pointed out by *R. Hirschl,* judicialization of politics has not ceased. He follows the escalating involvement of courts in the preserve of politics, from checking the legality of public administration procedures, through checking the constitutionality of the legislature, to so-called mega-politics. Mega-politics deals with making fundamental decisions on issues defining the very essence of the political community, such as for example the extent of an admissible delegation of powers by a Member State to the European Union (judgments of the Federal Constitutional Court), the admissibility of apartheid in the Republic of South Africa, or desegregation case law of the United States Supreme Court. In order to be able

---

55 Ehrenzeller, Bernhard: *Legislative Gewalt und Aussenpolitik.* Basel – Frankfurt am Main: Helbing & Lichtenhahn, 1993, p. 116.

56 Ehrenzeller, 1993, pp. 124-125.

57 In Czech literature Ondřejková, Jana: *Smíšená forma vlády a Evropská unie.* [*Mixed Form of Governance and the European Union*] Právník, vol. 2010, no. 7. More generally dealt with in the past by Manin, Bernard: *The Principles of Representative Government.* Cambridge: Cambridge University Press, 1997. According to B. Manin the mixed constitution is associated with the representative democracy itself by its (aristocratic) principle of selection as opposed to democratic equality, the symbol of which is election by drawing lots.

to conceptually deal with such a rise to power without the use of sword or purse, *Hirschl* uses the term new constitutionalism.[58]

Those who criticise this development claim that the situation has moved from excluding courts from political processes, through to their involvement, ending up with their hegemony. This means that the courts are politicized,[59] and also the list of things that parties may compete for in elections becomes reduced (with reference to vague prohibitions of a constitutional nature – typically: it is a human right).[60] This is enhanced in those cases where the courts are supposed to "communicate" with each other. Such court dialogue, worshipped in the European Union, is sometimes questioned by raising the objection that judges should decide based on law rather than considering the reactions of other courts with whom they are marking out the playing field (the judge of the Federal Constitutional Court *S. Bross* in his time). This is why political constitutionalism is defined in opposition to legal constitutionalism, talking about the importance of open political processes, participation, and deliberation.[61]

The role of courts on the European continent is associated with a decreasing importance of law. The modern state and legality belong together, because legality is a way of conducting bureaucracy,[62] which symbolizes the modern state. In the 19th and 20th century laws were increasingly profiled as instruments of state policy, which was criticised for its contradiction with the ideal typical attributes of generality, stability and foreseeability (cf. major criticism of *F. A. Hayek*). These qualities of law fell prey to the connection between law and state policy. There was a growing number of laws and these were often amended: in the Czech

58 E.g. Hirschl, Ran: *The New Constitutionalism and the Judicialization of Pure Politics Worldwide*. Fordham Law Review, 2006.

59 The political nature of the decided question will not disappear just because it is being decided by an independent and impartial body relying on non-political authority.

60 Exclusions from the political process are not related only to human rights, but recently have been associated also with constitutionalisation of various debt brakes. Nevertheless prohibitions of budget deficit again proclaim a certain form of economic and social policy as excluded within the given constitution and by doing so they limit what is politically possible. This is not to say that states should fall into debt, but it is a question however whether the dynamic political will should be replaced with static constitutional regulation. The issue clearly is a lack of belief in the ability of voters as well as politicians to resist the temptation of buying votes by means of social policy.

61 Bellamy, Richard: *Political Constitutionalism. Republican Defence of the Constitutionality of Democracy*. Cambridge: Cambridge University Press, 2007.

62 Schmitt, Carl: *The Leviathan in the state theory of Thomas Hobbes: meaning and failure of a political symbol*. Chicago: Chicago University Press, 2008, p. 66.

environment there were discussions about a legislative whirlwind, and in Germany about normative flooding. The legal order, burdened by high dynamics and contradictions, invites creative judicial reconstruction of meaningful rules. Constant judicial decisions thus *de facto* attain the nature of a source of law. It may not be easy for the law-maker to win out against judicial decisions. This is even more true in situations of conflicting legal orders - national, international and European - where the weight of the judicial branch formulating a relevant rule for the given case is growing.

IV.2.4 Weakening of public space, rights of individuals and minorities

The growing role of courts goes hand in hand with a weakening of public space where consensus may be sought, partners convinced, and politics fostered. For various reasons we have already touched upon, the political processes partially deteriorate. However we are less concerned because we rely less on the political processes. The above is also related to the concept of rights policy, or possibly rights rhetoric. The substance of rights policy consists of substituting the requirement of what we would like to have with the claim that we are entitled to it.[63] It is similar to the characteristic of something being utopian according to Polish political scientist *M. Bankowicz*, who describes it as passing our wishes and desires off as reality.[64] The difference may be that in our case we could come across a court which will recognize a fact so far undreamt of (e.g. the right of persons of the same sex to marry) in a new reading (typically) of human dignity.

Desire requires seeking support within a community, while making a claim about a right requires convincing a court. In the first case the public is moulded, while in the second case an individual asserts himself. In politics we have opponents who dissent, but in a legal dispute people who deny our rights. Deriving further rights, or expanding the reach of existing rights from their general wording in the human rights catalogues not only usually interferes with someone's freedom to act without restriction (various antidiscrimination practises), but also drains politics. If something is an inalienable right, it cannot be the subject

---

63 "Rights policy" is dealt with more descriptively by M. Shapiro. He describes the growing range and number of rights as a reaction to the growing scope and intensity of government. See Shapiro, Martin: *The Success of Judicial Review and Democracy*. In: Shapiro, Martin, Stone Sweet, Alec: *On Law, Politics and Judicialization*. Oxford: Oxford University Press, 2002, p. 180.

64 Bankowicz, Marek: *Kritikové marxismu*. [*Critics of Marxism*] Brno: Barrister & Principal, 2013, p. 48.

of a political fight and it cannot appear as a goal in an election campaign. Then it is of course necessary to enquire what may, and what should, be subject to decisions of the majority.[65]

The perspective of rights is close to the perspective of a private individual, rather than a citizen who is interested in the common project. *F. Furet,* when commenting on *Proudhon's* position, says that the basis of the modern society is legal individualism and democratic abstraction.[66] *H. Arendt* nicely illustrates the concept of "public happiness", having an impact at the times of the foundation of the US, which attracted excellent men to aspire toward public recognition by engaging in politics. Gradually this was replaced by a different concept of private happiness, for which the state creates space.[67] Nevertheless, the idea of a "general treasury" belonging to someone else, which exists for the people to get what they want out of it through defiance, has never prevailed there. The state as a "general treasury" whose citizens are private individuals focusing only on their rights is a weak state in terms of the capacity to assert itself.[68] Such a state does not have support, however paradoxically this does not mean that citizens will cease to expect that the state will take care of them.

We are living in a world of not only expanding individual rights, but also expanding minority rights, and the list of minorities may be very long or infinite. It is in fact growing. Legal conclusions may be reached upon reference to such substantial components of human identity that a lack of respect for them results in the jeopardising of self-respect, awareness of oneself, and human dignity. Such a component may typically be gender, including indefinite or unclear gender (the so-called third gender and transsexualism), race, ethnicity, sexual orientation or religion - i.e. things that are not negotiable, that are not subject to change or compromise. Non-negotiable identity seeking recognition stands in opposition

65 The shift of decision-maker from law-making bodies to courts is also demonstrated in the status of public and political debate. Does it make sense to discuss issues if the result of the discussion cannot be reflected in political decision? Concerning these questions cf. also Glendon, Mary Ann.: *Rights Talk. The Impoverishment of Political Discourse*. New York: The Free Press, 1991.

66 Furet, 2007, p. 281.

67 Arendt, Hannah: *O revoluci.* [*On Revolution*] Praha: Oikoymenh, 2011, p. 118 et seq. In belle-letres this difference is clear in the famous Galsworthy's The Forsyte Saga, where the family lives consistently only for themselves, until Soames' daughter marries a man with political ambitions and aspiration for reform.

68 Public support may strengthen the activities of constitutional bodies: a popular president versus unpopular parliament, a constitutional court punishing the political class, and so on.

to negotiable interests that have at least implicitly a lower position; these are interchangeable. In the US there is a more pronounced emphasis placed on gender and race components of identity, whereas in Europe attention is focused on religious components, generally in relation to Islam.

An issue arises of course at the point where the consequences of a specific identity contradict the general rules that are interpreted only as an expression of identity different from a specific identity (masculine, white, Christian etc.). Assuming that all identities are equally valuable, why should one subordinate to another? There should be an exception to the general rule, which is typically in the case of conflict with special requirements arising from the freedom of expression of religious belief (riding a motorbike in a turban instead of wearing a helmet, or, in connection with the photograph on an ID card, the extent of covering the face, and so on). The latter case is, loosely speaking, a case of deciding between equality before the law and reducing the harshness of a law that has a different effect on various groups, and possibly also a case of comparing rights with public goods. However it is far from being always a zero-sum game.

An alternative consists in creating autonomous legal regimes for different groups defined by cultural identity. This is another variation on personality, mentioned earlier as a medieval feature. There are no exceptions from the general rule, but rather a general rule is absent – there are simply several legal regulations. *M. C. Nussbaum* points to the British model of respect for the autonomy of religious groups in India, including the regulation of status issues and family law. Founders of independent India opposed this autonomy in the name of equality and human dignity, primarily because of the status of women.[69] The good consisting of respect for the identity of the community was opposed by the good of equal respect for individuals.

A common pitfall of both approaches is "confinement" in an identity, which an individual may wish to abandon. The majority, in an effort to achieve tolerance toward the minority, leaves such an individual subject to minority rules

69 Nussbaum, Martha C.: *Personal Laws and Equality: The Case of India*. In: Ginsburg, Tom (ed.): Comparative Constitutional Design. Cambridge: Cambridge University Press, 2012. The British approach was in line with the general model of non-interference unless it is necessary. In relation to other cultural identities it was based on benevolent neutrality: there was no need for a hierarchy because there was an unswerving feeling of British superiority – everything else was secondary. On this topic cf. interesting interpretations of Czech political philosopher P. Barša – Barša, Pavel: *Politická teorie multikulturalismu.* [*Political Theory of Multiculturalism*] Brno: Centrum pro demokracii a kulturu, 1999.

that may not necessarily be advantageous for him. If on the other hand an individual can freely combine the advantages of both general and minority status the original discrimination, which those going before faced, becomes completely inverted.

It was mentioned above that the public space is weakening, and it is necessary to add that this is a shared space. In other words, its participants must feel mutually themselves to be "we" and not "we" and "them." Whereas in the past there were discussions about the fragmentation of political society (political pillars and political camps), now cultural (religious) distinctions are pointed out. And these distinctions may be associated with questioning elementary value consensus, and perhaps also the consensus on the manner of solving disputes.[70] Without such consensus there is not one single society, but rather there are several societies.

IV.2.5 Technological development

Another variable determining the role, strength and possibilities of state consists in technological development.[71] First, it is a challenge for the regulatory capabilities of the state.[72] Second, the internet has created the potential for extensive surveillance by the state of its citizens. Third, the internet provides the same means to non-state entities, which means that the monopoly of state has been broken up. Camera systems, the interception of telephone calls and the monitoring of electronic communications are definitely not the privilege of state. It seems that in Germany in the 1970s this formed part of the discussion on the "death of the state," which was contributed to by terrorism among other things - which, by breaking up the state monopoly on the use of force, endangered the basic

70 G. Sartori distinguishes three levels of consensus in democratic politics: basic (basic values), procedural and policy consensus. From the point of view of democracy he emphasises procedural consensus. For cohesion of the community the most important consensus is that relating to fundamental values and ideas (freedom, equality, human dignity and so on). Cf. Sartori, Giovanni: *Teória demokracie.* [*Theory of Democracy*] Bratislava: Archa, 1993, p. 92 et seq.

71 This is, of course, related also to the above-mentioned nature of public space. The development of the internet allows us to create our own information world without even leaving the home. There is no need to meet someone, to get to know them or to communicate. The importance of the space as such is disappearing. Cf. Bauman, 1999, p. 26 et seq.

72 Including the already mentioned issue of determining the end of life when medicine is capable of substituting the life functions by equipment.

mission of the state, i.e. to ensure security.[73] *W. Reinhard* takes heed of the lack of clarity of this effect when he says that the fight against terrorism has strengthened the state (the great surge) due to obtaining a means for fighting against it and achieving their acceptance.[74] Concern about a state capable of total surveillance later resulted in discussion about the efficient "size" of state.

Not only do states no longer monopolise technical resources for interfering with the privacy of citizens, they also no longer monopolise other activities that used to be related with such technical means. The modern state emerged as a centralistic and centralised state. Contemporary states on the contrary tend toward various forms of decentralisation (Great Britain, Spain, Italy and so on). This is an intra-state component of the multi-level model of governance we have come across in the context of European integration, and possibly also with contemplations of global government. The state, in the sense of a central state, is limited by the transfer of competencies downwards. It does not matter in this context whether this is due to mechanisms of "democratisation through democracy," i.e. decision-making as close to citizens as possible in order to increase their participation - or whether the main goal is only practical decision-making.

IV.2.6 Outsourcing of state

In addition to that, we also see the delegation of public administration to private entities, where it is not clear whether they can do only what they are permitted to do by law (they hold public authority), or whether they can do anything that is not prohibited by law (they are private persons, after all). This does not necessarily only have to apply to civil public administration: for example, in Iraq in addition to "real" American soldiers there were also mercenaries and employees of security agencies. This is a specific case of "outsourcing": the public authority purchases various services on the market instead of the authority rendering the service itself. This however increases the dependence of the public authority on non-state entities.

IV.2.7 Unregulated social authority

Non-state entities will constitute the last item on our list. The idea of a constitutional state is the idea of a state limited by constitutional rules in order

73 Möllers, Christoph: *Der vermisste Leviathan. Staatstheorie in der Bundesrepublik.* Frankfurt am Main: Suhrkamp Verlag, 2008, p. 44 et seq.

74 Reinhard, 2007, pp. 110-111. It will never be a surge comparable to the conditions behind the iron curtain, where the state was at the same time exclusive or dominant employer. Therefore there was no way and nowhere to escape.

to prevent it from degenerating into a tyranny endangering human freedom. Human freedom may be endangered by any authority, not only the state authority. The transfer of authority outside of the state reduces the reach of constitutional regulation.[75] Outside of states, unregulated social authority is growing: in addition to usual (neo)corporativist models there are the activities of multinational corporations that have already been mentioned. In Eastern Europe there is the phenomenon of the so-called oligarchs, and Western Europe is talking about the "Berlusconisation" of politics. These are cases of people so wealthy that what is to them mere "pocket money" exceeds the possibilities of political parties to compete with them in an election campaign in the case that they decide to enter into politics. But even if they do not, they are capable of creating barriers to the economic plans of the government (the movement of investments, media campaigns, corruption and so on). They become a risk factor for the soundness of democracy when they enter into the media market and politics, where they combine various means of influencing the will of the state. *H. McKinders's* idea that whoever controls mass media controls the voters, and whoever controls the voters controls the entire political process, is still relevant.[76] Warning against a concentration of media power was one of the pressing topics of *K. R. Popper* toward the end of his life. He dealt with the topic in his lecture on the occasion of taking on an honorary doctorate of Charles University in Prague. Oligarchs in a certain sense attain a position above the law which sometimes results in the state becoming tempted to get rid of them by means not completely compatible with the ideals of the rule of law. Here the rule of Aristotle applies: if someone defies the average he does not wish to submit to general rules. And so we can finish with a question: Is the state really the biggest danger to human freedom?

V. Partial summary

Before we proceed with individual chapters of analysis, we would like to summarise the factors that seem to limit the authority of the modern state, in comparison with the ideal-typical form of state.

---

75 This is noted by Grimm, 2012, in relation to the transfer of powers to the European Union. It results in an effort to constitutionalise the EU or international community, however such constitutionalisation is often criticised for being only technical in nature: we will find limiting rules, however not necessarily a legitimisation entity.

76 Loewenstein, 1969, p. 361. One of the wealthiest businessmen in the Czech Republic founded a political movement, then purchased several newspapers and a radio station. He was successful in the parliamentary elections and is currently a minister of finance.

1. International law (the number and nature of treaties, enforcement mechanisms, *jus cogens*).
2. Human rights as far as these entitle the international community to interfere in the internal affairs of a state.
3. European law and European integration in general (multi-level governance), in particular in the situation of conflict of interest of individual tiers.
4. Globalisation.
5. Estrangement of citizens from the state and its representatives.
6. Human rights as a limit of established authority.
7. The strengthening of the judicial branch at the expense of the political branches.
8. Conversion of political requirements into legal (rights policy, rights rhetoric).
9. Policy of protecting (minority) identity.
10. Development of technologies.
11. The strengthening of unregulated social authority.

Pavel Ondřejek

International law limits on state power. Limitation of state power by international law at the beginning of the 21st century

Modern international law, as it emerged at the end of the Thirty Years' War, gave rise to conditions for the co-existence and co-operation of states.[1] During this period a purely power-based view of international relations underwent a transformation and gradually the concepts of state sovereignty, international liability and other important attributes of international law developed. Whenever speaking about the sovereignty of states it is necessary to remember that this is a relative concept, as even sovereign states were limited by obligations that they took on within their autonomous law-making processes.[2]

An important development in international law commenced after the Second World War (for *L. Weinrib* this period was characterised by its acknowledgment of the innate human dignity of every person without exception and a focus of the legal order on human rights and natural law values; she refers to this as the "*post-war paradigm*").[3] Within international law the first catalogues of human rights were adopted as well; the importance of these rights was then further elaborated by the judgments of the International Court of Justice,[4] as well as the decisions

---

1 Shaw, Malcolm N.: *International Law*. 6th ed., Cambridge: Cambridge University Press, 2008, p. 1282. In Czech literature the formation of international law from the perspective of theory of law is described by P. Maršálek - Maršálek, Pavel: *Právo a společnost*. [*Law and Society*]. Praha: Auditorium, 2008, p. 89 et seq.

2 In Czech academic literature the issue of state sovereignty is dealt with in detail by the main author of this monograph. Kysela, Jan: *Ústava mezi právem a politikou. Úvod do ústavní teorie.* [*Constitution between Law and Politics. An Introduction to Constitutional Theory*]. Praha: Leges, 2014, pp. 138-197.

3 Weinrib, Lorraine E.: *Postwar Paradigm and American Exceptionalism*. In: Choudhry, Sujit (ed.): *The Migration of Constitutional Ideas*. Cambridge: Cambridge University Press, 2006, p. 86.

4 The very first judgment of this court: the Corfu Channel case (United Kingdom v. Albania) of 1949 deals with the issues of human rights. The judgment of the International Court of Justice is available at http://www.icj-cij.org/ and its commentary is available for example in Bedi, Shiv: *The Development of Human Rights Law by the Judges of the International Court of Justice*. Oxford: Hart Publishing, 2007, pp. 105-108.

of other emerging judicial and quasi-judicial bodies. The importance of human rights obligations arising from international law increased significantly after the International Court of Justice constructed the doctrine of obligations of states *erga omnes*, on which human rights are based.[5] In addition to these obligations the doctrine of international law acknowledges a special category of rules having more legal force than other rules, with the result that such rules are binding on states irrespective of whether they express a willingness to be bound by them – so-called *jus cogens*.[6]

It thus becomes clear that the effect of various sources of international law on states varies. International agreements bind those states that express their will to be bound by them; the rules of customary international law apply to states that acknowledge them as legally binding; while *jus cogens* rules apply peremptorily, irrespective of the will of states. According to some authors they are a manifestation of the process of constitutionalisation of international law.[7]

The principle of the sovereign equality of states is usually considered the basic principle for the functioning of international law in terms of the position of states.[8] Such equality, as already indicated in the introduction, does not have the same parameters as the equality of citizens of a state before the law. This is exemplified by the construction of certain powers of the permanent members of the United Nations Security Council. The arrangement is understandable, considering the necessity to deal with the post-war situation. As a result of a bipolar

5 The judgment in Barcelona Traction, Light and Power Co, Ltd. (Belgium v. Spain) from 5 February 1970, available at http://www.icj-cij.org/. For a commentary see Bedi, pp. 157-161.

6 Shaw, 2008, p. 124.

7 The phenomenon of constitutionalisation of international law as interpreted by J. Klabbers does not imply the creation of global constitutionalism, nor the construction of a constitutional order similar to that of a state. In his interpretation Klabbers points out that international law gradually adopts certain elements that are characteristic of modern constitutionalism on the level of states (the division of power in international organisations, the *rule of law* doctrine, guaranteed human rights, procedural rights, and guaranteed due process before international courts, and so on) – see Klabbers, Jan, Peters, Anne, Ulfstein, Geir: *The Constitutionalization of International Law*. Oxford: Oxford University Press, 2009, p. 4. The starting point is the theory of constitutionalism as a limitation of public power (*limiting government*) instead of constitutionalism as a theory of the basis of public power (*foundational constitutionalism*) – see also Krisch, Nico: *Beyond Constitutionalism. The Pluralist Structure of Postnational Law*. Oxford: Oxford University Press, 2010, p. 40 et seq.

8 Shaw, 2008, p. 214.

division of the world it became clear in the early years following 1945 that the idea of wide international co-operation was not realistic. After the collapse of the Eastern Bloc, actual co-operation among states started to increase primarily in the field of economics. The dynamically developing forms of co-operation caused various authors to contemplate more radical changes of international law. *N. Krisch* writes about *post-national law*, which is characterised by closer formal and informal overlapping of international and national regulatory and decision-making mechanisms.[9] Other authors speak in a similar context about globalised law,[10] or transnational law.[11] Even these characteristics however cannot blur the differences which continue to exist between the systems of international and national law: the absence of heteronomous rule-making, an enforcement system influenced not only by law but also by political decision-making, with a dominant role played by five permanent members of the United Nations Security Council, and in many cases the nonexistence of an obligatory jurisdiction of courts as bodies deciding disputes over applicable law.[12]

Since the Second World War we have witnessed changes in public power within states as well as changes within the entire international community. It may seem that these processes should complement each other as they are directed toward the same goals. This, however, does not happen in some cases (as will be detailed below). We see the reasons for this in the growing efficiency of international regulation, as a result of which national mechanisms and political processes often become side-tracked. This may result in tension between constitutional and international law.[13]

The purpose of this chapter is to describe in more detail selected limits on state power which originate from international law. In order to understand these limits we focus at the beginning on changes in international law from the point

---

9 Krisch, 2010, p. 4.

10 Berman, Paul Schiff: *From International Law to Law and Globalization*. Columbia Journal of Transnational Law 43, 2004-2005.

11 Koh, Harold Hongju: *Transnational Legal Process*. Nebraska Law Review 75, 1996, pp. 181-207.

12 Rosenne, Shabai: *Three Central Elements in Modern International Law*. In: Rosenne, Shabtai: *Essays on International Law and Practice*. Leiden, Boston: Martinus Nijhoff Publishers, 2007, p. 621. Similar ideas concerning international law are expressed by H. L. A. Hart. Hart, H. L. A.: *The Concept of Law*. 2nd ed., Oxford: Clarendon Press, 1994, 213 et seq.

13 Krisch, 2010, p. 3. Perhaps the most obvious example is the law of the European Union, which is dealt with in chapter 3. International law examples are described at the end of this chapter.

of view of the changing sources of its legitimacy, and then proceed to discuss the status of judicial and quasi-judicial bodies. Last but not least, we look at changes in international law regulation and its impact on national legal orders.

Even though it is the aim of this chapter to describe the limits on state power, it becomes clear, from the above brief description of the development of post-war international law, that this system has maintained certain remnants of the Concert of Great Powers. It is practically impossible for the international community to enforce the international obligations of the permanent members of the United Nations Security Council using mechanisms of international law. The impact of obligations arising from international law therefore differs in the case of individual states. The extent to which states are limited by international law obligations is less in the case of states that can utilise their exclusive position in specific international organisations to further their own objectives (this may be exemplified by dominant army and political groupings from the period of the Cold War, of which still exists the North Atlantic Treaty Organisation, with a dominant role played by the USA). Such states may use international law to strengthen (rather than to limit) their own power.

I. Changing sources of legitimacy of international law

There is no consensus among different authors on the definition of the concept of legitimacy which we refer to in this chapter. Authors generally agree that there are several contexts and therefore also several meanings of the concept of *legitimacy*.[14] When assessing legitimacy from a legal point of view the primary issue is the justification of validity of a certain legal rule, or law as a whole.[15] Legitimacy therefore creates a link between power and law.[16] In international law, as opposed to national law, there is stronger relation between the legitimacy of law and the legitimacy of institutions making the law (in cases when the rule-makers are not the states themselves).[17]

---

14 For example J. Klabbers uses examples of international law to describe input legitimacy and output legitimacy, substantive law and procedural legitimacy – see Klabbers, Peters, Ulfstein, 2009, p. 37 et seq.

15 Gerloch, Aleš: *Teorie práva*. [*Legal Theory*]. 6th ed., Plzeň: Aleš Čeněk, 2013, p. 256.

16 Shaw, 2008, p. 62.

17 Cf. Buchanan, Allen: *Legitimacy of International Law*. In: Besson, Samantha, Tasioulas, John (eds.): *The Philosophy of International Law*. Oxford: Oxford University Press, 2010, p. 80.

Traditional international law is characterised as law created by sovereign states, without which it could never have come into existence.[18] International law bases the legitimacy of its sources, including both international agreements and international customs, on the consent of states.[19]

The positivist idea that everything legal is legitimate collapsed when in the 20th century law became a crime, using the words of *J. Přibáň*.[20] The role of human rights in international law has been growing since the end of the Second World War, and more intensely since the beginning of the 21st century. The traditional paradigm of this legal system, characterised by the co-operation of sovereign states in some cases, yields to ensuring the rule of law and guarantees in the field of human rights protection irrespective of the consent of a given state.[21] Human rights may constitute an important source of legitimacy in international law similarly as in national law.

We will attempt to describe the changing sources of legitimacy of international law using the example of criticism of UN Security Council resolutions imposing sanctions on individuals supporting terrorism.

UN sanctions mechanisms existed already at the time of the Cold War, even though they were imposed only to a relatively limited extent (the only examples of that time were sanctions against Rhodesia in 1966 and against the Republic of South Africa in 1977).[22] Following experience with the negative consequences of sanctions against Yugoslavia, Haiti and Iraq at the beginning of the 1990s, which resulted in the economic isolation of these countries and related adverse effects on the civilian populations, the entire system of sanctions was criticised even by UN officials themselves. The sanctions mechanism was later converted into a form of so-called *targeted sanctions*, or using a euphemism, *smart sanctions*, imposed more frequently after 11 September 2001, against persons who

---

18 Wolfrum, Rüdiger: *Legitimacy and International Law from a Legal Perspective: Some Introductory Considerations*. In: Wolfrum, Rüdiger / Röben, Volcker: *Legitimacy and International Law. Beiträge zum auslandischen öffentlichen Recht und Völkerrecht*. Vol. 194, Berlin, Heidelberg, New York: Springer, 2008, p. 3.

19 Ibid., p. 6.

20 Přibáň, Jiří: *Lesk a bída právního pozitivismu*. [The Splendors and Miseries of Legal Positivism] In: Přibáň, Jiří, Holländer, Pavel et al.: *Právo a dobro v ústavní demokracii*. [*The Law and the Good in Constitutional Democracy*]. Praha: Sociologické nakladatelství, 2011, p. 29.

21 Cf. Tamanaha, Brian: *On the Rule of Law: History, Politics, Theory*. Cambridge: Cambridge University Press, 2004, p. 127 et seq.

22 Farrall, Jeremy M.: *United Nations Sanctions and the Rule of Law*. Cambridge: Cambridge University Press, 2007, p. 3.

were reasonably suspected of having a connection with a terrorist organisation.[23] This new type of sanctions did not have a negative impact on the general population of a state, since the sanctions were targeted at specific persons who were restricted from travelling abroad and whose property was seized.[24]

The measures of the Security Council against individuals suspected of connection with terrorist groups have been widely discussed in recent years in Europe as well as in other countries of the world,[25] which apply their own human rights standards regarding implementation measures of UN Security Council resolutions.

In the European Union the dispute concerning the applicability of human rights standards against persons affected by sanctions of the UN culminated in a case before the Court of Justice of the EU regarding the complaint of a citizen of Saudi Arabia, *Yassin Abdullah Kadi*, who challenged a secondary act of EU law implementing a resolution of the UN Security Council.[26] Two years before the first judgment of the Court of Justice of the EU in the case of *Kadi*, the UN made partial modifications to procedural guarantees for persons subject to sanction mechanisms on the basis of Security Council Resolution 1267 (which included persons associated with the Taliban, Al-Quaeda and Usama bin Laden). The UN Secretariat established a contact point whereby individuals may lodge a complaint against their being listed by the Sanctions Committee under abovementioned resolution 1267. Every complaint is then passed on to the state of which the individual is a citizen, and that state submits the complaint to the state which proposed listing the individual. The Sanctions Committee may vote on

---

23 Krisch, 2010, p. 155.

24 Farrall, 2007, p. 219. This type of sanction was used also at the beginning of the 21st century by states and international organisations (e.g. sanctions against the representatives of Ukraine or Russia from the part of EU or the USA).

25 A well-known example is the decision of the Federal Court of Canada of 4 June 2009 in the case *Abousfian Abdelrazik v.Canada (Ministry of Foreign Affairs)*, 2009 FC 580, in which the Canadian federal judge compared the situation of a listed person to that of Josef K. in Kafka's *The Trial*: "*who awakens one morning and, for reasons never revealed to him or the reader, is arrested and prosecuted for an unspecified crime.*" – quoted from Krisch, 2010, p. 159.

26 Judgment of the Court of Justice of 3 September 2008 – joined cases C-402/05 P and C-415/05 P *Yassin Abdullah Kadi and Al-Barakaat International Foundation v. Council and Commission*, judgment of the Court of Justice of 18 July 2013 – joined cases C-584/10 P, C-593/10 P and C-595/10 P *European Commission et al. v. Yassin Abdullah Kadi (Kadi II judgment)*.

withdrawing the person's name from the list upon the request of any state.[27] As becomes clear from the brief description of the process of removing a person from the list of the Sanctions Committee, with the exception of the actual lodging of the complaint by the individual, the entire subsequent process is subject to the voting of states represented in this committee and is therefore far from review by an independent judicial body.

The very slight progress toward strengthening the procedural rights of persons accused of association with terrorist groups is understandable from the point of view of international politics. Allowing the defence of such persons logically provokes disapproval on the part of the Security Council, since such defence could be perceived as legitimising the acts of terrorists and could also create space for the public justification of terrorist acts.[28] From the point of view of the Court of Justice of the EU even after some minor changes to the process of removing persons from the sanctions list,[29] such process is not deemed to be compliant with the standards of human rights in the EU.[30]

The above example may be viewed from various angles. This is why we chose it as an illustration of the expanding sources of legitimacy of international law, which may operate in a contradictory manner such as in this case (where legitimacy on the grounds of human rights standards on the one hand and on the grounds of the consensus of states on the other hand is concerned). It is clear

---

27 For details see Farrall, 2007, p. 222.

28 Ibid., p. 219.

29 Cf. Krisch, 2010, p. 159.

30 Para. 135 of the judgment of 18th July 2013 (*Kadi II*) states: "*It follows from the criteria analysed above that, for the rights of the defence and the right to effective judicial protection to be respected first, the competent European Union authority must (i) disclose to the person concerned the summary of reasons provided by the Sanctions Committee which is the basis for listing or maintaining the listing of that person's name in Annex I to Regulation No 881/2002, (ii) enable him effectively to make known his observations on that subject and (iii) examine, carefully and impartially, whether the reasons alleged are well founded, in the light of the observations presented by that person and any exculpatory evidence that may be produced by him.*" After a detailed review of individual facts justifying listing Y. A.Kadi on the sanctions list of the above-mentioned regulation the Court of Justice of the EU summarises as follows: "*It follows, from the analysis set out in … this judgment, that none of the allegations presented against Mr Kadi in the summary provided by the Sanctions Committee are such as to justify the adoption, at European Union level, of restrictive measures against him, either because the statement of reasons is insufficient, or because information or evidence which might substantiate the reason concerned, in the face of detailed rebuttals submitted by the party concerned, is lacking.*"

though that the consensus of states in current international law does not constitute sufficient conditions for the legitimacy of any rule of international law.[31]

II. International law as a system of evaluation of compliance with general principles

International law is not only a system assessed from the point of view of compliance with standards existing in individual states (most often standards of human rights protection). Since international law itself creates its own standards it may also become an assessing system that evaluates compliance with the standards of the legal systems of the states themselves.

In these cases it is possible to distinguish enforcement of the implementation of obligations accepted by states. In such a case the role of international law is less controversial as it is only a consequence of the existence of an international law obligation.[32] By contrast, those cases where international standards influence national law directly without such effect resulting from preceding international obligations of the state may be deemed more controversial. Here we will focus primarily on these latter cases, as they limit states in a more considerable manner because the state cannot influence these standards.

The first example of this type is the penetration of doctrines that originate from or are more often applied in the judgments of international courts into the national legal orders of states which did not previously apply such doctrines. This process is often subject to controversy regarding the limits to the acceptance of foreign doctrines.[33] In Europe the situation may be illustrated by

---

31 Buchanan, 2010, pp. 92-93.

32 However, even in this respect the role of states as "masters of treaties" is no longer fully performed. The powers of control are often held by bodies of international organisations which have been vested with individual powers of control by states. The role of international non-governmental organisations that assess whether states comply with international standards (such as Transparency International, Human Rights Watch, Oxfam International, Amnesty International and so on) keeps growing. Even though their role in the implementation of human rights is appreciable, there are also critical comments concerning the potential abuse of such organisations in promoting particular interests as well as their lack of accountability – see Alston, Philip, Goodman, Ryan: *International Human Rights*. Oxford: Oxford University Press, 2013, p. 1503 et seq.

33 A classic example is the doctrine of exceptionalism in US doctrine – Ignatieff, Michael (ed.): *American Exceptionalism and Human Rights*. Princeton: Princeton University Press, 2005.

discussions on taking on doctrines applied by the European Court of Human Rights or the Court of Justice of the European Union, and more specifically by discussions concerning application of the principle of proportionality in disputes involving human rights in the UK. Traditionally the doctrine of proportionality in this legal system was rejected by both British courts and jurisprudence in purely national disputes. The doctrine was considered a very strict model of review, contradictory to the tradition of the sovereignty of British parliament.[34] In recent years though it seems not to be sustainable any longer for British courts to apply to similar disputes two different standards with a different intensity of review depending on whether the procedure involves a European element or not.[35] The British example clearly shows that the influence of international doctrines goes well beyond a mere model for comparison or the "transplanting" of foreign theories operating exclusively through the force of convincing arguments.

Another example of such influence of international doctrines also concerns the international law of human rights. It consists in indirect political pressure in cases where individual states breach international standards in respect of these rights. It would certainly be possible to find many examples of the violation of international human rights standards in non-democratic states, however the importance of such political pressure is best exemplified by a situation where the state that fails to comply with the human rights standard is the most powerful state in the world.

In the case of *Medellín v. Texas*[36] the Supreme Court of the United States excluded any direct effect of the Vienna Convention on Consular Relations in the national law of the US and stated that the judgment of the International Court

---

34 British courts traditionally reviewed the rationality of decisions of an administrative body rather than strict proportionality. Cf. the details in Ondřejek, Pavel: *Princip proporcionality a jeho role při interpretaci základních práv a svobod.* [*The Principle of Proportionality and Its Role in the Interpretation of Fundamental Rights and Freedoms*]. Praha: Leges, 2012, p. 181 et seq. commenting on the precedent in this field: *Associated Provincial Picture Houses Ltd. v. Wednesbury Corp.* (1948) 1 KB 223.

35 Craig, Paul: *Unreasonableness and Proportionality in UK Law*. In: Ellis, Evelyn (ed.): *The Principle of Proportionality in the Laws of Europe*. Oxford: Hart Publishing, 1999, p. 105. The European element may be related to both the application of the Convention for the Protection of Human Rights and Fundamental Freedoms, and the law of the European Union. Both these systems use the principle of proportionality.

36 Judgment of the Supreme Court of the US from 25th March 2008 in the case of *Medellín v. Texas* 128 S.Ct. 1346 (2008).

of Justice has no effect on the national proceedings at that time in progress. This dispute gave rise to criticism of the US system of criminal law.

The facts of the case were as follows: *José Ernesto Medellín*, a Mexican citizen who confessed to committing the murder of two girls in Texas, was sentenced by a court in Texas to undergo the death penalty. At the time of committing the crime the convict was 18 years old. After being arrested he was advised of his rights however he was not informed of the fact that he was entitled to have the consular office of Mexico informed of his arrest under Article 36 of the Vienna Convention on Consular Relations. After his conviction *J. E. Medellín* appealed, among other things also on the grounds of violation of the Vienna Convention on Consular Relations.[37]

In parallel with this national dispute in 2003 Mexico filed an application to the International Court of Justice in the Hague against the US because in the case of *Medellín* and 50 other cases the US did not respect the duty arising from the Vienna Convention on Consular Relations. The International Court of Justice decided in 2004 in favour of Mexico and in the case known as *Avena* ordered, among other things, a review of the judgments and sentences in 51 cases of citizens of Mexico, including that of *J. E. Medellín*.[38] The USA reacted to the decision of the International Court of Justice by renouncing the Optional Protocol to the Vienna Convention on Consular Relations, which contains a provision on the obligatory jurisdiction of the International Court of Justice in disputes arising from the said convention.[39]

The subsequent dispute before the US courts started as an appeal in a criminal case but turned into a test case against the US criminal system which permits the death penalty;[40] in this particular case this fact was at least as important as the issues of US compliance with international law obligations.

The judgment of the Supreme Court of the United States in *Medellín v. Texas* confirmed that the obligations arising from the Vienna Convention on Consular Relations and from the Statute of the International Court of Justice are not directly applicable and that the decision of the International Court of Justice has

---

37 McGuinness, Margaret: *Three Narratives of Medellín v. Texas*. Suffolk Transnational Law Review 31, 2007-2008, p. 228.

38 Judgment of the International Court of Justice of March 31, 2004 in the case of Mexico v. United States of America *Avena and other Mexican nationals*), available at http://www.icj-cij.org/docket/files/128/8188.pdf.

39 McGuinness, Margaret: *Medellín v. Texas, 128 S.Ct. 1436 (2008). Case Comment.* American Journal of International Law 102, 2008, p. 623.

40 McGuinness, 2007-2008, p. 228.

no influence on US criminal proceedings. Also because of that *J. E. Medellín's* defence was not successful and he was executed in August 2008.[41] This meant that the USA did not comply with the judgment of the International Court of Justice in the above-mentioned case of *Avena and other Mexican nationals* (Mexico against the United States), which provoked a wave of criticism.

Even though it is not possible to argue that the death penalty is a violation of international law, certain aspects of the US criminal justice are subject to criticism by non-governmental organisations as well as some judicial bodies. In the case of *Soering,*[42] the European Court of Human Rights considered the extradition of a German citizen to the US, where he might be sentenced to death, to be a violation of Article 3 of the Convention for the Protection of Human Rights and Fundamental Freedoms (prohibition of torture). The reason for such decision of the European Court of Human Rights did not subsist in the possibility of *Mr. Soering* being sentenced to death, but rather on the grounds of the practice in the US of maintaining long waiting times between conviction and execution (the so-called *death row phenomenon*).[43]

With respect to the fact that the decision of the international court in the case of *Medellín* was not reflected in the US courts, we may in this case see a certain parallel with the above-mentioned decision of the European Court of Justice in the case of *Kadí*. In both cases the supremacy of international law over the legal system in which the case was decided (in the case of *Medellín* US law, in the case of *Kadí* Community law),[44] was rejected. The US legal system may be contrasted

---

41 Application instituting proceedings: Request for the interpretation of the judgment of 31 March 2004 in the case concerning *Avena and other Mexican nationals* (*Mexico v. United States of America*) of 5 June 2008, available at http://www.icj-cij.org/docket/files/139/14582.pdf, p. 28.

42 Judgment of the European Court of Human Rights of 7 July 1989 *Soering v. United Kingdom* (Application No. 14038/88).

43 De Wet, Erika: *The Emergence of an International and Regional Value System*. Leiden Journal of International Law 19, 2006, p. 619. The authors of a representative Czech commentary on the Convention for the Protection of Human Rights and Fundamental Freedoms speak about "death row syndrome" – see Kmec, Jiří, Kosař, David, Kratochvíl, Jan, Bobek, Michal: *Evropská úmluva o lidských právech. Komentář*. [*European Convention on Human Rights. A Commentary*]. Praha: C. H. Beck, 2012, p. 415. The criticism in this case as well as in other cases also objected to sentencing juvenile offenders to death.

44 European law may be considered as generally more open toward international law (even though in EU law too there are cases of rejection of the direct effect of international treaties – extensively discussed regarding the effect of WTO law) – cf. Von

with the successful enforcement of EU law or the system of the Convention of the Council of Europe for the Protection of Human Rights and Fundamental Freedoms within the member states of these respective international entities. As we will show below, the opinions of the US courts and the Court of Justice of the EU cannot be deemed *a priori* illegitimate, yet at the same time it would be a mistake to consider the current international law as unenforceable.

The pressure to enforce international standards of human rights may be exerted also indirectly, not exclusively through denunciatory judgments. The expressed disagreement with the decision in *Medellín* has created and will continue to create pressure on the US criminal system and may result in important changes in the society.[45]

III. Growing importance of international institutions and the international judiciary in particular

The main reason for the formation of international organisations traditionally consisted in the fact that certain forms of regulation were either impossible to be introduced on a national level, or it was inefficient to introduce them on a national level.[46] In the course of the 20th century international organisations improved in many respects the efficiency of their activities and became less dependent on their member states.

Requirements for efficient decision-making resulted in numerous international organisations in the elimination of unanimous decision-making, or even in the circumvention of national constitutional procedures for the approval of changes to international treaties.

It is logical that the more contracting states an international organisation has, the more complicated the adoption of changes in basic documents becomes, because every individual state has a veto with respect to the proposed changes.

Bogdandy, Armin: *Pluralism, direct effect, and the ultimate say: On the relationship between international and domestic constitutional law.* International Journal of Constitutional Law 6(3&4), 2008, p. 405.

45 Cf. the decision of 17 May 2010 in the case of Graham v. Florida 560 U.S. 2010, in which the Supreme Court declared unconstitutional the administration of life imprisonment without parole for an offence not amounting to the intentional killing of a person committed by juvenile offenders. See Cohen-Eliya, Moshe, Porat, Iddo: *Proportionality and Constitutional Culture.* Cambridge: Cambridge University Press, 2012, p. 89.

46 Klabbers, Peters, Ulfstein, 2009, p. 45.

Recently the International Organisation for Migration (IOM) changed the manner of passing amendments to its founding treaty (Constitution). The original provision stipulated that amendments to the Constitution would enter into force after approval by two thirds of members of the IOM Council and at the same time two thirds of member states upon approval in constitutional procedures, with the exception of cases where the amendments involved new obligations for member states. In such a case these amendments entered into force only with respect to those member states that approved the amendments.

A reviewed IOM Constitution from the year 1998, which entered into force at the end of 2013, contains an amended rule under which amendments to the IOM Constitution involving major changes to the IOM Constitution or new obligations for member states enter into force upon adoption by two thirds of members of the IOM Council and the consent of two thirds of its member states in compliance with their national regulations. Other changes are adopted by a two-thirds majority of votes in the IOM Council. Therefore it is realistically possible that new obligations might be imposed on states without the states approving such obligations on an international or national level. This may involve rather substantial obligations, such as a change to the sources of funding of the international organisation or the scope of its privileges and immunities.

It remains to be answered whether accepting such regulation on an international level constitutes a transfer of powers from a state to a supranational body or not, and if so, under what conditions such a transfer should happen. This relates to the issue of democratic legitimacy, which should form the basis of the functioning of public power.

Another phenomenon resulting in the weakening of the modern state by international entities consists in emancipation from state power. The fact that the number of international institutions is growing may in some cases be justified by the advantages of creating such institutions as international law entities rather than forming legal entities under national law. This involves primarily the awarded privileges and immunities on the basis of treaties with the state on whose territory the international entity has its headquarters and with other states (which is advantageous both from an economic and political point of view). This may be illustrated by the example of educational institutions. Recently the International Anti-Corruption Academy was formed as an international organisation with its headquarters in Austrian Laxenburg; another example from the past is the European University Institute (an organisation formed on the basis of an international treaty from 1972 by the then Member States of the European Communities).

A separate example perceived as a model for building an international organisation on a completely different basis is the formation and development of the European Communities.[47] The major change was that the institutions themselves under European law stipulated and enforced the conditions of direct effect and the supremacy of EC legal rules over the legal order of its Member States. When describing this phenomenon *Charles Leben* speaks about successful international law.[48]

A strengthening of the roles of international organisations is also related to dynamic development of the international judiciary.[49] In his analysis of international tribunals *Cesare Romano* states as the principal reasons for this phenomenon the fall of the Iron Curtain and the related end of distrust in international courts on the part of Eastern Bloc states, the development of international regional economic organisations, a growing role of non-state actors in international relations, and finally procedural changes enabling national courts to initiate proceedings before international courts concerning the interpretation of international treaties.[50]

The development of international judiciary goes hand in hand with expanding obligations of states arising from international treaties (see below), which naturally results in the international courts deciding, in addition to traditional disputes between two states (for example border disputes), also many other issues that such courts formerly did not deal with (this may involve disputes initiated by natural persons or legal entities seeking to enforce their rights against states, or for example disputes concerning the environmental impact of specific measures taken by a state).[51]

It is impossible to separate the requirements for decisions in international relations disputes from the issues of legitimacy of supranational judicial bodies.

---

47 The perspective of political aspects of European integration up until 1990 is presented by J. Weiler using the economic categories of "Exit" and "Voice" developed in the work of Albert Hirschman: Weiler, J. H. H.: *The Transformation of Europe.* Yale Law Journal 100, 1990-1991, p. 2410 et seq.

48 Leben, Charles: *Hans Kelsen and the Advancement of International Law.* European Journal of International Law 9, 1998, p. 298.

49 For the purposes of this analysis we will not deal with arbitration tribunals whose activities only to a limited extent resemble the functions of permanent international courts of justice.

50 Romano, Cesare: *The Proliferation of International Judicial Bodies: the Pieces of the Puzzle. New York University Journal of International Law and Politics* 31, 1998-1999, p. 728 et seq.

51 Klabbers, Peters, Ulfstein, 2009, p. 126.

A pluralist view of the situations of conflict between international and national courts over direct effect or an internationally-compliant interpretation of national law leads *A. von Bogdandy* to the conclusion that international courts should leave these issues to the decisions of national constitutional courts, because constitutional courts, at least in liberal democracies, have a higher level of legitimacy.[52]

In spite of all the changes in international law since the end of the Second World War it is still not possible to claim that all disputes on an international level must be decided by courts; in sensitive issues there should be room left for a political solution.[53] In certain issues of international relations a dyadic model of dispute resolution prevails over the triadic one.

IV. International obligations of the state and the effect of international law in national law

The role and effect of international law was for a long time affected by discussions concerning the relationship between international and national law. Legal positivists at the turn of the 20th century were generally of the opinion that both systems are strictly separate, and hence took the stance of legal dualism, because, among other things, reflections on the penetration of international law into national legal systems were contradictory to the concept of state sovereignty at that time.[54] Later *H. Kelsen*, who represents normative legal theory, argued in favour of a monistic theory of relationship between these normative systems, where with reference to a tiered structure of legal order he understands international and national law as a monistic system with the supremacy of international law.[55]

Contemporary reflections on the relationship between international and national law increasingly incline toward pluralist models. For example *A. von Bogdandy* considers reflections on monism and dualism to be obsolete, because

52 Von Bogdandy, 2008, p. 403.

53 Kinsbury, Benedict: *Foreword: Is the Proliferation of International Courts and Tribunals a Systemic Problem?* New York University Journal of International Law and Policy, vol. 31, 1998-1999, pp. 695 – 696. See also in Malíř, Jan: *Judicialization of international relations: Do international courts matter?* The Lawyer Quaterly 3 (3), 2013.

54 Shaw, 2008, p. 131.

55 "... *It is necessary to understand international law as a legal order standing above the state legal orders and surrounding them to form a single universal community; which theoretically guarantees the integrity of law in the system of individual legal tiers layered one above the other.*"– Kelsen, Hans: *Ryzí nauka právní.* [*The Pure Theory of Law*] Brno, Praha: Orbis, 1933, p. 37.

there is a growing trend toward a *coupling* of both legal systems taking place at the level of political institutions when creating the law, as well as at the level of administrative and judicial institutions when applying the law.[56] *In the application of law* this phenomenon becomes manifest for example in the penetration of doctrines recognised by international courts within the interpretation of national catalogues of human rights. *At the level of rule-making* it is possible to mention the example of rules of international organisations regulating air traffic. To take the example of the Czech legal order, these rules are directly applicable, and the reason for their national binding effect is the law.[57] Consent to such rules is expressed on behalf of the Czech Republic by representatives delegated as members of bodies of international organisations. With respect to the possible weakening of democratic control processes it makes sense to explore in more detail the relation between the delegated representative and political representation (for example the existence and compliance with the mandate; the member of the government who approved the mandate is accountable for this to the parliament). Such questions have so far attracted only very limited attention in spite of the fact that the absence of accountability results in the delegitimising and therefore weakening of state power.

The growing importance of functions that are delegated by the state to the supranational level provoke reactions in relation to the democratic control of transfer and exercise of such powers. This is why the constitutions of many states (European ones in particular) have started to include a category of international treaties enabling the transfer of powers to a supranational entity. This category of treaties appears in West Europe states in the context of integration into the European Communities as early as the end of the Second World War.[58] A similar

---

56 Von Bogdandy, 2008, p. 401.

57 Cf. Section 102 (2) of Act No. 49/1997 Sb., to regulate civil aviation, as amended, which stipulates as follows: (2) Airport and aviation building operators, persons authorised to operate aviation services, operators of aviation activities and other persons involved in civil aviation are obliged to comply with aviation rules issued in accordance with international treaties, that form part of the legal order, by (a) the International Organisation for Civil Aviation, (b) Joint Aviation Authorities under European Communities regulations and (c) the European organisation for the safety of air navigation EUROCONTROL, in the wording adopted by the Czech Republic represented by the Ministry of Transport. The rules are published in Aeronautical Information Publication and are available at the Ministry of Transport and the Authority.

58 Kokott, Juliane: *The Basic Law at 60 – From 1949 to 2009: The Basic Law and Supranational Integration*. German Law Journal 11(1), 2010, p. 104.

provision has existed in the Czech Republic since 2002 and was originally intended for integration into the EU. Later this process of national approval of international treaties was applied also in the case of adoption of the Rome Statute of the International Criminal Court in 2009.[59]

There is a question, which has already been identified in Czech specialist literature, whether the group of treaties transferring powers from the bodies of the Czech Republic to international organisations or institutions might in fact be wider. It is possible to mention the above example of rules of international organisations in civil aviation.[60] Doubts may arise in relation to the simplified process of adopting changes typical of various international treaties in environmental protection.[61]

The number of various "simplified" approval processes is growing at a similar pace to the growing number of international integration treaties which transfer certain more or less important powers to international institutions. This development is not only an invitation to consider the extent to which states are willing to limit their powers in favour of supranational bodies, but primarily to reflect on institutional guarantees of control over the exercise of such powers.

---

59 Print reference no. 423, 5th term of the Chamber of Deputies of the Parliament of the Czech Republic available at www.psp.cz.

60 Another example mentioned by J. Kysela and Š. Hůlka is the European Agreement concerning the International Carriage of Dangerous Goods by Inland Waterways (ADN Agreement), under which harmonising rules are adopted by the supranational body in a procedure which enables such rules to be binding also on contracting parties that did not consent to them. Kysela, Jan, Hůlka, Štěpán: *Mezinárodní smlouvy – jejich klasifikace, sjednávání, ratifikace a právní účinky.* [International Treaties – Their Classification, Negotiation, Ratification and Legal Effects]. Právní rozhledy 6, 2005, pp. 198-199.

61 Annexes to these treaties contain for example a list of protected animals or a list of hazardous chemical substances. We may mention as an example the Rotterdam Convention of the Prior Written Consent Procedure for Certain Chemicals and Pesticides in International Trade (so called Rotterdam Convention) which contains in Annex III a list of these hazardous substances which is regularly expanded by decisions of the executive body of this Convention. The rule for entry into force of the updated list of substances in Annex III is different from the rule applicable to entry into force of changes to other parts of this convention: a change in Annex III is approved by consensus at a Conference of the Parties and enters into force on the day identified in the decision. Change approved in the course of 6th Meeting of the Conference of the Parties in Geneva on 10th May 2013 entered into force on 10th August 2013, however this change of the annex was still debated in the Parliament of the Czech Republic in May 2014.

Jan Grinc, Jana Ondřejková

The State and the European Union

I. Transformations of the state and its importance within the European Union

European integration counts among the most important historic movements of our times. The European Union has been significantly transforming the very fundaments of the organisation and functioning of the institutions of its Member States. Therefore, European integration falls within the wider framework of globalisation and other phenomena related to the "hollowing out" of the state - which still commands the strongest means of power, including a monopoly on legal violence, but the scope of its real power has been narrowing and it cedes a range of its decisions to other entities.[1]

Unlike many other manifestations of globalisation, European integration is a desired and controlled phenomenon. It was established to ensure prosperity and peaceful co-operation among the states of post-war Europe and the welfare of their citizens. The path leading to this aim was to be the self-limitation of states and their submission to common decisions, which conformed to the post-war development of international law. Although the European integration was conceived as an idea of federalisation, it was created as a functionalist project of supranational economic regulation, and has only gradually grown into other areas where the Member States considered it beneficial to act jointly.[2] All the subsequent integration steps were connected with conferring new competences upon the European level, and with the deepening or widening of competences that had already been conferred. At the same time, many features functionally equivalent to federalism have developed within the institutional and legal framework of integration.[3] While for the states of the first enlargement of the EU and for some others, accession to the European Communities was to a great extent a question

1 Cf. e.g. Sieber, Ulrich: *Rechtliche Ordnung in einer globalen Welt. Die Entwicklung zu einem fragmentierten System von nationalen, internationalen und privaten Normen.* Rechtstheorie 41(2), 2010, pp. 151-198.

2 Cf. e.g. Lindseth, Peter L.: *Power and Legitimacy. Reconciling Europe and the Nation-State.* Oxford and New York: Oxford University Press, 2010, pp. 61-74.

3 Cf. Schütze, Robert: *From Dual to Cooperative Federalism. The Changing Structure of European Law.* Oxford: Oxford University Press, 2013, pp. 133-151.

of economic calculation, for many of the states of Southern and Central-Eastern Europe it was and still is a symbol of their political and economic transformation and stabilisation.

The impact of European integration on the state can be explored from many perspectives. We will deal with only some of these perspectives and present an overview with elaborations into topical issues, rather than a detailed analysis. First of all, the expectations and benefits connected with integration enabled politically a significant self-limitation of individual states (I.1). At the same time, integration changes the power relationships among the Member States' constitutional bodies (I.2). We, however, presume that the state, as a form of organisation of society based on the principles accepted in the European-American context, remains in spite of all the specific features of the European Union an important criterion of its further development (I.3). In the second part of the text we focus on two institutes of EU law aimed at the protection of values attributed to the post-war European state – the national identity clause laid down in Article 4(2) of the Treaty on European Union (TEU) (II.), and the principle of subsidiarity contained in Article 5(3) of the Treaty on the Functioning of the EU (TFEU) (III.).

I.1 Limitation of Member States' powers

Membership of the European Union results in self-limitation of the state (through the act of accession and revisions of the founding treaties) in terms of its possibility to further democratically shape itself.[4] Accession limits the state's political decision-making in many areas where competence has been conferred upon the Union and the aims of policy to be effected by the Union have been determined. There is no point in mentioning all of these areas. Let us rather look at the forms this limitation takes, since it also affects the areas which have remained prevailingly within the competence of the Member States.

Firstly, there is the standard duty to observe obligations resulting from international treaties establishing the EU. In some areas these obligations amount to a duty to refrain entirely from any legislative activity (the area of exclusive competence of the EU), and in many others they significantly narrow the state's room for manoeuvre (the four market freedoms). Often, these duties are rather general – for example the principle of sincere cooperation in Article 4(3) TEU - moreover, unlike common international obligations, they are interpreted rather

4 Judgment of the German Federal Constitutional Court from 30 June 2009, 2 BvE 2/08, para. 252 (Lisbon Treaty).

autonomously by the Court of Justice of the European Union (CJEU),[5] which enforces them through sanction mechanisms such as the infringement procedure.

The second form of limitation is the suppression of national legislation by legal acts adopted at the Union level that enjoy primacy (regulations), or which determine binding goals to be implemented as part of national law (directives). Member States usually take part in the adoption of such acts in the Council, however many legal acts may be adopted against the will of an individual Member State (voting by qualified majority in the Council) or merely by a decision of the Commission. Thus, directives under Article 288 TFEU shall leave national authorities with the choice of form and methods to achieve the desired result, but in reality they are very close to regulations in terms of the complexity and detail of their specifications.[6] When transposing these, the parliament and the executive face not so much a political choice, but rather the risk that their creativity will endanger a proper transposition. The share of EU law on the legal order of Member States, i.e. the extent to which they are affected by the European element, can hardly be calculated,[7] but it is enormous.

The mentioned forms of limitation of Member States have been subject to very detailed attention of legal and political science. In addition to these, an informal and tentative co-operation of policies, which have remained prevailingly within the competence of Member States, has developed in recent decades. This takes the form of recommendations, comparison surveys, setting goals and assuming political obligations at the European level, and the supervision of their

---

5 Kysela, Jan: *Ústava mezi právem a politikou – Úvod do ústavní teorie.* [Constitution between Law and Politics – Introduction to the Theory of Constitution] Praha: Leges, 2014, pp. 179-180.

6 E.g. Prechal, Sacha: *Directives in EC Law.* Oxford: Oxford University Press, 2005, p. 14; Hilf, Meinhard: *Die Richtlinie der EG – ohne Richtung, ohne Linie?* Europarecht 28(1) 1993, pp. 1-22.

7 Hitherto, attempts were summarised by Zbíral, Robert: *Analýza míry vlivu EU na vnitrostátní legislativu: Srovnání situace v ČR s jinými členskými státy.* Právník 150(11), 2011, pp. 1049-1076 [The Analysis of the Degree of Influence of the EU on National Legislation: A comparison of the situation in the Czech Republic and in other Member States]. When comparing the number of legal acts of the EU and the Member States, we arrive at an 80 percent share of EU law in the Czech Republic and Germany; when focusing on national legal acts with a European element (transposing acts and other acts accompanying or implementing EU law) we achieve a range of between a 10 percent and a 45 percent share in various states. Cf. also references in Zbíral to works by Elisabeth Töller.

realisation at a national level.[8] The EU is to act here as a catalyst for the exchange of experience and the transmission of successful policies.[9]

Many of these processes are covered by the formalised mechanism of the European Semester,[10] which has been in operation every year since 2011. This is a tool for the co-ordination of the economic policies of the Members States of the EU (Article 5 TFEU), aimed at the approximation of their economic performance and preventing conflict between national economic policies and overall European priorities. It is closely linked to the Stability and Growth Pact, i.e. supervision of the budgetary policies of the Member States. Its main tools are country-specific recommendations adopted by the Council upon the Commission's proposal, and the mechanism of prevention and correction of macroeconomic imbalances, which may affect the most sensitive political areas– taxes and social matters, employment, health care, education, science and research.[11] Although under primary law the EU bodies may adopt only recommendations in this area (Article 121 TFEU), regulations governing these procedures enable the imposition of financial sanctions on Eurozone states if they fail to follow such recommendations.[12] Such sanctions are imposed by a so-called reverse qualified majority in the Council: if there is no qualified majority in the Council opposing the proposal of the Commission, the proposal is deemed to be adopted. This raises doubts concerning compliance of the relevant regulations with the

8 Sometimes the so-called *open method of co-ordination* is summarily mentioned, by means of which the EU "*exerts influence on domestic policy through common EU guidelines, benchmarks and recommendations combined with national reporting, monitoring and surveillance, and peer review.*" Armstrong, Kenneth A.: *The new governance of EU fiscal discipline.* European Law Review 38(5), 2013, p. 602. In the most general sense also the current *Europe 2020 Strategy* may be included here.

9 Duina, Francesco, Oliver, Michael J.: *National Parliaments in the European Union: Are There Any Benefits to Integration?* European Law Journal 11(2), 2005, pp. 173-183.

10 Article 2-a of amended Council Regulation (EC) No 1466/97 of 7 July 1997 on the strengthening of surveillance of budgetary positions and the surveillance and co-ordination of economic policies (so-called preventive arm of the Stability and Growth Pact).

11 Cf. Dawson, Mark, de Witte, Floris: *Constitutional Balance in the EU after the Euro-crisis.* Modern Law Review 76(5), 2013, p. 833.

12 Especially Regulation (EU) No 1174/2011 of the European Parliament and of the Council of 16 November 2011 on enforcement measures to correct excessive macroeconomic imbalances in the euro area. Similar sanctions can be found in the area of surveillance of budgetary policy of the Member States.

Treaties,[13] or at least the observation that differences between various categories of Union competences are being blurred.[14] In order to enforce the implementation of recommendations, the Commission may suspend payments from the Cohesion Fund, and, since 2014, also from other European funds.[15]

The European Semester fits into the supervisory model of fiscal integration set out in the Maastricht Treaty and the Stability and Growth Pact, where the principal powers concerning taxes and public expenditure are left with the Member States, but their exercise is monitored and guided from the centre. Thus, the Union avoids heading for fiscal federalism as per the US model, where the centre collects a crucial amount of taxes and the main tool for the regulation of individual Member states' economies is the massive federal budget.[16]

The European Semester reflects the fact (which is the essence of functionalist theory) that the integration of certain areas, to be effective, gradually requires the adjustment or integration of related policies. This manifests itself in the legal restrictions of the related policies (free movement rules restrict states' decisions on social policy)[17] and their more or less intensive co-ordination (the stability of a common currency should be one of the benchmarks of a Member State's economic policy), which should create conditions for the unhindered implementation of European policies rather than change their setting. The resulting

13 Häde, Ulrich: *Rechtliche Bewertung der Maßnahmen im Hinblick auf eine 'Fiskalunion'.* Berliner Online-Beiträge zum Europarecht, No 77, 2012, pp. 3-5. According to Kysela, this construction may originate from a so-called *guillotine* set out in Article 49(3) of the French Constitution, which provides that the Prime Minister may connect the passing of an act with a confidence vote, meaning that the act is passed if the government wins confidence. In both cases it is a tool boosting capacity of action. Kysela, 2014, pp. 295-297.

14 Armstrong, 2013, p. 612.

15 Article 23 of Regulation (EU) No 1303/2013 of the European Parliament and of the Council of 17 December 2013 (General regulation on the funds covered by the Common Strategic Framework).

16 Hinarejos, Alicia: *Fiscal federalism in the European Union: Evolution and future choices for EMU.* Common Market Law Review 50(6), 2013, pp. 1621–1642. Approximately 20 percent of the GDP of the US passes through the US budget, while only one percent of EU Member States' total GDP passes through the EU budget. Dawson, de Witte 2013, p. 828 comment: "*While allowing national control over welfare and labour policies is increasingly seen as economically unwise, the Europeanisation of such policy areas is also normatively unattractive, threatening the constitutional balance upon which EU integration has rested, and which is indispensable for its long-term authority and stability.*"

17 Dawson, de Witte, 2013, pp. 823-826.

limitation of national policies may, undeniably, lead to the erosion of those functions of the state which are democratically exercised through the national policies.[18]

This logic was manifested in its extreme through the way in which European Union proceeded during the financial crisis. A partial waiver of obligations and the grant of financial support to over-indebted states, with the aim of restoring the financial stability of monetary union, were conditional on the implementation of stringent reforms. This was negotiated by the so-called Troika, consisting of the European Commission, the European Central Bank, and the International Monetary Fund, and set down in Memoranda of Understanding. It reminds of the characteristic scheme of insolvency law, where the creditors take over the management of the debtor. On the basis of the memoranda, autonomous decisions of the state on its social policy were (temporarily) ruled out, and economic and social rights were infringed – such rights being binding under EU law and international law both on EU bodies and Member States. Moreover, this happened through acting beyond the competence of the EU bodies.[19] It is also worth mentioning that *ad hoc* resolutions of the "Greek crisis" have inspired the new general legal framework of the EU.[20]

It comes as no surprise in this context that European integration is frequently viewed from the perspective of the sovereignty of states. The debate, however, is conceptually rather unclear. Often used as a starting point is the argument

---

18 In this context, social policy is frequently mentioned. E.g. Ashiagbor, Diamond: *Unravelling the Embedded Liberal Bargain: Labour and Social Welfare Law in the Context of EU Market Integration.* European Law Journal 19(3), 2013, pp. 303-324. There has been criticism that free movement and harmonisation of the market push the regulatory competition among the Member States to the area of tax and social policies and there follows the "race to the bottom" and the destruction of the welfare state. Fisahn, Andreas: *Europäische Union in der Legitimationskrise.* Kritische Justiz 42(2), 2009, pp. 104-115, here p. 111. Cf. also Bickerton, Christopher J.: *European Integration: From Nation-States to Member States.* Oxford: Oxford University Press, 2012, pp. 131-134.

19 Fischer-Lescano, Andreas: *Troika in der Austerität. Rechtsbindungen der Unionsorgane beim Abschluss von Memoranda of Understanding.* Kritische Justiz 47(1) 2014, pp. 2-25; cf. also Dawson, de Witte, 2013, pp. 823-826; Potacs, Michael: *Vom Wert des Rechtes in Europäischen Union.* Journal für Rechtspolitik 50(1), 2012, pp. 23-30.

20 Regulation (EU) No 472/2013 of the European Parliament and of the Council of 21 May 2013 on the strengthening of economic and budgetary surveillance of Member States in the euro area who are experiencing or threatened by serious difficulties with respect to their financial stability.

that the Westphalian concept of sovereignty is no longer applicable, or, in other words, that the understanding of sovereignty as unlimited, unconditional, exclusive and ultimate power within a certain territorial community was always a fiction rather than a reality.[21] Instead of a binary understanding of sovereignty as indivisible (either Member States, or the European Union, are sovereign), terms such as divided, shared or pooled sovereignty are used.[22] Thus, sovereignty may be identified with a certain extent of competence belonging to a subject, with a certain degree of political autonomy in the exercise thereof, with the effective realisation of functions of the state (the necessity of joint actions as the only means for the states to enforce their powers in reality) or with the claim that the EU legal order is not derived from the legal orders of the Member States. But the question remains: what is such understanding of sovereignty good for, also if considered within the more general debate on the sovereignty of states in international law?[23] It may be more meaningful to understand sovereignty principally as a power which has competence over competences (*Kompetenz-Kompetenz*) and which makes final decisions.[24] The sharing of competences among states or their conferral upon supranational institutions should not be confused with the conferral or sharing of sovereignty.[25] The final decision on the development of integration, including a possible withdrawal from the integration project, is,

---

21 E.g. Přibáň, Jiří: *Multiple Sovereignty: On Europe's Self-Constitutionalization and Legal Self-Reference*. Ratio Juris 23(1), 2010, pp. 41-61, here p. 51.

22 Ibid; Keohane, Robert O.: *Ironies of Sovereignty: The European Union and the United States*. Journal of Common Market Studies 40(4), 2002, p. 743-765.

23 According to these conceptions we could designate as 'sovereign' the international, the EU and the national legal order, and possibly also autonomous legal orders within a state. Kysela 2014, p. 159. Belling, Vojtěch: *Legitimita moci v postmoderní době. Proč potřebuje Evropská unie členské státy?* [Legitimacy of Power in a Post-Modern Era. Why does the European Union Need Member States?] Brno: Mezinárodní politologický ústav Masarykovy univerzity, 2009, p. 147. According to Belling these approaches represent a resignation on the concept of sovereignty.

24 Grimm, Dieter: *Die Zukunft der Verfassung II: Auswirkungen von Europäisierung und Globalisierung*. Suhrkamp: Berlin, 2012, pp. 275-292. Kysela, 2014, pp. 138-139, 159, 179-185.

25 Jackson, Robert: *Sovereignty in World Politics: a Glance at the Conceptual and Historical Landscape*. Political Studies 47(3) 1999, pp. 431–456, here pp. 450-454; Kysela, 2014, p. 184; Pavlíček, Václav: *Suverenita v procesu integrace (retrospektiva a perspektiva)* [Sovereignty in the Process of Integration (Retrospective and Perspective)] In: Pavlíček, Václav (ed.): *Suverenita a evropská integrace* [Sovereignty and the European Integration]. Praha: Univerzita Karlova v Praze, 1999, pp. 42-46.

under the current state of the law, dependent on the will of the Member States. This does not conflict with the fact that the European Union represents a conferral of public power to a subject other than the state, that is unprecedented in its scale and intensity, or the fact that ideas regarding legitimate goals, tools and manners of state functioning have undergone significant changes since the end of the Thirty Years' War.

Although formally, from the point of view of their competences, all states are limited to the same extent, decision-making at EU level cannot conjure away the geopolitical reality of unequally strong Member States. Larger Member States can enforce "their" solutions using their legally (the weight of a vote in the Council) or effectively greater negotiating power than others. In recent years, the dominance of the German-French tandem, manifested mainly in the European Council,[26] has been the subject of discussion. Thus far reflections on the limitation of Member States are relative.

I.2 The impact of integration on the constitutional systems of the Member States

As regards the impact of European integration on the structure of state power and relations among state bodies, two main areas of questions come to the fore.

The first, which we will not explore in detail, concerns the functioning of administrative and judicial systems. EU law is generally enforced by means of national administrative bodies and courts in conjunction with the procedure of preliminary ruling. This mechanism challenges, to a certain degree, the roles and doctrines of individual national bodies of legal protection due to the absorption of EU law doctrines.

The second area of questions concerns a shift in the balance of power in the Member States from parliaments to executive power. This is a more general feature of post-World War II development in West European states which cannot be attributed solely to European integration.[27] However, it has played a principal role in the EU and has also had an impact on the functioning of all states that

26 It has become an informal initiator of legislation and a creator of compromise agreements on important legislative proposals. See also the European Council Conclusions of the latest four years. Dinan, Desmond: *Governance and Institutions: Impact of the Escalating Crisis*. Journal of Common Market Studies 50 (Supplement s2), 2012, pp. 88-89; Puetter, Uwe: *Europe's Deliberative Intergovernmentalism: The new role of the Council and European Council in EU Economic Governance*. Journal of European Public Policy 19(2), 2012, pp. 161-178, here p. 170 et seq.

27 Lindseth, 2010.

have later acceded to the EU. The essence of the shift is that European legislation is proposed by the supposedly technocratic Commission and approved primarily by the Council, which is composed of the governments of the Member States, while the involvement of their parliaments is not required. So the term "deparliamentarisation of governance"[28] has been used. National parliaments were represented in the European Parliament until 1979, but the parliament had only a consultative function at that time and the range of topics dealt with at European level was quite limited when compared with the current situation. The national parliaments of many Member States did not start to show an interest in European integration affairs before the late 1980s, and they have since been trying to catch up and adapt their procedures and competences.[29]

Peter Lindseth describes how the interwar economic crisis - which was resolved both in the US and in European democracies by the marginalisation of parliaments and the transfer of legislative functions to the executive - influenced the post-war arrangement of European states and the shape of European integration.[30] From the beginning this corresponded with the political practice of the Council, based on diplomacy, behind-the-scene negotiations, and an effort to reach consensus. It is frequently remarked that negotiations in the Council and its bodies are seen as a search for solutions to problems rather than a political debate leading to the settlement of national interests. This practice has been transforming into group solidarity of European political and diplomatic elites.[31] It is characterised by the ability to adopt a decision, but it lacks transparency and is hardly open to parliament or other public control.

Placing governments along with a professional, independent and impartial Commission in the very centre of European policy-making should result in the professional production of effective policies which are not blocked by

28 For example Lindseth, 2010, pp. 202-203 distinguishes between a weaker concept of deparliamentarisation, which criticises the decline of power of national parliaments, and a stronger concept, which considers European integration as a danger to democracy as such.

29 Cf. e.g. Maurer, Andreas, Wessels, Wolfgang (eds.): *National Parliaments on their Ways to Europe: Losers or Latecomers?* Baden Baden: Nomos, 2001.

30 Lindseth, 2010, pp. 74-91.

31 E.g. Bickerton, 2012, pp. 29-38, 47-48; Harlow, Carol: *Accountability in the European Union*. New York: Oxford University Press, 2002, pp. 33-36. Negotiation mechanisms in the Council are comprehensively described by Zbíral, Robert: *Teorie a praxe vyjednávání v Radě Evropské unie*. [Theory and Practice of Negotiation in the Council of the European Union]. Brno: Mezinárodní politologický ústav Masarykovy univerzity, 2008.

local rent seekers.[32] But many authors believe that the purpose of the transfer of competences to Brussels is also to make the government more independent of its electors[33] and that the decision to confer competences to the European level is frequently motivated by executive, party and other particular interests.[34] For national governments, the European Union represents a lever for pressing and petrification of certain political lines even against national resistance.[35] Governments may utilise obligations resulting from EU membership as a kind of trump against political opposition and public opinion, enabling them to dictate agenda with less effort and avoid responsibility for unpopular decisions.[36] The expression "perversion of democracy" has been coined, to describe how EU institutions enable governments to shake off national mechanisms of political responsibility and parliamentary control.[37] Although the strengthening of the role of the European Parliament within the legislative process has progressively weakened the Council as a body, the Council certainly has not become a second, weaker chamber of the European system.

---

32 Moravcsik, Andrew: *Why the European Community Strengthens the State: Domestic Politics and International Co-operation*. Paper presented at the Conference of Europeanists, Chicago, USA (April 1994), and quoted by Wincott, Daniel: *Does the European Union Pervert Democracy? Questions of Democracy in New Constitutionalist Thought on the Future of Europe*. European Law Journal 4(4), 1998, p. 424.

33 Wincott, 1998, pp. 424-427; Bickerton, 2012, p. 67 mentions the separation of the political process from the will of the people.

34 Schäfer, Armin: *Die demokratische Grenze output-orientierter Legitimation*. Integration 29(3), 2006, pp. 194-196. According to Bickerton, 2012, pp. 12-14 this strategy enabled the deconstruction of the post-war national corporatist state through the technocratisation of politics. Convergence criteria for economic and monetary union became instruments for isolating social partners and weakening opposition in the process of reforms (pp. 131-134).

35 Schäfer, 2006, pp. 194-198. According to Schäfer the Council and the European Council do not represent fully the interests of the Member States. He mentions the fact that to turn the helm of an existing European policy is very difficult due to very detailed primary law and procedural difficulties. This applies also to the possible collective withdrawal of some conferred competences.

36 Harlow, 2002, pp. 33-36. Poiares Maduro, Miguel: *A New Governance for the European Union and the Euro: Democracy and Justice*. In: European Parliament: *Challenges of multi-tier governance in the European Union. Effectiveness, efficiency and legitimacy. Compendium of Notes*. Brussels, 2013, p. 46: "*It is well known that national governments sometimes transfer unpopular decisions from the national to the European level as a way of transferring the political costs of those decisions.*"

37 Wincott, 1998, p. 412.

I.3 Importance of the state for the European Union?

As we have stated before, the real extent and the intensity of competences of the EU are unparalleled among any other non-state entity exercising public power. At present, the European Union intervenes in almost all areas of national policy. At the same time, the exercise of this power is organised differently than that of state power, with negotiations among governments and bureaucratic expertise emphasised. Thus, the European Union has been approximating the state, and yet it principally differs from it. The key to their mutual relationship is the issue of legitimacy of public power.

The modern state has evolved in the European-American context as a form of organisation of society, where in the creation and enforcement of law, i.e. in the exercise of state (public) power, basic principles are applied which make such public power, including its extreme forms (monopoly of violence), socially legitimate. These principles include namely the sovereignty of the people, government of the people by the people and for the people, legality of state power, protection of individual rights including fundamental rights and freedoms, division of power, constitution as the criterion of legal order, and state efforts to provide dignified social conditions. An entity exercising public power to an extent close to that of the state should logically be subject to the same rules, the objectives of such entity included. Thus, the state should be a measure for the Union, although the Union has not yet achieved the quality of state. The position of *Mark Dawson* and *Floris de Witte* holds true, namely that "*The EU, just like the nation state, is but a social artefact. It does not serve a divine greater good, but rather provides a framework to facilitate the attainment of the objectives of its constituents – whether citizens or nation states.*"[38] Features providing legitimacy to state power have not been surpassed and should form the basis for the institutional shape and functioning of the Union.[39] It should be ensured that their implementation in the Member States is protected from the intrusive bearings of EU law.

The fulfilment of democratic principles is considered to be the most poignant problem concerning the exercise of public power at the EU level. *Jiří Přibáň* comments that ratification of the Treaty establishing a Constitution for Europe made it impossible to ignore the fact that the democratic legitimacy of the Union is embedded in the Member States. This leads to two questions: how far can the EU powers reach without undermining this democratic legitimacy, and to what extent may EU competences expand without any institutional underpinning in

38 Dawson, de Witte, 2013, pp. 818-819.

39 Cf. Georgiev, Jiří: *Doslov.* [Afterword] In: Belling, 2009, pp. 169-171.

the form of a democratically legitimate political government?[40] A great many works are devoted to the issue of a democratic deficit in the EU. A classic definition of the problem is provided by *Simon Hix*, who states that a democratic deficit can be seen in 1) the growth of power of the executive (the Commission and the Council) along with the weakening of national parliaments (their will is not respected); 2) a too weak European Parliament and continuing dominance of the Council; 3) the non-existence of real European elections (only referenda on the European Union are held; elections in Member States usually ignore European topics and elections to the European Parliament function rather as a continuous public opinion poll regarding national policy); 4) great remoteness between the EU and the citizen who does not understand the EU (the Commission is neither a government nor a bureaucracy, it does not derive from the Parliament, while the Council is the only law-making body which decides in secret ballot,[41] and European policy is apolitical); and 5) as a result the EU enforces policies which do not enjoy the support of the majority of citizens in the majority of the Member States.[42]

Frequently the objection is expressed that the European Union cannot be measured against the democracy criteria applicable to a state.[43] Those who point to the democratic deficit allegedly idealise democracy at the Member State level and do not consider the fact that the idea of representative democracy is more suitable for 18th century states than it is for the governance of complex, post-industrial societies,[44] and that purist visions of democracy correspond neither with history nor with the current situation in a number of Member States.[45] But these objections set aside the fact that not even constitutional theory is a description of real situations. It is always the measuring of reality against ideal categories and the degree of their satisfaction in constitutional practice. We could also

---

40 Přibáň, Jiří: *The Self-Referential European Polity, its Legal Context and Systemic Differentiation: Theoretical Reflections on the Emergence of the EU's Political and Legal Autopoiesis.* European Law Journal 15(4) 2009, p. 453.

41 This applies in fact even after the coming into force of the Lisbon Treaty.

42 Hix, Simon: *The Political System of the European Union.* Basingstoke: Palgrave, 2005, pp. 177-178.

43 E.g. Schütze, 2013, p. 68. Cf. also Weiler, Joseph H. H.: *The political and legal culture of European integration: An exploratory essay.* International Journal of Constitutional Law 9(3-4), 2011, p. 682.

44 Dehousse, Renaud: *Beyond representative democracy: Constitutionalism in a polycentric polity.* In: Weiler, Joseph H. H., Wind, Marlene (eds.): *European Constitutionalism Beyond the State.* Cambridge: Cambridge University Press, 2003, pp. 137, 154.

45 On these arguments see Wincott, 1998, pp. 413-416.

remark that the EU has been unable to imitate even those imperfect practices of political control and executive accountability in the Member States.[46]

According to the second classic objection to the notion of democratic deficit, EU legitimacy should lie in the effective satisfaction of social needs and the resolution of problems (output legitimacy; government for the people) rather than in the democratic creation of political will (input legitimacy). Indeed, it is a variation of the slogan "bread and circuses."[47] Generally, it is combined with the thesis of Pareto efficiency of European policies,[48] which are created non-politically and technocratically. We can hear the echo of criticism of mass democracy from the turn of the 19th and 20th centuries.[49]

The main rebuttal argument is that output legitimacy, i.e. whether the government acts for the benefit of the people, is always ultimately assessed in the political and election process, i.e. by input legitimacy. *Armin Schäfer* states that output legitimacy can only be validated if the standard of "good governance" has been defined, which, in a number of policy areas, cannot be done *ex cathedra*, but rather has to be done in a democratic process. Such a process must define political objectives (what policy should be followed) and only then is it possible to examine how effectively they are fulfilled. The need for dealing with varied preferences and the determination of priorities in the democratic process cannot be neglected using the excuse that decisions aimed at prosperity for all may be excluded from political contestation.[50] Such considerations can lead as far as the Jacobin objective government of the political avant-garde, which is able to recognise the needs of the people and so does not need to ask for their opinion.[51] But to assess whether European policy is Pareto efficient is also difficult. It undoubtedly is at the most general level (peaceful co-operation), but does the same apply to the outcomes of concrete policies and regulations? The more so, as European (and national) elections do not result in a change in political line, do not compel representatives to adjust their activities to the will of the electorate, and such representatives are not held accountable for political failures at the European

46 Weiler, 2011, pp. 679-680.

47 Ibid, p. 682.

48 Within the context of EU policy Pareto efficiency is a redistribution of goods that makes at least one member state better off and no member state worse off.

49 Cf. Hix, 2005, pp. 178-180.

50 Schäfer, 2006, p. 199 et seq., cf. Laffan, Brigid: *The Politics of Identity and Political Order in Europe.* Journal of Common Market Studies 34(1), 1996, p. 83; Belling, 2009, pp. 139-140.

51 Kysela, 2014, pp. 90-96.

level.[52] What we miss is a responsive government, and the risk of agency capture and path-dependent policy has been growing. The chances that "remote" European policy will be dominated by particular concentrated interests seem higher than they might at national level.[53] Moreover, a leaning toward output legitimacy slows down the process of creation of a European political identity.[54] Thus, the importance of a politically isolated "government for the people" for legitimacy is limited.

The solution to democratic deficit cannot be found in a sudden adjustment of the Union institutions' structure to reflect those of a state, because legal form without political context (Europe-wide public opinion, a developed political space, adequate culture of conduct of EU bodies) will only be an empty shell.[55] The creation of real pan-European political parties could be deemed a principal indicator of changes, however there has been no prospect of this yet.[56]

It is often argued that there is no "European people" (demos) as a prerequisite for a legitimate and consequently functioning democracy at the European level.[57] But the question is whether the formation of a political community (state) is the result of self-awareness of the people, or the other way around. We could

52 Weiler, 2011, pp. 679-680. Mair, Peter: *Popular Democracy and the European Union Polity*. In: Curtin, Deirdre, Wille, Anchrit (eds.): *Meaning and Practice of Accountability in the EU Multi-Level Context*. Connex Report Series No. 7, Mannheim, 2008, quoted according to Schäfer, 2006, p. 197; cf. also Harlow, 2002, p. 169, which underlines the absence of real political competition.

53 Harlow, 2002, p. 180 links the risk to the fact that regulatory functions of the Commission are aimed at highly specialised technological branches. Similarly Hix, 2005, pp. 65-69, notes that the Commission is not an apolitical body. It has its own political preferences and institutional interests; it can set agenda and benefit from information asymmetry. Cf. also Schmidt, Susane K.: *Only an Agenda Setter? The European Commission's Power over the Council of Ministers*. European Union Politics 1(1), 2000, pp. 37-61. In extreme, the fragmented network of regulatory institutions, often featuring various forms and degrees of "political independence," can transform into a *sectoral state* (Sektoralstaat), where various policy areas will be controlled by those who are the largest stakeholders or who are most closely related to them – cf. Lindseth, 2010, p. 264.

54 Hix, 2005, p. 178-180.

55 Cf. Belling, 2009, pp. 135-136.

56 Ladrech, Robert: *National Political Parties and European Governance: The Consequences of 'Missing in Action'*. West European Politics 30(5), 2007, pp. 945-960; cf. also Hix, 2005, p. 180-192.

57 Judgment of the German Federal Constitutional Court from 12 October 1993, 2 BvR 2134/92, 2 BvR 2159/92, paras. 98 and 99 (Maastricht Treaty). Belling, 2009, pp. 95, 133-138.

argue that the European people will be born "out of necessity" only in a politically integrated European Union. This, of course, conforms to many historic examples,[58] however the formation of states, where the political nation gradually crystallised later, was generally not democratic or free from violence precisely for these reasons, and so the question is really whether the EU should follow such a path. Legal and social integration go hand in hand and influence each other. But legal integration can only proceed as quickly as social integration is able to keep up with its pace. Otherwise, there would be the threat of an overhang of competences above the legitimacy necessary for their exercise, bringing dangerous consequences for democracy. Thus, the Member States continue to play the key role in democratic legitimacy of the EU.[59]

Strict compliance with the principles of the rule of law and protection of fundamental rights, as probably the main common denominator of output legitimacy, should be an important source of legitimacy of public power exercised by the Union. There is no persuasive argument why standards applying to the Member States should not apply to the Union as well.

Regarding the protection of fundamental rights, deficiencies may be found in EU procedural law, which has systematically preferred economically active and transnationally mobile entities[60] and their individual interests over collective values and public goods.[61] Even after the changes brought about by the Lisbon Treaty, EU law sometimes fails to provide access to the CJEU as the administrative court, and fails to satisfy the requirements of a modern system of legal protection.[62] Problematic is the promotion of market values to the constitutional

---

58 Scicluna, Nicole: *EU Constitutionalism in Flux: Is the Eurozone Crisis Precipitating Centralisation or Diffusion?* European Law Journal 18(4), 2012, p. 497.

59 Cf. also Dawson, de Witte, 2013, p. 836: "*it is precisely because Europe cannot dispose of a transnational political system that incorporates each citizens' voice equally, that we must protect the capacity of citizens to make their voices heard within the national political settlement.*"

60 Goldoni, Marco: *Constitutional Pluralism and the Question of the European Common Good.* European Law Journal 18(3), 2012, p. 400. Somek, Alexander: *The Argument From Transnational Effects I: Representing Outsiders Through Freedom of Movement.* University of Iowa Legal Studies Research Paper Number 09-23, 2009, p. 27. Chalmers, Damian: *Democratic Self-Government in Europe. Domestic Solutions to the EU Legitimacy Crisis.* Policy Network Paper, 2013, pp. 11-12.

61 Weiler, 2011, p. 691; cf. also Poiares Maduro, Miguel: *Europe and the constitution: What if this is as good as it gets?* In: Weiler, Wind, 2003, pp. 78-79.

62 Thiele, Alexander: *Das Rechtschutzsystem nach dem Vertrag von Lissabon – (K)ein Schritt nach vorn?* Europarecht 45(1), 2010, pp. 30-50.

level,[63] and the resulting perception of fundamental rights as a restriction on these values, which must be subjected to the test of proportionality.[64] The Lisbon Treaty no longer leaves the issue of the position of fundamental rights within EU law entirely with CJEU case law, but problems have persisted. The Charter of Fundamental Rights of the EU is a Pandora's Box, containing a labyrinth of general provisions which do not provide unequivocal guidelines for the determination of the relevant extent and standard of protection. It means that the protection will continue to depend mostly upon the practical approach of the CJEU, which was criticised in the past. EU accession to the European Convention for the Protection of Human Rights and Fundamental Freedoms is a long-distance run and is subject to the Protocol No. 8 attached to the Lisbon Treaty, which requires, inter alia, that the accession does not affect the competences of the Union or the powers of its institutions, which seems to be a sign of an attempt to ensure a "special" treatment of EU law in the international system of the protection of human rights. So far, the unsatisfactory situation created by the decision of the European Court of Human Rights in the Bosphorus case has persisted; the decision *de facto* exempted acts of EU law from the competence of the Convention and thus gave immunity to the public power of states parties exercised within the European Union.[65]

EU legislation is also characterized by a compromise approach to fundamental rights. Among the most recent proposals, we should mention the proposal of

---

63 Bickerton, 2012, pp. 127-128.

64 From economic and social rights cases C-438/05 *International Transport Workers' Federation and Finnish Seamen's Union v Viking Line* [2007] ECR I-10779, C-341/05 *Laval un Partneri Ltd v Svenska Byggnadsarbetareförbundet* [2007] ECR I-11767 and others; see Ashiagbor, 2013.

65 European Court of Human Rights judgment from 30 June 2005, *Bosphorus Hava Yollari Turizm ve Ticaret Anonim Şiketi v Ireland* 2005-VI; 42 EHRR 1, especially paras 154-158. The European Court of Human Rights formally confirmed the responsibility of the contracting parties for the exercise of powers conferred to other public authorities, but established a general presumption that actions of member states under obligations from EU law will be considered as justified under the Convention, as long as the EU is considered to protect fundamental rights in a manner comparable to the Convention. In order to rebut this presumption, individual applicants have to demonstrate that the protection of their fundamental rights in the EU legal system has been, in their particular case, "manifestly deficient". See e.g. Besselink, Leonard F. M.: *The EU and the European Convention of Human Rights after Lisbon: From 'Bosphorus' Sovereign Immunity to Full Scrutiny?* (January 13, 2008). Available at SSRN: http://ssrn.com/abstract=1132788

a Monti II regulation related to the *Viking* and *Laval* case law, and subsequently criticised for violating the international obligations of member states,[66] or the proposal for a regulation establishing the European Public Prosecutor's Office, which was affected by very poor drafting.[67] Also, there is a proposal for a regulation on the statutes and financing of European political parties and foundations, which, in its initial wording, sharply contradicted the standards of the regulation of the right to political association in the Council of Europe member states.[68] As we will see, especially the national parliaments are very sensitive to these issues.

Problematic in the European Union has been the treatment of the principle that public power is bound by law, which is the central feature of the rule of law and in the form of the principle of conferred powers (Article 5 TEU) one of the main elements of the legal order of the Union. Instead, we can see a strongly instrumental conception of law in practice.[69] At the same time, this predominance of utility leads to the diluting of the value of the legal order, which ceases to be a binding framework for political decision-making (and which can be changed by prescribed procedures) and becomes a mere substance or material, which

---

66 COM (2012) 130. See Bruun, Niklas, Bücker, Andreas, Dorssemont, Filip: *Balancing Fundamental Social Rights and Economic Freedoms: Can the Monti II Initiative Solve the EU Dilemma?* The International Journal of Comparative Labour Law and Industrial Relations 28(3) 2012, pp. 279–306.

67 COM (2013) 534. About a half of the provisions of this proposal are dedicated to secondary topics, such as the protection of personal data, databases, financing and relations to other EU institutions, while the regulation of the powers and procedural rules for the public prosecutor is fragmentary, often ambiguous and takes very lightly the problem of the functioning of these rules in the context of national criminal procedure laws. This is insufficient, especially considering that criminal proceedings are one of the most exposed situations concerning fundamental rights. See also Hamran, Ladislav, Szabová, Eva: *European Public Prosecutor's Office – cui bono?* New Journal of European Criminal Law 4(1-2), 2013, pp. 40-58.

68 COM (2012) 499. This proposal entrusts the European Parliament with the power to decide on applications for the registration of European political parties and their access to financing from the EU budget, as well as with the power to de-register them (resulting in the loss of a European legal personality and status) and impose other sanctions. In a democratic rule-of-law state, this would not be acceptable. Furthermore, the registration is conditioned by the observance of European values not only in the political party's programme, but also in the actions of its members. Judicial remedies against the decisions of the European Parliament will not suspend the effect of sanctions.

69 Snyder, Francis: *The unfinished constitution of the European Union: Principles, processes and culture.* In: Weiler, Wind, 2003, pp. 69-72.

can be shaped according to needs, and which serves as a formal justification of the legality of currently promoted measures.[70] *Peter Lindseth* has provided an interesting analysis of the roots of this situation. According to him, the CJEU has never considered itself as an institution whose primary goal is to control whether the limits of competences of the EU institutions are observed. He describes the connection between the *effet utile* doctrine and the approach of representatives of inter-war functionalism to the interpretation of law. The consequences are the expansive case law concerning the Union competences and the Member States' duties on the one hand and insurmountable procedural demands on complainants prejudiced by the acts of European institutions on the other.[71] Specifically, he demonstrates the extensive interpretation of competences of the Union as well as the absence of consistent judicial monitoring of compliance with the principle of conferral. This applies namely to the use of the most general competence provisions (particularly current Articles 114 and 352 TFEU). With respect to the fact that proposals according to Article 114 TFEU (the approximation of rules on the internal market) are decided by the Council by a qualified majority rather than unanimously, the Commission gives priority to the use of this provision over some special and more concrete provisions in order to weaken possible opposition in the Council.[72] Thus, it strongly shifts the balance laid down in primary law and makes it more difficult to safeguard individual states' interests in the Council, despite such safeguarding being absolutely legitimate.

We may sum up by stating that the integration process in Europe is in principle a potentially state-forming process.[73] As such, it cannot be driven beyond a certain limit solely by functionalist arguments without corresponding cultural and political movements taking place in the society.[74] If, among other things because of this insufficient democratic background, the EU lacks some attributes

---

70 Potacs, 2012, pp. 23-30.

71 Lindseth, 2010, pp. 133-152.

72 Ibid, pp. 216-220. Similarly Schütze, 2013, pp. 133-151 and Weatherill, Stephen: *The Limits of Legislative Harmonization Ten Years after Tobacco Advertising: How the Court's Case Law has become a 'Drafting Guide'*. German Law Journal 12(3), 2011, pp. 827–864, which speaks of "competence creep."

73 Bross, Siegfried: *Überlegungen zur europäischen Staatswerdung*. Juristenzeitung, 2008, pp. 227-232.

74 Lindseth, 2010, pp. 266-269; cf. also Hix, 2005, pp. 173-174, who writes about outdated conception of "permissive consensus" of citizens of the Member States in relation to the integration. Wincott, 1998, p. 428 comments: "*The images of the political movements which helped to secure civil, political and social rights over the last two or three centuries seem out of place in the European Union context.*"

of state power, fails to fulfil certain functions of the state, and especially fails to systematically protect certain values, it must respect the fact that these functions are exercised, or values protected, by the Member States and it must not prevent them from doing so.[75]

EU law recognises a number of mechanisms which should lead to this aim. These are the principle of conferred competences, including more detailed competence provisions which exclude certain issues from EU law, a rigid procedure for changing treaties, the right of veto or over-representation of smaller states in the decision-making process, the principle of proportionality, and so on.[76] Key among them is the duty of the European Union to respect national identity and the basic functions of Member States (Article 4 (2) TEU), and to observe the principle of subsidiarity in its actions (Article 5(3) TEU). These provisions should complement the functionalist canon of principles and effects of EU law through limits protecting the self-determination of political communities, which still represent the principal building blocks of European integration. Their application, which we will look at further, has been problematic so far, to say the least.

II. National identity

Authors who focus on the issue of national identity of the EU Member States base their reasoning primarily on the scarce and fact-specific case-law of the CJEU on the one hand, and broad statements of the Member States' constitutional courts on the other.[77] Article 4 (2) TEU is therefore not just interpreted,

---

75 Chalmers, 2013, pp. 11-12 states that the EU does not secure *individual autonomy* of entities which are not active across borders, *local tradition* which is perceived as a "whimsical idiosyncrasy" rather than a central feature of democracy, or *distributive justice* in a general sense (political choices made within tax and social policies). In the context of free movement, EU law demands transnational solidarity of social systems, but consequently can violate the fulfilment of functions of the systems within individual states or toward their citizens that do not participate in cross-border activities. Cf. e.g. Balthasar, Alexander: *Nichtdiskriminierung und Unionsbürgerschaft in einem Staatenverbund. Zugleich eine Auseinandersetzung mit (vornehmlich) dem Urteil des EuGH vom 13.04.2010, C-73/08 (Bressol).* Zeitschrift für Öffentliches Recht 66(1), 2011, pp. 41-75.

76 Dawson, de Witte, 2013, pp. 821-822.

77 This development was probably most influenced by the Lisbon (2009) and Honeywell (2010) decisions of the German Federal Constitutional Court that were followed by the Ilonka Sayn-Wittgenstein judgment of the CJEU of 22 December 2010. In chronological order, see e.g.: Besselink, Leonard L. F. M.: *National and constitutional identity*

but is reconstructed through this perspective of judicial competence. The following section aims to discuss possibilities of more general "identity protection"[78] in legislative procedure and the application of EU law by EU and Member States' institutions.

II.1 Legal concept of constitutional and national identity

For this purpose we may distinguish between two main legal[79] understandings of constitutional identity: constitutional identity as a reflection of constitutional subject,[80] and constitutional identity as the perpetuation of a constitution in legal and political development.[81] The former is connected with the different types of nations, i.e. "the People" who gave themselves their respective constitutions. The latter relates to the so-called eternity clauses and inviolable core of the constitutions.

At the intersection of the two theories lies a critical assessment: who can amend the present constitution, and to what extent. Or, in other words, who are the People and what are the powers of their representatives in the legislative, executive and judiciary. Without plunging into a wide-ranging doctrinal debate, we can refer to the notion of "legitimacy advantage": the more direct the link to the People, the

---

before and after Lisbon. Utrecht Law Review, 3/ 2010, pp. 36 et seq., Bourgorgue-Larsen, Laurence (ed.): *L'identité constitutionelle saisie par les juges en Europe*. Paris: Editions A. Pedone, 2011, Mayer, Franz C.: *Rashomon in Karlsruhe: A reflection on democracy and identity in the European Union*. I-CON 3-4/2011, pp. 757 et seq., von Bogdandy, Armin, Schill, Stephan: *Overcoming absolute primacy: respect for national identity under the Lisbon Treaty*. Common Market Law Review, 48/2011, pp. 1417 et seq., Besselink, Leonard F. M.: *Respecting Constitutional Identity in the EU* (comments on case C-208/09, Ilonka Sayn-Wittgenstein – note of the author). Common Market Law Review, 49, 2012, pp. 671 et seq., Guastaferro, Barbara: *Beyond the Exceptionalism of Constitutional Conflicts: The Ordinary Functions of the Identity Clause*. Yearbook of European Law, 1/2012, pp. 263 et seq., Saiz Arnaiz, Alejandro, Alcoberro Llivina, Carina: *National Constitutional Identity and European Integration*. Cambridge: Intersentia, 2013.

78 In contrast with the more limited concept of the '*prerogative of Member States to express national identity*' proposed by Gerhard van der Schyff in *The constitutional relationship between the European Union and its Member States: The role of national identity in article 4(2) TEU*. European Law Review, 5/2012, 563 et seq.

79 For other terminological meanings see e.g. von Bogdandy, Schill, 2011, pp. 1427-1429.

80 See Rosenfeld, Michael: *The identity of the constitutional subject: Selfhood, citizenship, culture, and community*. Routledge: London, 2010.

81 See Jacobsohn, Garry J.: *Constitutional identity*. Cambridge, USA: Harvard University Press, 2010.

more fundamental change may be implemented, and vice versa. If we omit those rare cases where constitutional courts would protect the constitution even against the popular will as expressed in a valid referendum, then the most telling example is the reasoning of the German Federal Constitutional Court in the Lisbon-Urteil: *'The Basic Law does not grant powers to bodies acting on behalf of Germany to abandon the right to self-determination of the German people in the form of Germany's sovereignty under international law by joining a federal state. Due to the irrevocable transfer of sovereignty to a new subject of legitimation that goes with it, this step is reserved to the directly declared will of the German people alone.'*[82]

National identity as a legal term used in Article 4 (2) TEU can relate to constitutional identity in several non-exclusive ways: first, as a socio-political notion that includes constitutional identity as one of its components, with the other parts being e.g. national history, language, state, patriotism or a specific emphasis on various historically conditioned values that usually find their expression in the national constitution (human dignity, laïcité, sovereignty of parliament, the protection of unborn children, welfare state, neo-corporatism, etc.).

Second, constitutional identity contains the legally regulated aspects of national identity that enjoy higher protection from arbitrary change by organs of *pouvoir constitué*. Here we can mention institutions that cannot be amended without constitutional reform, such as the form of state (republic or monarchy), vertical division of powers (unitary state or federation), horizontal division of powers (among different branches of government and/or other agencies), and constitutionally protected values (fundamental rights including social and economic rights). Or, from the other end, as *Besselink* puts it, "*the notion of* 'national identity' *has over time acquired a legally more relevant flavour by its reformulation as* 'constitutional identity'."[83]

The last reading of national identity which we will briefly explore is that of CJEU decisions and the scholars who found their theories mainly on the broad acceptance of such case law.[84] First and foremost they stress that the protection of national identity does not mean the protection of state sovereignty.[85] Quite to the

82 Lisbon decision of the German Federal Constitutional Court of 30 June 2009, section 228.

83 Besselink, 2010, p. 37.

84 These scholars ground their reasoning in selected decisions that include Case C-208/09, *Ilonka Sayn-Wittgenstein*, of 22 December 2010, and Case C-391/09, *Runevič-Vardyn*, of 12 May 2011.

85 Cf, von Bogdandy, Schill, 2011, p. 1425. Because of the high number of references to this article, we will use it for a demonstration of the typical aspects of the third approach.

contrary, they claim that *"the national identity* [of the Member States] *needs to be construed as that of States that are members of the EU."*[86] In line with CJEU case law on the transfer and/or modification of state powers which, allegedly, has been at least tacitly accepted[87] by Member States, such scholars understand national identity as *"a gateway that opens EU law vis-à-vis domestic constitutional law."*[88] In practice it lays down a legal basis for the reflection of the decisions of Member States' constitutional courts that curtailed the reach of the principle of primacy of EU law. They propose only modest adjustments to the CJEU approach, which has so far refrained from expressly referring to national court decisions as being external to the jurisdiction of the CJEU. According to the proposed "European composite constitutional adjudication,"[89] the CJEU should ensure that in its proceedings the relevant views of the respective constitutional court regarding aspects of national identity of the Member State in the issue are taken into consideration.

The main difference between the second and third understanding consists in the interpretation of Article 4 (2) TEU: while the second interpretation favours national identity as enshrined by particular Member States, the third brings national identity almost exclusively into the scope of EU law and, more importantly, the jurisdiction of the CJEU. We would like to point out several shortcomings of the current restrictive approach of the CJEU that are also transposed to theories based on such case law. As a consequence, we would like to propose a broader and stronger meaning of national identity as a legal limitation on proposed EU legislation and as a decisive factor in the application of EU law.

II.2 Constitutional identity as a part of the limits on EU law and EU institutions

In our view, there are important arguments against the assumption that national identity could be at most a legitimate "rule of reason" exception. From its first

86 von Bogdandy, Schill, 2011, p. 1426 and references mentioned therein.

87 This seems to be the prevalent understanding, even if there are many countervailing arguments that while the Member States did not block the further integration in general, they indeed tried to constrain the Court of Justice and Commission by adding further conditions for their action in cases the Member States considered to be "potentially dangerous," the insertion of the protection of national identity being one such condition.

88 von Bogdandy, Schill, 2011, p. 1431.

89 Ibid. p. 1447 et seq.

codification[90] in the TEU (1992), national identity was given special standing. Article F of the Maastricht Treaty formulated in the same way the requirement for the respect of national identities (paragraph 1) and of fundamental rights as guaranteed by the ECHR, and as they result from common constitutional traditions, as general principles of (then) Community law. According to the preceding Article E, under these conditions and for these purposes the European institutions should exercise their powers. To affirm the corner-stone and at the same time politically sensitive requirements of Article F, this was excluded from the jurisdiction of the Court of Justice, together with other provisions of the then second and third pillar, by Article L of the Maastricht Treaty.

A few years later even stronger safeguards for Member States seemed necessary. In the short summaries of the preparatory work on the so-called *Christophersen clause* the intention of the drafters is very clear: during a meeting of 6th September 2002, a large majority of the working group on complementary competences was in favour of incorporating a clause on the protection of national identity as a *"valid alternative to the proposals to include ... a list of States' competences or even to draft a charter of Member States' rights."*[91] In its final report of 31st October 2002 the group explained in detail why it insisted on clarification and a broader meaning of the national identity clause. However, in the spirit of constitution making that overtook the Convent, the final report relativised previous intentions through an added commentary: *"the provision* [is] *not a derogation clause"* and will *"not constitute a definition of Member State competence."* Nevertheless, at the plenary session on 8th November, many (in report anonymous) speakers expressed reservations even to this moderated approach.[92]

The final text of Article I-5 CT[93] led to different readings, especially in connection with the following Article, I-6 CT: *"The Constitution and law adopted by the institutions of the Union in exercising competences conferred on it shall have*

90 For a more detailed overview see Besselink, 2012, p. 678.

91 Summary of the meeting on 6 September 2002, CONV 251/02, p. 3, available at: http://european-convention.europa.eu/pdf/reg/en/02/cv00/cv00251.en02.pdf

92 Summary report of the plenary session – Brussels, 7 and 8 November 2002, CONV 400/02, p. 13, available at: http://european-convention.europa.eu/pdf/reg/en/02/cv00/cv00400.en02.pdf

93 *"The Union shall respect the equality of Member States before the Constitution as well as their national identities, inherent in their fundamental structures, political and constitutional, inclusive of regional and local self-government. It shall respect their essential State functions, including ensuring the territorial integrity of the State, maintaining law and order and safeguarding national security."*

primacy over the law of the Member States." An inspiring divergence occurred in commentaries on the consequences of these articles by *M. Maduro* on the one hand, and *M. Kumm* and *V. Ferreres Comella* on the other.

M. Maduro argues that already on the basis of Article 6 TEU (1992), competence for the protection of the Member States' constitutional values in the realm of the EU law has been transferred to the CJEU and national constitutions may no longer constitute the referential scope for the review of EU law.[94] Furthermore, had the Constitutional Treaty been ratified, Article I-6 in connection with Article-I-5 would have had the effect of "*previous systemic compatibility between the EU and national constitutions*" that would "*authorise the primacy of EU norms over national norms, including constitutional norms.*"[95] Different reasoning is offered by *M. Kumm* and *V. Ferreres Comella*, according to whom Article I-5 CT would empower national courts to "*set aside secondary EU law when it fails to respect national constitutional identities, and to do so* as a matter of EU law."[96]

The subsequent development to the Lisbon treaty does not need to be rewritten here. The wording of the clause on national identity was complemented by a specification that "*in particular, national security remains the sole responsibility of each Member State*" and new paragraph 1 of Article 4 states that "*competences not conferred upon the Union in the Treaties remain with the Member States.*" In connection with the strengthening of the principles of proportionality and subsidiarity and the transfer of the reference to the principle of primacy from the draft Constitutional Treaty to a declaration of the Intergovernmental Conference, the arguments of *M. Kumm* and *V. Ferreres Comella* gain more traction. Moreover, they point our attention back to an important question: is there any reason to distinguish the national identity clause from other limits on the scope of EU law and powers of its institutions?

---

94 Compare AG Maduro's opinion delivered in Case C-127/07, *Arcelor*, on 21 May 2008, in particular paragraphs 16 and 17: "*Community law having thus incorporated the constitutional values of the Member States, national constitutions must adjust their claims to supremacy in order to comply with the primordial requirement of the primacy of Community law within its field of application.*"

95 Maduro, Miguel: *The importance of being called a constitution: Constitutional authority and the authority of constitutionalism.* International Journal of Comparative Law, 2-3/2005, p. 348.

96 Kumm, Mattias, Ferreres Comella, Victor: *The primacy clause of the constitutional treaty and the future of the constitutional conflict in the European Union.* International Journal of Comparative Law, 2-3/2005, p. 479.

There indeed were times when the reach of EU law seemed for some scholars to be limitless.[97] However, this was never generally accepted by academia[98] nor by judicial practice.[99] One such limit was, from its first express codification, the protection of national and then constitutional identity, which was intended to modify the precedent of Costa.[100] In contrast with a "mere" declaration of primacy that had to be omitted from the Lisbon Treaty due to insufficient political and public acceptance, the codified protection of national identity was further developed. This legal and political development did not seem to impress the CJEU enough to change its previous divergent case law. When compared with evolving decisions on fundamental rights - which were nevertheless criticised for an insufficient level of respect to and protection of non-economic rights[101] - respect for national (constitutional) identities remained as narrow as possible,[102] as if the Maastricht and Lisbon Treaties had not come into force. The CJEU in substance seems to follow its previous case law that regards national identity as a part of the unwritten rule of reason principle (and pays lip service to the new Article 4 (2) TEU at best[103]) which, if recognised,[104] is subject to a substantially biased[105] proportionality test.

97 *"There simply is no nucleus of sovereignty that the Member States can invoke, as such, against the Community."* Lenaerts, Koen: *Constitutionalism and the Many Faces of Federalism*. American Journal of Comparative Law, 1990, p. 220.

98 From the 1990s (Dashwood, Alan: *The Limits of European Community Powers*. European Law Review, 1996, pp. 11 et seq.) until present (Barnard, Catherine, Odudu, Okeoghene: *The outer limits of European Union law*. Oxford: Hart, 2009).

99 From the Italian Frontini case (1973), through the review of the Lisbon Treaty, and beyond.

100 Besselink, 2010, p. 48.

101 Scharpf, Fritz W.: *Legitimacy in the Multi-level European Polity*. In: Dobner, Petra, Loughlin, Martin: *The twilight of constitutionalism?* Oxford: Oxford University Press, 2010, pp. 112 et seq.

102 Chalmers, Damian: *Democratic Self-Government in Europe*. Policy Network Paper, p. 5. Available at: http://www.policy-network.net/publications_download.aspx?ID=8362

103 Compare the structure of the reasoning in the decisions of cases C-208/09, Ilonka Sayn-Wittgenstein, of 22 December 2010, and C-202/11, Anton Las, of 16 April 2013, where the argument regarding national identity serves only to reassert the possibility to claim the previously recognised type of exception.

104 See the differences between AG Maduro's opinion, that was developed upon the issue of respect for constitutional identity, and the ECJ judgment in the case of Michaniki (C-C-213/07 of 16 December 2008), which did not distinguish between national laws and the constitution.

105 Reich, Norbert: *How proportionate is the proportionality principle? Some critical remarks on the use and methodology of the proportionality principle in the internal*

Because of the express codification of the protection of national identity, the path-dependence of CJEU case-law that continues to provide a lower level of protection[106] is untenable as being based on *une certaine idée de l'Europe* which has become too removed from the current TEU text.[107] The authors are aware that since possibilities are limited for Member States to have a legally acceptable influence on the CJEU,[108] and other factors connected with judicialisation[109] also play a significant role in judicial empowerment vis-à-vis other governmental bodies, a change will not be immediate. However, it is inevitable in the long term. It could be brought about by the institutional and procedural adjustments that are subject of the third part of this sub-chapter.

II.3 Applicable mechanisms of effective protection of national identity within the existing EU treaties framework

Article 4 (2) TEU, similarly to its predecessor, creates a legal obligation for each EU institution to respect further specified national identity and correspondingly allows the Member States to control the fulfilment of this obligation at different stages of legislative and application process. However, upon brief survey one can see that most of these possibilities are not exploited effectively or at all, and the trust is bestowed on the CJEU and national courts. Could such neglect be overcome and respect for national identity improved?

Starting from the drafting of secondary EU legislation by the Commission there is no commitment nor policy paper similar to fundamental rights protection (Strategy for the effective implementation of the Charter of Fundamental Rights

---

market case law of the ECJ. In: Micklitz, Hans-W. – de Witte, Bruno: *The European Court of Justice and the autonomy of the member states*. Cambridge: Intersentia, U. K., 2012, pp. 83 et seq.; Scharpf, 2010.

106 See Chalmers supra.

107 Most recently see J. Weiler's critique of *"Lenaerts mill"* in Weiler, Joseph H. H.: *Epilogue: Judging the Judges – Apology and Critique*. In: Adams, Maurice, de Waele, Henri et al. (eds.): *Judging Europe's judges: the legitimacy of the case law of the European Court of Justice*. Oxford: Hart, 2013, p. 237.

108 Even in comparison with other supreme courts – Komárek, Jan: *Judicial Lawmaking and Precedent in Supreme Courts*. LSE Legal Studies Working Paper No. 4/2011. Available at: http://ssrn.com/abstract=1793219

109 Hirschl, Ran: *The New Constitutionalism and the Judicialization of Pure Politics Worldwide*. Fordham Law Review, 2006, pp. 721-754, available at: http://fordhamlawreview.org/assets/pdfs/Vol_75/Hirschl_November.pdf.

by the European Union – COM (2010) 573 final, and Operational Guidance on taking account of Fundamental Rights in Commission Impact Assessments – SEC (2011) 567 final) whereby fulfilment thereof would be evaluated periodically. The task of creating such a 'constitutional identity assessment' document could be assigned to the Commission by the European Council. The counter argument that national identity can only be defined by Member States alone cannot free the Commission from its obligation set out in the TEU. On the contrary, it would provide more transparency as to how the Commission applies Article 4 (2) TEU. Understandably, the Commission's interest is not to tie its hand too much, but issues insufficiently covered by such a policy paper could be still dealt with and assessed by national parliaments and Member States' bodies in general, as the Commission's policy paper would not be binding on them.

This leads us to the second step: assessment by the national parliaments within the mechanism of subsidiarity control, which seems to have growing success (see the following subsection). If we adopt a certain interpretation of the principle of subsidiarity, as some national parliaments have, it is possible for national parliaments to more directly invoke respect for national identity.

The third venue is linked to the Member States' representation at Council (and in some cases the European Council) meetings. If the relevant quotas for the suspension of a problematic proposal are not met within the direct national parliaments' involvement, those chambers concerned may attempt to influence the government position in order to repeat their objections and to modify or block the proposal at Council level. Another situation where parliamentary adoption or approval of the government's position presents an important tool is when the European Parliament modifies the proposal in such a way that could intrude on national identity. The influence of national parliaments vis-à-vis their governments was strengthened also through new rules of procedure initiated by the changes brought about by the Lisbon Treaty.

After adoption of a controversial proposal, Member States' bodies may nevertheless attempt to implement and apply it in conformity with the national constitution. Although the CJEU interprets the principle of primacy as covering not only the national courts (as was the original reading of the Costa ENEL case) but also all Member States' bodies[110] when applying EU law, national constitutions as interpreted by national constitutional courts set boundaries to this loyalty to

110 For a short summary of the case law and its critique see the Opinion of AG Ruiz-Jarabo Colomer delivered on 25 June 2009 in Case C-205/08 Umweltanwalt von Kärnten v Kärntner Landesregierung, para. 51-52.

the "other master."[111] The combined effect of precaution during the making of EU law and deference to national identity in its application can lead to the minimisation of possible conflicts even before any controversy reaches the national court or the CJEU. Only in concrete and serious conflicts such cases would be brought before the courts. Given the specific and often non-transferable character of national identity, individual decisions should not have precedential effect, except for the method of adjudication that would effectively reflect the current relevance of Article 4 (2) TEU.

The above-mentioned key points in the process of making and application of EU law could be accompanied by permissible political (in the form of declarations, statements etc.) and doctrinal pressure on the CJEU to update its decisional matrixes and to put them in line with the amended treaties. The minimum requirement could be that the CJEU takes national identity expressly into account every time constitutional matters at Member State level are contained or touched upon in proceedings, not only when the notion is raised by an authorised party. This of course does not presume the outcome, but signals that the CJEU respects Article 4 (2) TEU and the obligation set therein.

A more ambitious outcome would be the complete abandonment of the current proportionality test and treating legitimate national identity claims as those that cannot be "balanced." Reasoning as to the legitimacy of constitutional provisions at issue would have to be much more persuasive than the current seemingly technical proportionality test. A moderate result could be the reformulation of the proportionality test as a more balanced test, for example by balancing both sides and assessing the legitimacy of the interference of the EU law at issue with the national constitutional law. For this reason, institutionalised cooperation with the Member States' constitutional courts, which would enable them to express their opinion on national identity in cases which have not yet reached them in the national judicial process hierarchy, would be very useful.[112] However, as the courts decide on controversies, it is wise to avoid these already in the process of law-making and application by carefully implementing the obligation to respect national identity stemming from Article 4(2) TEU.

---

111 See e. g. Wendel, Mattias: *Lisbon Before the Courts: Comparative Perspectives*. European Constitutional Law Review, 1/2011, pp. 96 et seq.

112 Especially in situations of national *guerre des juges* where the government may follow its own interests in proceedings before the CJEU, as happened in the so-called Slovak pensions case: Král, Richard: *Questioning the Recent Challenge of the Czech Constitutional Court to the ECJ*. European Public Law, 2/2013, pp. 271 et seq.

III. The Principle of Subsidiarity

III.1 The principle of subsidiarity in the EU law

The idea of subsidiarity as a guideline for the organisation of society and the determination of the optimal role of the state has been present in European political and legal thinking at least since Aristotle.[113] Its principal formulation is found in Catholic social doctrine contained in Quadragesimo Anno, an encyclical issued by Pope Pius XI in 1931, which warned against the hazards of exaggerated collectivism and individualism.[114] The principle of subsidiarity was introduced in EU law as a general principle by Article 3b of the Maastricht Treaty in 1992. This gave it a specific purpose and meaning and the form of a legal rule associated with a legally binding effect.[115]

The current Article 5 TEU lays down three fundamental principles governing the activities of the Union: the principle of conferral, the principle of subsidiarity and the principle of proportionality.[116]

The principle of subsidiarity represents a rule restricting the exercise of competences conferred upon the EU. Even if the adoption of certain measures falls within the competence of the Union, such competence may not be exercised if it means an infringement of the subsidiarity principle. Subsidiarity and proportionality can be described as rules of self-limitation of public power,[117] which are

---

113 Estella, Antonio: *The EU Principle of Subsidiarity and its Critique*. Oxford: Oxford University Press, 2002, pp. 76-80.

114 Particularly Articles 79 and 80 of the encyclical: "*Just as it is gravely wrong to take from individuals what they can accomplish by their own initiative and industry and give it to the community, so also it is an injustice and at the same time a grave evil and disturbance of right order to assign to a greater and higher association what lesser and subordinate organizations can do.*" Cf. Schütze, 2013, 244-245.

115 Schilling, Theodor: *Subsidiarity as a Rule and a Principle, or: Taking Subsidiarity Seriously.* Harvard Jean Monnet Working Paper No 10/1995, sections I.A. and III.. Available at: http://centers.law.nyu.edu/jeanmonnet/archive/papers/95/9510ind.html Otherwise the principle of subsidiarity in the form of a political principle should primarily be a guideline for the decision on conferral of competences on the Union.

116 The principle of subsidiarity is worded as follows: "*in areas which do not fall within its exclusive competence, the Union shall act only if and in so far as the objectives of the proposed action cannot be sufficiently achieved by the Member States, either at central level or at regional and local level, but can rather, by reason of the scale or effects of the proposed action, be better achieved at Union level.*"

117 Cooper, Ian: *The Watchdogs of Subsidiarity: National Parliaments and the Logic of Arguing in the EU.* Journal of Common Market Studies 44(2), 2006, p. 284.

binding for the interpretation of competence rules.[118] The adoption of a legal act infringing the principle of subsidiarity will be contrary to primary law and such an act will be declared void.[119]

The motivation for incorporating the subsidiarity principle into EU law was the fear of excessive centralisation as well as of the intrusion of EU law into traditional competences of the Members States in the course of ever faster and deeper integration. This was connected with 1) the widening of objectives and powers of the then Community by the Single European Act and the drafted Maastricht Treaty, which increased the possibility for conflict between European and national policies; 2) the enlargement of the Community, which logically decreased the weight of each Member State; 3) the growth of the number of cases where the Council was to decide by qualified majority rather than unanimity, which deprived states of the right of veto; and also 4) the strengthening of the competences of the European Parliament, which was able to intervene much more in the compromises arrived at by the Council, and force changes.[120] The principle of subsidiarity was supposed to be significant for the dynamics of competence rules in EU law, to counter the EU "competence creep".[121] It was expected to become the guarantee of protection of political decision-making at Member State level.

Soon, the toothlessness of the provision on subsidiarity became apparent in practice. Not long after the adoption of the Maastricht Treaty, the Commission was assigned the duty to justify the conformity of draft legal acts with the

---

118 Hahn-Lorber, Marcus. *Are There Methods of Reasoning on 'Meta-Legislation'? The Interpretation of Legislative Competence Norms within the Methodology of European Constitutional Law.* European Law Journal 16(6), 2010, p. 772.

119 Craig, Paul: *The ECJ and ultra vires Action: A Conceptual Analysis.* Common Market Law Review. 48(2), 2011, pp. 425-426 even states that a breach of the subsidiarity principle renders EU actions *ultra vires*. We, however, cannot concur with this conclusion, as it would mean that subsidiarity is a part of the principle of conferral of competences, which it is apparently not, within the logic of Article 5 TEU, or that any contradiction between secondary and primary EU law is a matter of a competence excess.

120 Cf. e.g. Bermann, George A.: *Taking Subsidiarity Seriously: Federalism in the European Community and the United States.* Columbia Law Review. 1994, pp. 348-369; Kocharov, Anna: *Subsidiarity After Lisbon: Federalism without a Purpose?* In: Azoulai, Loïc, Boucon, Lena, Millet, François-Xavier: *Deconstructing EU Federalism through Competences. EUI Workshop Proceedings – 14 June 2011.* EUI Working Paper Law 2012/6, p. 8; Craig, Paul: *Subsidiarity, a Political and Legal Analysis.* Legal Research Paper Series 15/2012, pp. 2-4.

121 Weatherill, 2011, p. 852 and the preceding works of the author.

subsidiarity principle according to defined criteria, however this had no significant impact on the activities of the Commission. Mere internal self-control, whereby the Commission itself produces the proposals and justifies their compliance with the principle of subsidiarity, proved to be insufficient.[122] Up until the present day, the duty to provide justification for its proposals from the point of view of subsidiarity has been frequently fulfilled by the Commission rather formally by means of an insubstantial panel speech.[123] Impact assessment raises doubts concerning neutrality,[124] and the internal rules for the implementation of such assessment are also subject to criticism.[125]

The approach of the CJEU was also lukewarm, as it did not find that the principle of subsidiarity drew any particular implications for other institutions and, indeed, simply confirmed the extensive interpretation of competence provisions of the Treaties presented by them.[126] It is true that there were only a few cases in which the claimants submitted well-grounded evidence of a breach of the

---

122 Calliess, Christian: *Schriftliche Stellungnahme zum öffentlichen Expertengespräch des Unterausschusses Europarecht des Rechtsausschusses des Deutschen Bundestages zum Thema Prüfung des unionsrechtlichen Subsidiaritätsprinzips am 16. Juni 2010*, p. 2. Retrieved via http://www.bundestag.de/bundestag/ausschuesse17/a06/ua_europarecht/anhoerungen/01_Subsidiaritaet/02_Stellungnahmen/Stellungnahme_Calliess.pdf (last visited 01-06-2014). Kiiver, Philipp: *The Early Warning System for the Principle of Subsidiarity. Constitutional Theory and Empirical Reality.* London/New York: Routledge, 2012, p. 136.

123 Puttler, Adelheid: *Stellungnahme zum Expertengespräch „Prüfung des unionsrechtlichen Subsidiaritätsprinzips" des Unterausschusses Europarecht am 16. Juni 2010*, p. 2. Retrieved via: http://www.bundestag.de/bundestag/ausschuesse17/a06/ua_europarecht/anhoerungen/01_Subsidiaritaet/02_Stellungnahmen/Stellungnahme_Puttler.pdf (last visited 01-06-2014) and Mellein, Christine: *Subsidiaritätskontrolle durch nationale Parlamente. Eine Untersuchung zur Rolle der mitgliedstaatlichen Parlamente in der Architektur Europas.* Nomos: Baden Baden, 2007, p. 132 concurrently speak of standardised building block text (*Textbausteine*).

124 Estella, 2002, pp. 126-127. Namely the United Kingdom parliament, when monitoring compliance with the principle of subsidiarity, very frequently questions the Commission's methods and manner of reaching conclusions.

125 Davies, Gareth: *Subsidiarity: The Wrong Idea, in the Wrong Place, at the Wrong Time.* Common Market Law Review 43(1), 2006, pp. 76-77.

126 See e.g. Estella, 2002; Weatherill, 2011; Martinico, Giuseppe: *Dating Cinderella: On Subsidiarity as a Political Safeguard of Federalism in the European Union.* European Public Law 17(4), 2011; Constantin, Simona: *Rethinking Subsidiarity and the Balance of Powers in the EU in Light of the Lisbon Treaty and Beyond.* Croatian Yearbook of European Law and Policy 4, 2008; Schütze, 2013, pp. 253-256.

subsidiarity principle, however the general reluctance of the CJEU to demand that the Commission present at least more detailed reasoning for draft legal acts became one of the main reasons for considering a new form of subsidiarity control involving national parliaments.[127]

The logical guardian of subsidiarity appeared to be the Council, whose ultimate role is to protect national interests. But, as we have already mentioned, it has not always been fully motivated to do so. Subsidiarity as a possible "defensive" argument of the Member States did not resonate well in the European Parliament either,[128] which has traditionally supported more integration and more competences for itself. Indeed, the absence of a real will to respect the principle of subsidiarity was admitted by representatives of EU institutions.[129] At the same time, it is not possible to say that the Union's activities have always observed the principle of subsidiarity.

As a result of this unsatisfactory situation the mechanism of *ex ante* control of compliance with the subsidiarity principle by national parliaments was included in the Treaty establishing a Constitution for Europe (CT) and later the Lisbon Treaty. The main argument was the proposition that national parliaments will be the most appropriate guardians of subsidiarity, as they are the most affected by its infringements and they represent a wider scope of opinions than the Council.[130]

III.2 Subsidiarity control by the national parliaments: the early warning mechanism and its interpretation

According to Article 5(3) TEU, the institutions of the Union shall apply the principle of subsidiarity as laid down in the Protocol on the application of the principles of subsidiarity and proportionality. The rules of the Protocol may be shortly summarized as follows: any draft legislative act should contain a detailed

---

127 Barber, Nicholas W.: *Subsidiarity in the Draft Constitution.* European Public Law 11(2), 2005, pp. 202-203, Martinico, 2011, p. 658.

128 Koch, Jessica, Kullas, Matthias: *Subsidiarität nach Lissabon – Scharfes Schwert oder stumpfe Klinge?* cepStudie 2010, p. 8. Available at: http://www.cep.eu/fileadmin/user_upload/Kurzanalysen/Subsidiaritaet/Studie_Subsidiaritaet.pdf

129 Fasone, Cristina: *Competing Concepts of Subsidiarity in the Early Warning Mechanism.* Luiss Guido Carli School of Government Working Paper Series. 4/2013 and quotations mentioned there. Available at: http://sog.luiss.it/it/ricerca/working-papers

130 Pabel, Katharina: *Die Kontrolle des Subsidiaritatsprinzips durch die Parlamente der Mitgliedstaaten.* Journal fur Rechtspolitik 19(3-4), 2011, p. 288; Pabel, 2011, p. 288, Kiiver: *The Early Warning System for the Principle of Subsidiarity*, 2012, p. 123; Weatherill, 2011, p. 852.

statement making it possible to appraise compliance with the principles of subsidiarity and proportionality, substantiated by qualitative and, wherever possible, quantitative indicators. Draft legislative acts shall take account of the need for any burden to be minimised and made commensurate with the objective to be achieved. Any national parliament or any chamber thereof may, within eight weeks of the date of transmission of a draft legislative act, send to the presidents of EU institutions a reasoned opinion stating why it considers that the draft in question does not comply with the principle of subsidiarity. The EU institutions shall take account of the reasoned opinions issued. Each national parliament shall have two votes (in bicameral parliaments, each chamber shall have one vote). Where reasoned opinions represent at least one third of all the votes allocated to the national parliaments (or one quarter in the case of a draft legislative act based on Article 76 TFEU), the draft must be reviewed (this is the so-called "yellow card"). After such review, the Commission or other author of the draft may decide to maintain, amend or withdraw the draft. Reasons must be given for this decision. Where reasoned opinions represent at least a simple majority of the votes ("orange card"), in addition to the Commission's duties, the Council and the European Parliament have to review the proposal's compliance with the subsidiarity principle and a majority of 55 percent of the members of the Council or a majority of the votes cast in the European Parliament may decide that the proposal will not be given further consideration. There is also a possibility for the national parliaments to bring an action for annulment to the CJEU on the grounds of a breach of the principle of subsidiarity.

The response to the introduction of the mechanism was mixed: some criticised its insufficiency and weakness, others were concerned over possible blocking the integration process.[131] Firstly, it is necessary to state along with *Philipp Kiiver* that the subsidiarity mechanism is no free exchange of opinions, but a formal communication framework intended to fulfil a specific purpose.[132] It represents an effort to promote respect for the subsidiarity principle within European legislative culture.[133] According to *Ian Cooper* the mechanism will be successful if it opens up a constructive debate between the Commission and national

---

131 Cf. e.g. Constantin, 2008.

132 Kiiver, Philipp: *The conduct of subsidiarity checks of EU legislative proposals by national parliaments: analysis, observations and practical recommendations.* ERA Forum 12(4), 2012, pp. 535–547.

133 Cooper, 2006, pp. 282-283. Similarly Kiiver: *The Early Warning System for the Principle of Subsidiarity,* 2012, pp. 3-4, Weatherill, 2011, p. 860.

parliaments and if the result of subsidiarity assessment depends on the quality of arguments of both sides.[134]

It was clear from the beginning that the content of the subsidiarity principle and the extent of its control under the Protocol will be construed by each institution in the way most favourable to its interests; the Commission and the European Parliament will construe it narrowly so that their activity is not restricted, national parliaments by contrast will construe it very extensively, and the Council will sway between, according to the actual aggregation of interests. So a clash among competing interpretations of the subsidiarity principle was to be expected[135] mainly between national parliaments and the Commission. At the same time it was said that if the Commission is going to argue with parliaments over interpretation of the extent of control, it will not be possible to establish a climate of real dialogue, which is so important for the success of the mechanism.[136]

The current practice of reasoned opinions has confirmed the tendency of national parliaments to interpret widely the extent of control within the Protocol (what are the legitimate reasons for adoption of a reasoned opinion).[137]

The subsidiarity test itself, which consists in an assessment whether "*the objectives of the proposed action cannot be sufficiently achieved by the Member States*" and, at the same time, whether these objectives "*can, by reason of the scale or effects of the proposed action, be better achieved at Union level,*" is rather unclear and has raised many questions.[138] If we return back to the proposition that subsidiarity is a tool for the interpretation of competence rules within the structure of public power based on democratic values, the assessment of "better"

---

134 Cooper, 2006, pp. 282-283, 293, 298.

135 Cooper, 2006, pp. 292-295, Kiiver: *The Early Warning System for the Principle of Subsidiarity,* 2012, p. 69.

136 Mellein, 2007, p. 203, Weatherill, 2011, p. 859.

137 Kiiver: *The Early Warning System for the Principle of Subsidiarity*, 2012, p. 98, Guastaferro, Barbara. *'EU value-added' to an 'EU non encroachment' test? Some Insights from National Parliaments' Reasoned Opinions.* Luiss Guido Carli School of Government Working Paper Series. 2/2013, p. 16. Available at: http://sog.luiss.it/it/ricerca/working-papers; Fasone, 2013, p. 17. Some authors even perceive the widening of the extent of subsidiarity control as a positive impetus for institutional balance in the European Union: Guastaferro, 2013, p. 16, Fasone, 2013, p. 13.

138 What exactly does "better" mean? What if the aim can objectively be achieved neither by the Union nor by the Member States? Does it make any sense to explore the efficiency of Union actions in relation to the "scale or effects of the proposed action," which will logically always be Europe-wide, so consequently we should always conclude that it is the EU which must act?

attainment of objectives cannot consequently be guided just by purely economic, technological efficiency, but must be guided also by considerations regarding which level can resolve the relevant problem in the most democratically sensitive manner.[139] The benefits of action at European level need to be balanced against their negative impact, namely the "costs" of a centrally proposed solution which does not take into account the different preferences of Member States,[140] or an unnecessary restriction of Member States' autonomy.[141] These issues are often said to be a part of the proportionality principle,[142] although they relate to the question of the appropriate level of regulation, which is typical of the subsidiarity principle. The proportionality principle as such is excluded from parliamentary control by the text of Protocol, which is sometimes considered illogical and erroneous.[143] At the same time the proportionality principle is partially contained in the definition of subsidiarity itself.[144] The two cannot be strictly separated.

It is generally accepted that infringement of the subsidiarity principle can be claimed on "procedural" grounds, with reference to insufficiently reasoned compliance.[145] It is not the role of national parliaments to make assumptions about relevant data and arguments of the Commission in order to dispute them.[146] If the reasoning is missing or if it is irrelevant to the subject matter of the proposal, it is possible to speak of a rebuttable presumption that the subsidiarity principle has been violated.[147]

---

139 Hahn-Lorber, 2010, p. 772, 776.

140 Koch, Kullas, 2010, pp. 2, 18-20. Similarly Mellein, 2007, pp. 234-235.

141 Schütze, 2013, pp. 263-264.

142 E.g. Craig, 2012, p. 19 et seq.

143 Cooper, 2006, pp. 282-283, 300-301, Calliess, 2010, pp. 13-14, Mellein, 2007, pp. 198-199.

144 Cf. the words "the Union shall act only if and *insofar* as..." in Article 5(3) TEU.

145 Mellein, 2007, in particular pp. 201-203, Kiiver: *The Early Warning System for the Principle of Subsidiarity*, 2012 and others.

146 Kiiver: *The conduct of subsidiarity checks of EU legislative proposals by national parliaments*, 2012.

147 Kiiver: *The Early Warning System for the Principle of Subsidiarity*, 2012, pp. 100-101. As an example we may mention the use of tautology that an EU institution can only be established by a legal act of the EU, in a proposal which does not establish such an institution but only changes its rules of operation to the prejudice of competences of Member States' authorities. See COM (2013) 535, Proposal for a Regulation of the European Parliament and of the Council on the European Union Agency for Criminal Justice Cooperation (Eurojust). Cf. also Schütze, 2013, pp. 253-254.

We can find strong arguments in favour of including the issue of competence in the subsidiarity check. The existence of EU competence represents a prerequisite with respect to the subsidiarity principle. If the Union lacks competence to adopt a certain measure, its actions are always in breach of the subsidiarity principle, as this principle cannot establish a competence for the Union.[148] If national parliaments were not able to accept a reasoned opinion, if they believed that the EU has no competence to act, then control of subsidiarity would lose all sense.[149]

In our opinion, to insist on a strict interpretation of the extent of subsidiarity control would be appropriate in case there was a risk of abuse of this tool with potentially paralysing effects on the EU legislative process. This is however not the case of the Protocol, which does not give the national parliaments any veto power or "red card". The destiny of the Commission's proposal depends firstly on the Union's legislator and secondly on the CJEU. The early warning mechanism has only the function of a warning and should result in a more exhaustive explanation of the policy of the Commission, or in the uncovering of the fact that there are no persuasive grounds for the adoption of a measure. The proposition that a wider approach to the extent of subsidiarity control could destabilise the institutional balance of the Union[150] should be denied.[151]

III.3 Subsidiarity control in practice

The first four years of operation of the early warning mechanism can be assessed rather sceptically. Taking subsidiarity seriously and achieving a pragmatic debate between the Commission and national parliaments are as yet far away. This

---

148 Kiiver, Philipp: *The Early Warning System for the Principle of Subsidiarity*, 2012, p. 98; Calliess 2010, pp. 13-14; Mellein 2007, pp. 200-201; Buschmann, Marco, Daiber, Birgit: *Subsidiaritätsrüge und Grundsatz der begrenzten Einzelermächtigung.* Die öffentliche Verwaltung 60(13), 2007, pp. 504–509.

149 Subsidiarity is specified also in individual provisions of the Treaties, such as various competence exclusions or clauses stressing the complementary character of the Union's actions. This concerns mainly the areas of social policy, education, culture, health care, and the former third pillar. Calliess, 2010, pp. 13-14. Legal acts in these areas of EU competence require especially detailed explanation.

150 Fabbrini, Federico, Granat, Katarzyna: *'Yellow card, but no foul': The role of the national parliaments under the subsidiarity protocol and the Commission proposal for an EU regulation on the right to strike.* Common Market Law Review 50(1), 2013 p. 117.

151 Cf. Kiiver, Philipp: *The Early Warning System for the Principle of Subsidiarity*, 2012 p. 147: "*[A]s long as the [early warning system] does not produce any terrible intrusive legal effects, a more creative approach to its political application is surely justified, without violating the letter of the law.*"

situation can be illustrated by the two "yellow cards," which were adopted in connection with the proposal for regulation "Monti II"[152] in May 2012 and the proposal for a regulation on the establishment of the European Public Prosecutor's Office[153] (the EPPO) in October 2013.

The abovementioned Monti II regulation attempted to resolve the conflict between market freedoms (free movement of services, freedom of establishment) and economic rights (collective action and right to strike). Instead of the current judicial conception of these rights as infringements of market freedoms, which must be subjected to a proportionality test, Article 2 provided that the exercise of market freedoms must respect economic rights, and vice versa. The proposal also contained several procedural rules for the resolution of collective disputes addressed to the Member States.

Reasoned opinions of national parliaments[154] contained the objection primarily that under Articles 153(5) and 352(3) TFEU the EU does not have the competence to harmonise the right to strike. They further argued that the submitted proposal does not lead to the attainment of the defined objective, i.e. clarification of the relationship between the above-mentioned rights and freedoms and the enhancement of legal certainty. Thus, the action of the EU has no added value. In light of the other provisions of the proposal, the parliaments were concerned about the violation of national mechanisms of collective bargaining and endangering international obligations of the Member States in the area of economic and social rights.[155]

The Commission replied to these reasoned opinions in a letter dated 12 September 2012, in which it stated that it "*has carefully assessed the arguments put forward by national Parliaments in their reasoned opinions, taking note that the concerns expressed relate in particular to the added value of the draft Regulation, the choice of the legal basis, [and] the EU competence to legislate on this matter,*" but that, however, it "*has not found that the principle of subsidiarity has been breached.*" In spite of this, the Commission decided to withdraw the proposal and reasoned that it would be

152 COM (2012) 130. Proposal for a Council Regulation on the exercise of the right to take collective action within the context of the freedom of establishment and the freedom to provide services.

153 COM (2013) 534.

154 For the full text of the reasoned opinions, see IPEX Database at http://www.ipex.eu/IPEXL-WEB/dossier/document/COM20120130.do. For a summary, see Bruun, Bücker, Dorssemont, 2012, pp. 299-300.

155 Cf. Bruun, Bücker, Dorssemont, 2012, p. 292 et seq.

unlikely to obtain the necessary political support either in the Council (where unanimity would be required) or in the Parliament.

The Commission thus simply maintained its statement; it did not recognise the arguments of national parliaments and did not attempt to deal with them by providing counter-arguments. In our opinion, such an approach does not respect the purpose of the Protocol. The Commission only conceived subsidiarity control as an indication of the Council's position and did not even try to engage in a real debate with the parliaments. It did not say whether it considered their objections relevant from the point of view of the subsidiarity principle yet unconvincing for some other reason, or whether it considered them to be irrelevant, and why. This may be interpreted neither as the Commission's approval of national parliaments' abuse of their control over the subsidiarity principle,[156] nor as a victory by the parliaments and the Commission's acceptance of their arguments.[157]

The second yellow card was shown to the Commission's EPPO proposal. This new EU agency should investigate crimes such as fraud damaging the Union's financial interests, bring actions before the criminal courts of the Member States, and also appear before them. Within individual national systems, the EPPO should have the same position as the national public prosecution, including the possibility to order various investigative measures and require co-operation with, or directly use Member States' authorities.

In this case, national parliaments challenged mainly the Commission's conclusion about the inability of the Member States to achieve an effective and equivalent level of prosecution of criminal offences against the financial interests of the Union and about the benefits of the proposal. They argued that criminal procedure is traditionally a matter of national competence and it is still primarily within the competence of the Member States. The Commission did not explain in what respect the current methods of judicial co-operation are insufficient and did not really consider the possibility of strengthening the existing institutions of Eurojust, Europol and OLAF, which many parliaments would prefer. The Commission did not state why the model of Eurojust as a collegium of public prosecutors delegated by the Member States is insufficient, or why the EPPO should have a monocratic and hierarchic structure. Neither did it consider possible improvements in the prevention of fraud that can be made at Union level.

---

156 As suggested by Fabbrini, Granat, 2013, p. 142, who, on the grounds of an extremely narrow interpretation of the extent of subsidiarity control, arrive at the conclusion that the arguments of national parliaments do not concern the subsidiarity principle.

157 As suggested by Fasone, 2013, pp. 23-24.

As regards the benefits of the proposal, the predicted increase in the clear-up rate of 25 percent was not substantiated by any relevant data. Whether it is possible to achieve a uniform level of successful prosecution, when the EPPO operates within 28 distinct judicial systems, also remains doubtful. On the other hand, parliaments stressed and explained in detail how the proposal violates the structures and principles of criminal law in their states and how it may endanger the efficiency of national criminal proceedings (jurisdictional disputes, giving priority to EPPO tasks over national investigation). At the same time the proposal lowers the standards of protection for accused persons by omitting to deal with many important procedural questions.[158]

In November 2013 the Commission issued a Communication on this yellow card,[159] where it stated that, having assessed the arguments of national parliaments, it had decided to maintain the draft regulation, but assured that it is going to take due account of reasoned opinions in the course of the legislative process. What exactly does this mean is unclear. We might speculate that if the Commission really wanted to take due account of the national parliaments' opinions, it could have modified the proposal according to the Protocol. The Commission is responding to the objections raised by national parliaments, which is a step forward, but it does not present new arguments and only negates reasoned opinions by repeating its propositions from the explanatory memorandum of the proposal. As regards the insufficient reasoning of the proposal, the Commission refers directly to benevolent case law of the CJEU and does not comment on the merits. The Commission finds the added value of the proposal in the decrease of need for legal assistance between Member States, the concentration of information on cases of fraud, the prevention of forum-shopping on the part of offenders, the duty imposed on the Member States' courts to admit evidence obtained under the law of another Member State, and in the EPPO's power to decide in which state proceedings will be held. The last two "advantages" significantly interfere with the rights of the accused. However, the arguments of national parliaments regarding the imperilment of fundamental rights protection and the functioning of Member States' judicial systems were specifically excluded by the Commission from the framework of subsidiarity control.

The Commission's reply to the second yellow card represents an improvement in the sense that the Commission stated which objections it found relevant from

158 For the reasoned opinions, see IPEX Database at: http://www.ipex.eu/IPEXL-WEB/dossier/document/COM20130534.do

159 COM (2013) 851.

the point of view of subsidiarity. Besides that, it only reiterated its initial arguments and avoided responding to some key counter-arguments.

We do not have space here for a detailed analysis of both proposals or for "judging" the dispute between the Commission and national parliaments. But it is clear that the parliaments' arguments cannot be dismissed as manifestly unfounded, particularly if we consider the reasoning of both proposals provided by the Commission.

National parliaments' control of the observation of the subsidiarity principle has the potential to contribute to the "good functioning of the Union" (Article 12 TEU). However, it faces resistance from the Commission, which does not perceive the principle of subsidiarity and the outcomes of the new mechanism as something which it should systematically consider in the interest of the Union, but rather as a bureaucratic exercise, an obstacle which needs to be overcome on the path to further integration. Some hope may be found in the co-ordination of national parliaments, which are increasingly discontent with the Commission's approach - not only toward subsidiarity check. Due to its responses to yellow cards, the Commission was criticised at inter-parliamentary forums such as the COSAC conferences and the question now is whether it will be able to go on and resist pressure from national parliaments, or whether it will start to fulfil its role under the Protocol and conduct a real dialogue with them.

Jan Broz, Pavel Ondřejek

Human rights limits on state power

I. Introduction

We live in an age of human rights.[1] Human rights have become – at least in terms of rhetoric – a central influence determining the transformation of modern Western society following the Second World War. Modern Western society puts at the forefront the individual with his or her inalienable rights, and is therefore seen as more individualistic than pre-modern society in which an individual was primarily someone who owed duties. Such a transformation inevitably also impacts the "classical architecture" of public law, which has since the end of the Second World War been facing new issues and challenges directly related to human rights.[2] Are human rights "trumps" that prevent the state from interfering with the elementary spheres of human existence?[3] If so, which aspects of the spheres of human life may be considered "elementary"? Or should human rights be conceived rather as approximative value propositions and the state strive to implement them in the widest possible scope?

Finding answers to these questions, as well as many other questions, is difficult due to the plurality of theories of human rights and the sources of their legitimacy. Further difficulties concern the existence of various methods for resolving mutual conflicts between human rights as well as conflicts with public goods, and the unclear relation between universal human rights and specific rights enshrined in the constitutions of individual states. An unclear approach to these issues does not only result in the delegitimising of state power, but also of human rights, which in such a situation cannot perform the role that they are expected to play. This fact indicates one of many paradoxes regarding these rights. Even though they are usually perceived as a pre-positive category independent of acknowledgement by the state power or by its positive legal order, in order to be able to exercise the rights in reality it is necessary to have a social mechanism that is capable of enforcing the rights. The social mechanism is

1 Bobbio, Norberto: *The Age of Rights*. Cambridge (UK): Polity Press, 1996.
2 Loughlin, Martin: *The Idea of Public Law*. Oxford: Oxford University Press, 2004, p. 114.
3 Dworkin, Ronald: *Taking Rights Seriously*. Cambridge (MA): Harvard University Press, 1978, p. xi.

traditionally the state, which historically primarily owed duties arising from constitutionally guaranteed human rights (human rights are traditionally exercised with so-called vertical effect, i.e. between the individual and the state).[4]

Human rights do not operate only within the legal orders of individual states. At least during the course of the Second World War it was possible to observe the growing importance of human rights in the field of public international law. Human rights currently operate on the one hand as a limit on the power exercised by international or supranational organisations, and on the other hand, at the same time they operate as a limit on state power that is put in place by international organisations.[5] International law obligations in the field of human rights protection may in certain cases even collide with the constitutional arrangement of the state. Such a situation recently occurred in Bosnia and Herzegovina, the constitution of which was drafted as a compromise within peace negotiations and contained a provision concerning the establishment of certain top state bodies by citizens of the so-called constituent peoples - that is, Bosnians, Croats and Serbs. The applicants, who were not among these constituent peoples and were thus in fact excluded from occupying a position in such state bodies, were able to obtain a declaration that the Bosnian-Herzegovian constitution was contrary to the European Convention for the Protection of Human Rights and Fundamental Freedoms.[6] The complexity of national political and social relations in Bosnia and Herzegovina still makes it impossible to make the required changes to the constitution in a manner that would be compliant with the standards of the Council of Europe. This raises a question concerning the role of international courts in the resolution of politically sensitive issues that have human-rights dimensions.

One of the paradoxes of the protection of human rights is the fact that even though human rights are perceived as a limit on state (or public) power, due to

---

4 Isensee, Josef: *Die heikle Weltherrschaft der Menschenrechte*. In: Breuer, Martin, Epiney, Astrid (eds.): *Der Staat im Recht. Festschrift für Eckart Klein zum 70. Geburtstag*. Berlin: Duncker und Humblot, 2013, pp. 1089 et seq.

5 Cf. chapters 2 and 3 dealing with international and European law.

6 The European Court of Human Rights declared a breach of Article 14 of the Convention in conjunction with Article 3 of Protocol No. 1 amending the Convention (non-discrimination in relation to the right to free election), and with article 1 of Protocol No. 12, amending the Convention for the Protection of Human Rights and Fundamental Freedoms (general non-discrimination). See the judgment of the Grand Chamber of the ECHR of 22nd December 2009 concerning the case of *Sejdic and Finci v. Bosnia and Herzegovina* (Application Nos. 27996/06 and 34836/06).

their legitimising role they might not only justify this power, but also contribute to its factual growth.[7] This does not apply only to the state but also to every community the purpose of which should be, among other things, the protection of human rights.[8]

The purpose of this chapter is to attempt to chart, within the above-described context, how human rights currently fulfil the role of domains within which the state cannot interfere using legislative or administrative measures. The chapter also discusses what the beneficiaries of these rights are entitled to claim against the state.

II. The origin and sources of legitimacy of human rights, and their relation to state power

Examining the origin and sources of legitimacy of human rights may seem to many to be impractical and far too academic. In our opinion this is not the case. Assuming that the application of law should be as coherent as possible, it is hard to avoid the issue that influences this characteristic. In other words, seeking the theoretical foundations of human rights is not a mere academic obsession, but rather consists in searching for the scope and limits of these rights - which are truly practical issues.

We may base our considerations on the German doctrine which differentiates between human rights (*Menschenrechte*) and constitutional rights (*Grundrechte*). The relationship between the two categories is not reflected in the valence or

7 Depending on whether we approach human rights as a political or legal category we may distinguish at least two different perspectives regarding their role. From the point of view of political theory, human rights rank among the most important phenomena to justify the existence of and specific activity on the part of the state, or, contrary to this, offer a legislative framework enabling criticism of the state's activities (Kysela, Jan: *Ústava mezi právem a politikou. Úvod do ústavní teorie* [*Constitution between Law and Politics. An Introduction to Constitutional Theory*]. Praha: Leges, 2014, p. 258). The theory of constitutional law, which is usually based on the precept of public rights, by contrast differentiates between the protective role of human rights, i.e. a prohibition of certain ways of exercising state power, and positive roles imposing a duty on the state to act in a certain manner (see part 2 of this chapter).

8 Here are only several examples from an extensive list of sources dealing with the legitimising role of human rights: Buchanan, Allen: *Justice, Legitimacy, and Self-Determination. Moral Foundations of International Law.* Oxford: Oxford University Press, 2004; Tasioulas, John: *Human Rights, Legitimacy, and International Law.* The American Journal of Jurisprudence 28(1), 2013, pp. 1-25.

value of rights that fall into these two categories, but rather in the different reasons for their validity.[9] Human rights are rights that are owed to every human being on the grounds of being a human. They are therefore natural, prepositive rights deriving their validity from human dignity rather than from the positive legal order of a particular society. This fact differentiates human rights from constitutional rights, the characteristic feature of which is their positive entrenchment in the legal order of a specific society.[10]

As mentioned above, *K. Stern* differentiates between the two categories with regard to the grounds of validity, rather than intensity or value. This is in line with the fact that the catalogue of constitutional rights generally includes human rights and possibly develops or complements these rights. What should be done, however, in those cases where a state does not have constitutional rights, or where the catalogue of constitutional rights is more limited than the catalogue of human rights that is independent of the state? According to *K. Stern,* in such a case it is necessary to give priority to the direct effect of human rights. This stems from their special quality as an "*immediately applicable supreme law from which constitutional rights may be derived.*"[11]

This approach raises various questions, the most important of which at this point is as follows. Imagine a hypothetical state, the constitutional order of which guarantees to citizens the right to choose between religion X, which is promoted by the state, or to declare that they have "no religion." Intuitively we may say that such a state violates the right of an individual to freely choose his or her religion, as well as the right not to be discriminated against. In spite of this, a significant majority of citizens may consider such an order to be legitimate if the majority in general consists of atheists benevolent toward people professing religion X. How could such people be persuaded of the universal validity of the human right of freedom of religion, i.e. the right of the people to also practise generally peaceful religions other than X (for example religion Y)?

Stern's answer to this question is unconvincing. Even though he bases his human rights theory on a specific understanding of human dignity, he does not claim that his conception is the only possible one: "*Irrespective of which justification one chooses for their [human rights] existence, it will always consist in their pre-state determinateness.*"[12] Such a statement is an "escape" from a normative

9 Stern, Klaus: *Staatsrecht der Bundesrepublik Deutschland. Bd. III/1. Allgemeine Lehren der Grundrechte.* Munich: C. H. Beck, 1988, p. 44.

10 *Ibid.,* p. 43.

11 *Ibid.,* p. 44.

12 *Ibid.,* p. 43.

level to a descriptive level, at which *Stern* points out the known weakness of all similar theories. These theories, which we may identify as *traditionalist,* or *foundationalist,*[13] agree on people being owed certain human rights due to the "simple fact" that they are human beings.[14] The dispute concerns what makes a human being a human being, and it is therefore also contentious what rights must be deemed human rights, and what their content and scope is.

Traditionalist, or more generally conceived *foundationalist* approaches, are thus exposed to two substantial issues. First, specifying human rights through various characteristics that define a human as a being endowed with these rights may result in the situation where a certain group or category of people will not be endowed with these rights precisely due to the fact that they do not possess the right characteristic (intellect, gender, race and so on). It may seem that such concerns were appropriate in past centuries,[15] however it is necessary to remember an important note of *R. Rorty* stating that genocides even in this period were generally not based on an intention to deny human rights, but rather on the assumption that the attacked group of citizens does not reach the qualities worthy of a civilised man endowed with these rights.[16] Therefore not only does

13 These two expressions are not synonymous. The term *traditionalist* is usually used for theories seeking the basis of human rights in the specific character of human nature. The term *foundationalist* is used for a wider group of theories trying to find a theoretical basis for human rights (this group includes for example a majority of contractualist theories). We use in this chapter the more general of these terms. See Beitz, Charles R.: *The Idea of Human Rights.* Oxford: Oxford University Press, 2009, pp. 103-104.

14 In this context Kysela, 2014, p. 260, points out the fact that in the English language (*natural rights*) and in German (*Naturrechte*) the conception of human rights is not fully differentiated from "naturality," which does not necessarily have to be viewed in a universalist manner, but may be perceived from the point of view of social Darwinism.

15 For example St. Thomas Aquinas derived the sanctity of human life and therefore also the prohibition on killing from the dignity of human existence arising from the capability of volitional conduct. Since this capability and therefore also dignity is derived from God (man as the image of God), an individual acting in an ungodly manner loses his dignity and may be subject to the death penalty. The right to live as well as other rights are not granted to everyone, but are only granted to people who are capable of volitional conduct which at the same time is not contradictory to God's requirements for human conduct. See Mahlmann, Matthias: *Elemente einer ethischen Grundrechtstheorie.* Baden-Baden: Nomos Verlagsgesellschaft, 2008, pp. 122-125.

16 Rorty, Richard: *Human Rights, Rationality, and Sentimentality.* In: id.: *Truth and Progress: Philosophical Papers.* Vol. 3. Cambridge (UK): Cambridge University Press, 1998, pp. 167-69.

the question "What rights are typical of people?" remain important, but also so do the questions "Who is endowed with human rights?" and "What makes a human being a human being?"[17]

A second and more general issue is entailed in the fact that these theories justify the existence of human rights using certain normative axioms that are not subject to any further justification. As we have indicated above, even though human rights are conceived primarily in an individualistic manner, they are at the same time a social phenomenon that must rely on acknowledgement through discursive practice. The simple statement "I have right X because simply I have it" may hardly constitute such an acknowledgement.[18] Theories attempting to justify the existence of human rights by reference to other more elementary values are always ultimately based on a doctrine, i.e. lacking final unchallenged justification.[19] If somebody justifies the existence of human rights, either in general or a specific catalogue of human rights, by reference for example to a certain conception of human dignity, we may ask him what justifies human dignity or what justifies this specific conception of human dignity. And this process may be repeated until all arguments are exhausted and it becomes evident that it is simply not possible to agree, on the basis of such arguments, upon the existence of specific human rights, their content, or their limits.

We may however choose a different approach consisting in a particular understanding of human rights as a manifestation of culturally shared sentiments, historical and social constructions, and so on. Perhaps the most well known theory of this category is *Rorty's* understanding of human rights using sentiments. According to *R. Rorty,* a departure from the conception of the rationality of Enlightenment also means a departure from *foundationalist theories,* raising questions concerning the substance and uniqueness of the human being, which are usually found in human intellect.[20] Instead of engaging in disputes concerning the issue of human nature as the basis of human rights, we should put our energy

---

17 We must note that this issue does not apply only to *foundationalist* theories but also to other theories discussed in the text.

18 We base our considerations on the fact that the existence of certain human rights is contentious in a specific community. Otherwise, if all members of a society intuitively perceived that "everyone has the right to X," it would not be necessary to prove this right.

19 See Freeman, Michael: *The Philosophical Foundations of Human Rights*. Human Rights Quarterly 16(3), 1996, pp. 495-6.

20 R. Rorty uses the term *foundationalist* for those theories whose authors attempt to derive the validity of human rights from premises that are considered true (and therefore valid and therefore final) independently of the intuition of morals. (Rorty, 1998, p. 171).

into "sentimental education," which is better suited, if appropriate examples are used, to the spreading of a general awareness of human rights as the rights of all people irrespective of their race, gender or education.[21]

The problem with *Rorty's* theory is that it does not say what rights should be promoted. We may expect that the majority of citizens will remain loyal to the values of the society in which they were socialised. In other words, a Frenchman should have a sentimental relation with the rights contained in the Declaration of the Rights of Man and of the Citizen, while a US citizen will have such a relation with the Bill of Rights. This brings us back to the issue of making a distinction between human rights and constitutional rights. The nature of constitutional rights is much closer to *Rorty's* conception of rights than the classic universal conception of human rights.[22]

In reaction to a growing scepticism concerning the potential for anchoring human rights in a satisfactory theoretical conception, theories may have tended toward a more analytical approach to the issue. One such approach to human rights is that of *J. Raz*, who presents a *political conception* of human rights. In his conception, "*human rights are those regarding which sovereignty-limiting measures are morally justified.*"[23] The problem of the political conception is that it is too focused on the second characteristic, i.e. the capability of human rights to legitimise the limits of state sovereignty. This reflects the emphasis placed on international law recognition and the institutional enforceability of these rights: "*Its essence as a political conception is that it regards human rights as rights which are to be given institutional recognition, rights which transcend private morality.*"[24] Human rights, as admitted by the author, then become almost undifferentiable

21 *Ibid.*, p. 176.

22 According to K. Stern the specific conception of constitutional rights is one of the specific national features of a country. Citing E. R. Huber, Stern says: "*There is clearly a strong relation between constitutional rights and the spiritual content present in a nation. This relation between a legal rule and spiritual fact is more direct in the case of constitutional rights than in the case of provisions concerning the form of government.*" Stern, Klaus: *Idee der Menschenrechte und Positivität der Grundrechte.* In: Isensee Josef, Kirchhof, Paul (eds.): *Handbuch des Staatsrechts der Bundesrepublik Deutschland. Bd. V. Allgemeine Grundrechtslehren.* 2nd ed. Heidelberg: C. F. Müller, 2000, p. 5.

23 Raz, Joseph: *Human Rights without Foundations.* In: Besson, Samantha, Tasioulas, John (eds.): *The Philosophy of International Law.* Oxford: Oxford University Press, 2010, p. 329.

24 *Ibid.*, p. 335. It is worth noticing the emphasis placed on institutional recognition of these rights which is used by Raz to relate the political conception with his interest theory of rights. See Raz, Joseph: *The Morality of Freedom.* Oxford: Clarendon, 1986, ch. 7 (esp. pp. 180-183).

from the prevailing international political morals.[25] If *J. Raz* criticises traditional theories for their inability to normatively criticise current international practice, it is highly disputable whether his own theory is capable of such criticism.

The political conception of human rights is quite close to a sociological justification of their validity, according to which these rights "*represent a legal reaction to historically specific, subjectively experienced relations between a person and the society and its institutions.*"[26] In this opinion the determining factor for the creation of human rights consists primarily in an injustice having been experienced.

Finally, even though the above and similar theories have been increasingly influential since the middle of the last century, it is not possible to say that traditionalist theories are on the decline. For example, according to prominent continental legal philosopher *R. Alexy*, human rights may be justified by a combination of arguments based on the essence of a person as a rational being capable of discourse and having a personality characterised by freedom, equality and dignity.[27]

And so we find ourselves in a situation where the majority of people are able to agree that there are certain human rights of elementary importance. What they cannot agree on though are answers to the questions of what the content of such rights is, what their origin (or the reason for validity) is, and whether there is a comprehensive theoretical conception of human rights.[28] This is not really encouraging if we wish to focus on the issues of interpretation and the application of human rights.[29]

---

25 Raz, 2010, p. 333. We would consider the term "political convention" to be more appropriate than "political morals" as used by J. Raz, which may tempt the reader to think in normative intentions, which does not seem to be very appropriate to this context.

26 Bárány, Eduard: *Pojmy dobrého práva* [*The Concepts of Good Law*]. Bratislava: Eurokodex, 2007, pp. 60 -61. Slovak expert in legal theory E. Bárány refers to a number of German authors supporting this thesis: H. Klenner, F. Ossenbühl or J. Habermas.

27 Alexy, Robert: *Menschenrechte ohne Metaphysik?* Deutsche Zeitschrift für Philosophie 52(1), 2004, pp. 15-24.

28 See the classical text Böckenförde, Ernst-Wolfgang: *Grundrechtstheorie und Grundrechtsinterpretation*. In: id.: *Staat, Verfassung, Demokratie. Studien zur Verfassungstheorie und Verfassungsrecht.* Frankfurt a.M.: Suhrkamp, 1991, pp. 115-145.

29 Practical issues related to concepts lacking clear definitions in the conception are currently raised for example by those criticising a lack of entrenchment of the concept of "human dignity." See for example McCrudden, Christopher: *Human Dignity and Judicial Interpretation of Human Rights.* European Journal of International Law 19(4), 2008, pp. 655-724; Mattson, David J., Clark, Susan G.: *Human dignity in concept and practice.* Policy Sciences 44(4), 2011, pp. 303-19.

III. Horizons and functions of human rights in legal orders

J. Raz is right in that, irrespective of whether we recognise the prepositive or even the suprapositive character of human rights, in order to be realistically able to invoke those rights it is necessary for them to be recognised by public power, i.e. the state, which will ensure their factual enforceability. First, this means that the existence of judicial bodies must be ensured (currently they exist not only on a state level), which make authoritative decisions in disputes in which individuals seek protection of their rights. In order to fully accomplish the ideal of human rights, which generally consists in providing for the development of the free individual under conditions of a democratic society,[30] it is necessary for human rights to be respected and at the same time to be implemented through the activities of all bodies with public power when making law, when applying it, and also in other forms of their activities. It is possible to state that too much emphasis on the judicial protection of human rights may be counterproductive in relation to the whole system of their protection due to the lower activity of other branches of government in this field - the legislative branch in particular.[31]

The enforceability of human rights was not matter of course for a long time. Even though it is possible to find reflections on human rights in the work of ancient philosophers and other ancient thinkers,[32] they were in the majority of states legally entrenched for the first time in the course of the 18th or 19th centuries. Constitutionally entrenched rights at that time represented only a moral declaration of state power, rather than its actual limitation. This criticism of the conception of constitutionally guaranteed rights was typical primarily for representatives of the normative school. For example, *H. Kelsen* pointed out

30 Bleckmann, Albert: *Staatsrecht. 2. Bd. – Grundrechte.* 4. ed. Köln: Carl Heymanns Verlag, 1997, p. 15.

31 In its strong form this argument results in a rejection of the existence of charters of constitutional rights, i.e. a rejection of the constitutional entrenchment of human rights, due to an inadequate growth in the power of constitutional courts at the expense of the legislative branch - which however does not in fact secure better standard of protection of these rights. See for example Waldron, Jeremy: *A Rights-Based Critique of Constitutional Rights.* Oxford Journal of Legal Studies 13(1), 1993, pp. 18-51; Allan, James: *Bill of Rights and Judicial Power – A Liberal's Quandary.* Oxford Journal of Legal Studies 16(2), 1996, pp. 337-352.

32 See for example a well-arranged selection of texts in Ishay, Micheline R.: *The Human Rights Reader: Major Political Essays, Speeches, and Documents from Ancient Times to the Present.* 2nd ed. London: Routledge, 2007.

that constitutional rights historically developed "*from a natural idea of certain absolute rules limiting the state and later became the content of positive law as they derived from an instance foreign to the state*."[33] In Czech jurisprudence there is a well-known statement made by an outstanding expert in the theory of public law, *František Weyr*, who said that a part of German literature considered "*the relevant constitutional provisions concerning the rights of citizens and freedoms and their guarantees to be mere academic principles, or 'monologues of the law-maker,' that do not have the nature of rules binding on courts and administrative authorities.*"[34] This is in contrast with French and American doctrine in the first half of the last century that recognised the binding character of human rights vis-à-vis courts and administrative authorities.[35]

The spread of the theory of constitutionally enshrined human rights as valid law which has superior legal force must be viewed as a manifestation of the "post-war paradigm" which is best illustrated by the development of constitutionality and constitutional judiciary in the post-war Federal Republic of Germany. This transformation must be considered another manifestation of the growing importance of the legitimising function of human rights in relation to state power.[36]

When speaking about the recognition of human rights by public bodies as a condition of the real application of these rights, we implicitly assume a consensus within the whole society regarding the existence of specific human rights. Such a recognition of human rights by society must take place on an abstract level, i.e. on the level of the existence of a right, not necessarily on the level of the resolution of a specific contentious case (we acknowledge that discrimination on

---

33 Kelsen, Hans: *Základy obecné teorie státní* [*Fundamentals of the General Theory of State*]. Brno: Barvič a Novotný, 1926, p. 48.

34 Weyr, František: *Československé ústavní právo* [*Czechoslovak Constitutional Law*]. Praha: Melantrich, 1937, p. 248.

35 Holländer, Pavel: *Filosofie práva* [*Philosophy of Law*]. 2nd ed. Plzeň: Aleš Čeněk, 2012, p. 215

36 There are however also opponents of this conventional statement in contemporary literature. Cf. Bedi, Sonu: *Rejecting Rights*. Cambridge (UK): Cambridge University Press, 2009. In Czech literature a similar attitude is taken by Matěj Gregárek, even though he uses different arguments. See his *Justifikace státu: legitimita, ospravedlnění a neradikální rámec filosofického anarchismu* [Justification of State: Legitimacy, Justifiability and Non-Radical Framework of Philosophical Anarchism]. In: Kosek Jan, Gregárek Matěj: *Stát, právo a (ne)spravedlnost. Dvě studie z právní filozofie [State, Law and (In)justice. Two Studies in Legal Philosophy*]. Praha: Právnická fakulta UK, 2012, pp. 47-98.

the grounds of race is not allowed, but certain measures may be deemed justifiable by the majority of the society).[37]

The state may apply its power with respect to individuals, however this application is limited with respect to human rights. These rights primarily create a defence against illegitimate or inappropriate interventions by the state or any other public power. In this context German constitutional theory speaks about so-called *defensive rights (Abwehrrechte)*, i.e. the rights of an individual against the state.[38] The content of this basic level of relation between the state and constitutional rights is the recognition of the validity of certain human right on the part of state and the consequent duty of the state to refrain from interfering with this right – in this context the term "negative obligations of the state" is used.

In a modern state the importance of human rights exceeds their defensive role. This is why modern constitutional theory points out also the positive obligations of the state arising from human rights, which are further classified as *duties to protect* and *duties to fulfil* human rights.[39]

---

37 It is possible to mention the example of the prevailing attitude of Czech society toward the judgment of the ECHR concerning *D. H. and others v. the Czech Republic* (judgment of 13 November 2007, Application No. 57325/00). Even though it is not possible to claim that the majority of citizens of the Czech Republic support discrimination on the grounds of race, the finding of the ECHR concerning the discriminatory treatment of Roma children who were, to a large extent and not always based on adequate criteria, transferred to special schools designed primarily for children with moderate mental retardation, provoked general disagreement in Czech society. On the issue of abstract agreement with constitutional clauses in general see Sunstein, Cass R.: *Constitutional Agreement without Constitutional Theories*. Ratio Juris 13(1), 2000, pp. 117-130.

38 One of the first known attempts to classify different statuses of human rights is the theory of G. Jellinek (*System der subjektiven öffentlichen Rechte,* 1892), which is still one of the basic sources of German theory. In practice the concept of defensive rights became known primarily thanks to the well-known decision of the German Federal Constitutional Court in the case of *Lüth*, in which the court stated the following: "*It is beyond any doubt whatsoever that the purpose of constitutional rights is primarily to protect the sphere of freedom of the individual: they are defensive rights (Abwehrrechte) of individuals against the state.*" BVerfGE 7, 198 at 204 cf. Stern, Klaus: *Idee und Elemente eines Systems der Grundrechte*. In: Isensee Josef, Kirchhof Paul (eds.): *Handbuch des Staatsrechts der Bundesrepublik Deutschland. Bd. V. Allgemeine Grundrechtslehren.* 2nd ed. Heidelberg: C. F. Müller, 2000, p. 70. More important in this judgment is, of course, its elaboration on the horizontal effect of human rights – see below.

39 Fredman, Sandra: *Human Rights Transformed. Positive Rights and Positive Duties.* Oxford: Oxford University Press, 2008, pp. 73 et seq.

Another angle that is currently undergoing the most progressive development consists in guaranteeing these rights and ensuring that nobody interferes with the rights. The state is charged with actively protecting constitutional rights that are recognised in the constitution. This role of constitutional rights is closely related to their *horizontal effect,* i.e. to the application of constitutional rights in private law relations in which formally equal persons engage. There are certainly more reasons for the development of the conception of horizontal effect of constitutional rights, however one of the most important could be the fact that it is becoming increasingly clear that private persons may in some cases cause much more damage to the human rights of an individual than a state might.[40]

The concept of horizontal effect covers a wide range of various effects of human rights, likened by *S. Gardbaum* to a scale where at one extreme are models acknowledging the full application of human-rights rules to private law relations, and at the other extreme there are models excluding the application of human-rights rules in private law.[41] German academic literature, which is probably the richest in this field and where the first conceptions of horizontal effect originated as early as shortly after the Second World War, usually distinguishes between direct and indirect horizontal effect of constitutional rights.[42]

H. C. Nipperdey, the president of the Federal Labour Court (*Bundesarbeitsgericht*) in Kassel from 1954 until 1963, is usually referred to as the "father" of direct horizontal effect. His main idea was that some constitutional rights should constitute principles of the organisation of the life of the whole society and therefore should have immediate importance also in social relations between individuals.[43]

Other representatives of German doctrine opposed the conception of direct effect of constitutional rights. One of the most important opponents was *G. Dürig*, who stated that constitutional rights should not have direct effect in

---

40 See Barak, Aharon: Constitutional Human Rights and Private Law. In: Friedman Daniel, Barak-Erez Daphne (eds.): *Human Rights in Private Law.* Oxford/Portland: Hart Publishing, 2001, p. 15. Cf. also the introductory chapter.

41 Gardbaum, Stephen: *The "Horizontal Effect" of Constitutional Rights.* Michigan Law Review 102, 2003-2004, p. 394.

42 Starck, Christian: *Human Rights and Private Law in German Constitutional Development and in the Jurisprudence of the Federal Constitutional Court.* In: Friedman Daniel, Barak-Erez Daphne (eds.): *Human Rights in Private Law.* Oxford/Portland: Hart Publishing, 2001, p. 97.

43 Schiemann, Gottfried: *Grundrechte im Privetrecht der Bundesrepublik Deutschland.* In: Tichý Luboš (ed.): *Základní lidská práva v jednotlivých právních odvětvích. Grundrechte und Einzelne Rechtsgebiete.* [*Fundamental Rights in Particular Legal Branches*]. Praha: Eva Rozkotová – IFEC, 2006, p. 46.

private law branches, but should have effect only through indefinite legal concepts.[44] Indirect effect of constitutional rights results in the recognition of the specificity of private law principles, in particular of the autonomous will of persons, which is supposed to result in a certain extent of independence of these branches from constitutional law.[45] Even though it may seem at first sight that indirect horizontal effect provides a lower standard of protection, the benefit of this approach consists in systemic arguments. If the role of constitutional rights were to be accentuated *ad absurdum*, we could reach the conclusion that specific rights and duties in individual branches of law are irrelevant because in the end legal relations would be regulated on the basis of abstract constitutionally protected rights interpreted by courts in specific cases.

The German Federal Constitutional Court, which faced the choice of conception of horizontal effect as early as the end of the 1950s in the well-known decision in *Lüth*, inclined toward the indirect horizontal effect of constitutional rights.[46] The court's arguments were based upon the constitutional rights radiating through the entire legal order and creating an objective order of values.[47]

The conclusions of German teaching became at the beginning of the 1990s a source of new Czech constitutional theory, and in particular a source of jurisprudence of the Constitutional Court, according to which: "*One of the roles of the*

44 These concepts and doctrines are referred to as "*Einbruchstelle*" (See Stern, 1988, p. 1532).

45 Ibid, p. 1543.

46 Judgment of the Federal Constitutional Court of the Federal Republic of Germany 7 BVerfGE, 198 of 15 January 1958 (*Lüth*). The facts of the case were as follows: Veit Harlan, a former prominent Nazi film director shot in 1950 a film which he intended to present at a film festival in Hamburg. Eric Lüth, an official of Hamburg city and an activist fighting against Nazi criminals, appealed to citizens to boycott the film by Harlan. Harlan filed a law suit against Lüth claiming compensation for the loss caused by a wilful act against good morals and he was successful in the court of Hamburg. Lüth filed an appeal against this decision to the Federal Constitutional Court which decided in his favour, and reversed the decision of the lower court because it was not in compliance with the constitutionally guaranteed freedom of expression. The Federal Constitutional court thus attributed major importance to the constitutional rights in the German legal order and confirmed the conclusions of the doctrine that emerged at the beginning of the 1950s. The most important works of H. von Mangoldt and F. Klein, G. Dürig, H. Krüger and other authors are summarised in Stern, 2000, pp. 50 – 51.

47 On argumentation of the court in the case of Lüth cf. Dreier, Horst: *Dimensionen der Grundrechte. Von der Wertordnungsjudikatur zu den objektiv-rechtlichen Grundrechtsgehalten*. Hannover: Hennies und Zinkeisen, 1993, pp. 10 et seq.

Constitution and in particular of the constitutional provisions concerning fundamental rights and freedoms consists in its "radiation" through the entire legal order. The purpose of the Constitution consists […] also in the necessity for state bodies, or the bodies of public power, to interpret and apply law with a view to protecting fundamental rights and freedoms."[48]

After more than twenty years of development of the democratic state which respects the rule of law, the basic theories on the role and effect of constitutional rights in the legal order seem to be accepted.[49] The role of constitutional rights in Czech law was strengthened by the legislature in a restatement of private law in 2012, the main outcome of which was a new Civil Code. One of its basic interpretation provisions constituted the duty to interpret every regulation of private law in accordance with spirit of the Charter of Fundamental Rights and Freedoms.[50]

IV. Constitutional rights and limitation of law-making power

The previous section stated that human rights exist in the legal orders of individual states as rights of individuals to be asserted against state power, and that the state power must respect them not only in applying the law, but also in making the law. This fact is however associated with a number of questions that turn to the issues of possible limitation of the legislative branch, usually elected in democratic election by bodies exerting a judicial review of this branch. Are

48 Judgment of the Constitutional Court reference no. III. ÚS 139/98 of 24 September 1998. The author of the judgment was Pavel Höllander, who was in the 1990s together with Vladimír Klokočka instrumental in transferring many principles of German constitutional theory into the decision-making of the Czech Constitutional Court.

49 Wagnerová, Eliška in Wagnerová, Eliška et al.: *Listina základních práv a svobod. Komentář* [*Charter of Fundamental Rights and Freedoms. A Commentary*]. Praha: Wolters Kluwer, 2012, pp. 1-32; Holländer, Pavel: *Základy všeobecné státovědy.* [*Fundamentals of the General Theory of State*]. Plzeň: Aleš Čeněk, 2012; Tichý, Luboš (ed.): *Základní lidská práva v jednotlivých právních odvětvích. Grundrechte und Einzelne Rechtsgebiete. [Fundamental Rights in Particular Legal Branches].* Praha: Eva Rozkotová – IFEC, 2006.

50 Section 2 (1) of Act No. 89/2012 Sb., the Civil Code, provides as follows: Every provision of private law may be interpreted only in compliance with the Charter of Fundamental Rights and Freedoms and the constitutional order in general, and with principles of this Act as well as with constant regard to the values thus protected. If an interpretation of a provision deviates only in its wording from this order, this order shall prevail. See Tichý, Luboš: *Obecná část občanského práva.* [*A General Part of the Civil Law*]. Praha: C. H. Beck, 2014, pp. 85-88.

constitutional courts capable of a responsible review of legal rules governing complex relations within the framework of complicated institutes? And if so, is such a review legitimate?

American legal philosopher *L. Fuller* in a paper published in 1978 dealt with the question of whether there are some types of tasks that it is generally inappropriate for courts to decide on.[51] His answer is positive, the courts in his conceptions should not decide on so-called *polycentric problems* relating to large numbers of people.[52] To illustrate this we may imagine decisions on the appropriateness of a reward for work done or decisions on the level of taxation that would be addressed by courts. Polycentric problems may be visualised according to *Fuller* as a spider web where pulling one strand makes the whole structure of the web move.[53]

Even though it is not possible to disregard the fact that also in continental legal culture the courts contribute through their decisions to creating law, it is necessary to keep in mind that they are not appropriate bodies for making the law. This fact is becoming clearer with respect to the growing competencies available to those bodies protecting constitutionality in individual states. Constitutional courts may, in an abstract review of constitutionality, review the compliance of legal regulations with the constitution, and if required they may repeal such regulations in their role as "negative law-makers." At the same time they may also for example assess the constitutionality of judgments of other courts or the decisions of executive bodies. Even though the extent to which the court contributes to creating the law - or even "makes" the law - differs in such cases, we cannot disregard the fact that constitutional courts in deliberation operate with a different "frame of mind," than the other branches of state power. The constitutional courts, whose primary role is to protect human rights, or constitutional rights, may often disregard for example financial, economic, or other impacts of their decisions, i.e. they do not have to take into consideration information that is considered by the executive branch and the legislative branch when making the

---

51 Fuller, Lon L.: *The Forms and Limits of Adjudication*. Harvard Law Review 92(2), 1978, p. 393. Fuller's meaning of "limits" is primarily the question of which social tasks should be attributed to courts; his meaning of "forms" is the organisation and management of the decision-making process in courts.

52 Ibid, p. 394 et seq. The concept of polycentric problems was taken from Polanyi, Michael: *The Logic of Liberty*. Chicago: University of Chicago Press, 1951. See also elaboration of this thesis in Rivers, Julian: *Proportionality and Variable Intensity of Review*. Cambridge Law Journal 65(1), 2006, p. 176.

53 Fuller, 1978, p. 395.

law. And what is more, such information does not necessarily have to be available to constitutional courts. On the one hand, there is a relatively high expectation on the part of society, often supported by political representatives, that the courts are the best to decide on complicated issues, while on the other hand, such decisions may often disregard some important facts and result in less acceptable conclusions.

The consequences of this general reflection may be seen in the self-restraint of the court in deciding certain types of issues relating not only to the parties to the proceedings, but also to the society at large – for example in disputes concerning the amount of taxes and fees, or mandatory insurance premiums, issues of the redistribution of public goods in society which have an impact on the implementation of social rights, and so on.

An example of a decision on a polycentric problem is a judgment of the Constitutional Court of the Czech Republic from 2010 concerning the constitutionality of the reduction threshold for the calculation of pensions. In this case the court dealt with the question of whether the reduction threshold stipulated by law excessively discriminated against high-income citizens by giving preference to the principle of solidarity (of high-income citizens with low-income citizens) over the principle of equivalence (which manifests in relating the amount of pension to earnings). The Constitutional Court in the end cancelled the reduction threshold because the system based on public insurance excessively weakened the principle of pensions being related to earnings.[54] In reaction to this the government changed the pension system in such a manner that the amount of funds spent on pensions remained the same and the principle of solidarity was reduced, which resulted in a reduction of pensions for low-income citizens and in an insignificant increase in the pensions of high-income groups.

In the appendix to the English-language edition of *A Theory of Constitutional Rights*, *R. Alexy* states that the legislative branch has structural discretion in making the law. Therefore it may create such law that the constitution does not prohibit and where the constitution does not promulgate different regulation.[55] This relates to the overall idea of the role of constitutional law within the legal order, where constitutional law creates a framework for legislative decision-making (*Rahmenordnung*), rather than a basis in the sense that all legal regulations

---

54 Judgment of the Constitutional Court of the Czech Republic ref. no. Pl. ÚS 8/07 of 23 March 2010.

55 Alexy, Robert: *A Theory of Constitutional Rights*. Oxford: Oxford University Press, 2002, p. 394.

would arise from the constitution and would only implement the constitution (*Grundordnung*).[56]

With respect to these facts we consider it appropriate to differentiate the intensity of review in cases where the court reviews the conformity of a legal regulation with human rights enshrined in the constitution and in cases of incidental review of specific acts of application of the law. This approach, however, means that in many cases the courts may reach several conclusions that are all in accordance with the constitution.

Arguments claiming that the judicial branch is not sufficiently capable of solving polycentric problems may be expanded upon with arguments that derive the necessity to limit judicial power from its insufficient democratic legitimacy.

The progressing value plurality of societies is also reflected in morally contentious questions that must be solved by courts in the present time: Should a woman have the right to have an abortion? Do we have the right to have someone else to put us to death upon our request? Is the fact that couples of a different sex can marry whereas couples of the same sex cannot contrary to the principle of non-discrimination?[57] In pluralistic societies there are no clear answers to these questions. According to *A. Scalia*, US Supreme Court Justice, such questions should not be decided by judges, in spite of the current practice. The solution should come from public political discussion.[58] Such an opinion, of course, is not the only possible one. For example *R. Den Otter*, on the basis of almost identical questions, reached the opposite conclusion. According to *Den Otter* the courts are best at handling exclusive public reasons generally accepted throughout society and which enable them to solve such contentious questions.[59] According to other authors the courts constitute the most appropriate environment for deliberating on such important topics due to their political independence and ability for *argumentative representation*, i.e. the ability to decide on the basis of arguments that are accepted by reasonable people on the basis of their

56 See Alexy, Robert: *On Constitutional Rights to Protection*. Legisprudence 3(1), 2009, p. 2.

57 Scalia, Antonin: *Mullahs of the West. Judges as Moral Arbiters*. Warsaw: Rzecznik Praw Obywatelskich, 2009, p. 10.

58 *Ibid.*

59 Den Otter, Ronald: *Judicial Review in an Age of Moral Pluralism*. New York: Cambridge University Press, 2009, pp. 128, 294. It is however necessary to note that in pluralistic societies there is often no consensus even on the level of principles, let alone the grounds for solving moral contentions arising from such principles.

rationality.[60] Irrespective of which of the presented theories we prefer, those who criticise the judicial review of constitutionality, such as *A. Scalia*, clearly point out that the assumption that judges are capable of solving these questions better than democratically elected legislators is, to say the least, questionable, and highly problematic from a democratic point of view.[61] It seems to be a necessary starting point to require the courts to consider a different approach depending on the nature of cases before them.

To conclude this chapter we return to the question which forms part of the main question raised by this book: *To what extent is the state weakened by human rights?* Even though the above paragraphs only indicate a number of problematic aspects of the answer to this question, it is clear that the answer will depend on many factors. First, the model of protection of human rights in the constitutional systems of individual states will be of key importance. The situation will differ in jurisdictions with judicial review of constitutionality and in jurisdictions where such review is not institutionalised. There will be major differences found also among states where there is such review. It is not only important whether there is a judicial institution with competence to review the compliance of legal acts with the constitutional order and the constitutional rights enshrined in it, but also what consequences the decision of such an institution may have,[62] and what the actual position of the institution in society is.

The second essential determinant relates to the scope of functions that the constitutional rights are expected to perform, i.e. whether the relationship of the state vis-a-vis constitutional rights is perceived as exclusively negative, or whether we ascribe to the state a positive obligation to protect and enforce those rights.[63] The function of constitutional rights is necessarily related to questions of methodology describing possible models for the solution of mutual conflicts

---

60 Alexy, Robert: *Balancing, constitutional review, and representation*. International Journal of Constitutional Law 3(4), 2005, pp. 578-581. Cf. Harel, Alon: *Rights-Based Judicial Review: A Democratic Justification*. Law and Philosophy 22, 2003, pp. 247-276.

61 To name at least one of many authors cf. primarily the works of J. Waldron: *Law and Disagreement*. Oxford: Clarendon, 1999; *The Core of the Case Against Judicial Review*. The Yale Law Journal 115, 2005-2006, pp. 1346-1406; *Judges as moral reasoners*. International Journal of Constitutional Law 7(1), 2009, pp. 2-24.

62 In present time it is possible to observe on the basis of this distinction a *strong* and *weak model of judicial review*. See in particular Tushnet, Mark: *Weak Courts, Strong Rights: Judicial Review and Social Welfare Rights in Comparative Constitutional Law*. Oxford: Oxford University Press, 2008.

63 See also Kysela, 2014, p. 266.

between constitutional rights, or conflicts between such rights and public (collective) goods, and also possibly methodology dealing with the possibilities of horizontal effect of these rights.

Nevertheless there is also the influence of other than purely juristic criteria. The plurality of theoretical conceptions and ideas shared by society on the scope and content of human rights represents another important factor manifesting in the activity of state power. At times of a prevailing moral disagreement it is possible to observe the status of delegitimisation of state power, where we see one of the main reasons for this phenomenon as being the very lack of consensus on the existence and importance of human rights.

The causes described in this chapter are certainly not the only ones. An important role is played for example by the "openness" of an individual state to the human-rights mechanisms of international law, which may be considered an important factor in the external limitation of state power mentioned in the introductory chapter of this book. Having described the determining factors, it becomes clear that the phenomena influencing the relationship between state power and human or constitutional rights are highly complex.

Michal Urban, Jan Kysela

Societal limits on the state

This chapter, which deals with societal limits of contemporary states, will chart those actions originating from society itself that limit the power of states and their representatives. We have identified two main groups of these limits. The first may be summarised under the heading of the distrust of people in (their) state. Irrespective of whether this takes the form of distrust in state institutions, political representatives, or the possibility to formulate a common public interest, this reflects the attitude of a considerable part of society that does not consider the state in which they live to be their state. There are many reasons for such an attitude, however the effects are quite similar: alienation from the state and low motivation to become involved in state administration and decisions both of legal and political character. The distrust limits political representatives by making their ideas and power more difficult to implement because they must be prepared for a certain degree of resistance on the part of society.

The second group relates to how the many activities formerly carried out by the state or at least kept under the close supervision of the state are now often taken on by specific groups of citizens or organisations which cannot be simply subordinated to the state. These are activities of civil society with its initiatives, associations, not-for-profit organisations and also direct participation in state decision-making in the form of referenda, and also the effort to introduce elements of corporativist organisation and various forms of outsourcing of state power, coupled with the changing role of political parties. What these activities have in common is that they usually involve new societal players in political decision-making, which on the one hand adds to the legitimacy of the decisions, but on the other reduces the stability of such decisions and sometimes – however paradoxical it may sound - deprives the decision of its representativeness, as will be explained further in this chapter.

I. Distrust in the state

Trust[1] represents an *"invisible institution"*[2] that is indispensable in every society. *F. Fukuyma* says of trust: *"Trust acts like a lubricant that makes any group or organisation run more effectively."*[3] Suffice it to imagine how our everyday behaviour would change if we *a priori* did not trust that other people and institutions would generally behave according to the rules and act in line with common sense. We would hardly cooperate with the police, deposit money in a bank, or even drive on the street. We are aware of the fact that police power is sometimes abused, that there is bank fraud (and there are financial crises), and that traffic accidents occur, but in spite of this we are generally convinced that all these activities are – at least for the moment – more or less safe. We trust them.[4]

Politicians too are aware of the importance of trust. In politics more than in any other field it is true that impressions are greater than reality. If a politician builds up a negative image in the media, he will pay for it, even though in the future he may turn out to be right (for example if the court acquits him in a criminal case or identifies information published to his detriment as defamatory). And vice versa, a built-up capital of trust is capable of protecting someone

---

1 Trust may be defined as *"a type of attitude and at the same time interpersonal relation resulting in a feeling of certainty based on the conviction that the partner in communication (person, institution) will meet certain expectations"* (Velký sociologický slovník 1, A-O. [Large Dictionary of Sociology 1, A-O] Praha: Karolinum, 1996, p. 231) or as *"relying on another person or institution not to abuse part of my freedom that I put in their hands by trusting them"* (Sedláčková, Markéta: *Důvěra a demokracie: přehled sociologických teorií důvěry od Tocquevilla po transformaci v postkomunistických zemích.* [*Trust and Democracy: Overview of Sociological Theories of Trust from Tocqueville to Transformation in Postcommunist Countries*] Praha: Sociologické nakladatelství, 2012, p. 96.). So it includes an element of relying on another person (or institution), mutuality (or at least expectation of mutuality), acceptance of the risk that our expectation will partially not be met or will not be met at all, and an outlook to the future – trust always turns us toward future events that are beyond our control.

2 Rosanvallon, Pierre: *Democratic Legitimacy: Impartiality, Reflexivity, Proximity.* Princeton: Princeton University Press, 2011, p. 8. Rosanvallon speaks primarily about legitimacy, however as will be shown in this chapter, legitimacy represents trust in the system.

3 Fukuyama, 2006, p. 29.

4 According to H. de Soto, varying degrees of trust in rules and institutions (contracts, registers etc.), or in specific persons, influence varying degrees of success of capitalism in the world. See Soto, Hernando, de: *The Mystery of Capital: Why Capitalism Triumphs in the West and Fails Everywhere Else*. New York: Basic Books, 2000.

who has not been telling the whole truth for a long time. We saw this quite clearly for example in 1998 during the now legendary affair of US President *Bill Clinton* and White House intern *Monica Lewinsky*. It was only after the president was publicly proven to have withheld important information that he had no choice but to stand in front of the TV cameras and apologise to the nation - not because he only then realised what he had done, but because it was the only way of winning back the trust of Americans.[5]

Not only democratic societies are built on the trust of their citizens. An authoritative regime also cannot survive for a long time without trust, even though it is true that such regimes may remain in power for a relatively long time only as a result of the passivity of their citizens.[6] There is nevertheless an important difference in the way that the trust capital is used in democratic systems and in non-democratic regimes. A non-democratic regime focuses, from the point of view of its acceptance, more on the outputs: it offers, or claims to offer, better economic performance, a higher level of security, and less corruption than the previous democratic regime. In contrast with this, democratic systems point out the inputs: more openness or sensitivity to the preferences of individuals, because without them the system cannot defend the constitutive thesis of self-government. Put more simply, they do not necessarily offer politics that is better than that of non-democratic systems, however it is politics that may be changed without violence. For this reason it must not be alienated and closed. If democratic systems lose the trust of their citizens then such loss becomes an immediate threat to the substance of their existence, since they do not have available the proven means of social control belonging to non-democratic regimes – violence, or at least a genuinely intended threat of using violence. As aptly noted by *M. Sedláčková*, "*...a democratic society built on free elections*

---

5 His current considerable popularity proves that his move (irrespective of whether it was honest or purely pragmatic) was successful. There is even a chance that he may return to the White House - not as a president but as a "first gentleman," together with his wife Hillary Clinton, who did not succeed in the primary elections against Barack Obama, but who perhaps has not given up on her candidature. The US example is, of course, specific due to the commingling of private and "official" morals, which would have surprised not only N. Machiavelli but also many contemporary French people.

6 Cf. Havel, Václav: *Moc bezmocných*. Praha: Lidové noviny, 1990. (Havel, Václav et al.: *The Power of the Powerless: Citizens against the State in Central - Eastern Europe*. London: Hutchinson, 1985) and a recent interpretation by a young Czech lawyer working at the London School of Economics, J. Komárek. Komárek, Jan: *Waiting for the Existential Revolution in Europe*. Jean Monnet Working Paper 04/2014.

and mutual co-operation of citizens is most paralysed by distrust – towards other people, towards democratic institutions, towards the system as such."[7] Without at least elementary trust it is not possible to build a democratic society or maintain it for a long time. This is true for the "old" democracies in the world as well as for countries recovering from long-term authoritarian or totalitarian governments – and the recovery may last for several decades.

Trust played an important role in the development of modern society. As stated by French sociologist *A. Peyrefitte*, the basic "*dynamic driver of modern society was and still is the existence of trust – trust of people in themselves, trust towards other people and towards jointly built permanent institutions which are capable of being trusted and on which we can pin our hopes.*"[8] This quotation also indicates that trust may be perceived and empirically measured on various levels. Generally three basic levels are distinguished, while the quotation from *Peyrefitte* only covers the first two. The first, most specific level covers general trust in other people (*social trust*), the second level observes the attitude of people toward selected institutions of the society (*institutional trust*), and the third, most abstract level explores the degree of trust of the public in the system as a whole (*systemic trust*), which is often referred to as legitimacy.[9]

Individual authors are not in agreement about the degree to which the levels of trust influence each other. Advocates of institutional theories (for example *P. Dasgupta* or *R. Hardin*) are convinced that trust in institutions is based on rational assessment of their operation, and so is not derived from social trust. Representatives of culturalist theories (such as *G. Almond, S. Verba, R. Inglehart,* and *R. Putnam*) consider institutional trust to be an extension of social trust, which arises from cultural norms and social networks.[10] Nevertheless, for our purposes it is not important to decide the above-mentioned theoretical dispute, but rather to observe whether the state, its representatives, institutions and citizens are trusted, whether people trust each other, and why trust is being lost.

---

7 Sedláčková, 2012, p. 10.

8 Petrusek, Miloslav: *Společnost pozdní doby.* [*Society of the Late Period*] Praha: Sociologické nakladatelství, 2006, p. 369. Trust is a key component of social cement. Cf. Elster, Jon: *The Cement of Society: A study of social order*. Cambridge: Cambridge University Press, 1989.

9 Cf. Sztompka, Piotr: *Trust. A Sociological Theory*. Cambridge: Cambridge University Press, 1999 and Barber, Bernard: *The logic and limits of trust*. New Brunswick: Rutgers University Press, 1983.

10 Sedláčková, 2012, pp. 155-178.

I.1 The case of the Czech Republic

The following text describes the situation in the Czech Republic 25 years following the fall of the communist regime, when the Czech Republic celebrated the 10th anniversary of its accession to the European Union. Even though our attention will focus on the Czech Republic, it serves mainly as a model that can be used to demonstrate phenomena common to the majority of countries in Central and Eastern Europe, and which, of course, are to a certain extent present also in traditional Western European democracies. We may state that in general the gap between those representing and deciding, and those who are subjects of those decisions, is deepening. Not only the deputies in national parliaments and the European Parliament, but also members of regional or local councils are generally perceived to be bad administrators who become involved in politics primarily because they wish to enrich themselves. There is a deepening feeling of alienation and a growing number of people who are under the impression that the state in which they live is not quite theirs - which clearly makes the exercise of state power more difficult.

A deepening of the gap or gulf between representatives and those who are represented is illustrated by the feeling of citizens that their representatives are only interested in them when they need votes in an election. Data from the last decade[11] of development in the Czech Republic shows that only slightly more than ten percent of respondents were of the opinion that elected politicians are interested in what people think.[12] On the other hand, only slightly more than a

11 This chapter is based on data collected by Centrum pro výzkum veřejného mínění Sociologického ústavu Akademie věd České republiky [Public Opinion Research Centre of the Institute of Sociology of the Academy of Science of the Czech Republic], which has the status of public research institution (CVVM SOÚ AV ČR, v.v.i.) and has been collecting important data on Czech society as part of a longitudinal research among the Czech population since 1990. The research centre repeatedly (usually at monthly intervals) asks selected questions of a representative sample of citizens. This is why we consider the surveys carried out by CVVM to be reliable, as they can reveal long-term trends. Some of their surveys are also published in a commented form (see e.g. the below-cited studies by L. Linek). CVVM, Naše společnost [Our Society], 2004-2014. Slightly more optimistic data is offered by Linek, Lukáš: *Zrazení snu? Struktura a dynamika postojů k politickému režimu a jeho institucím a jejich důsledky.* [*A Betrayed Dream? Structure and Dynamic of Attitudes to the Political Regime and its Institutions and the Consequences*] Praha: Sociologické nakladatelství, 2010, p. 100.

12 Response to the question "*Political parties are only interested in people's votes in election, rather than their opinions.*"

half of respondents were in their own opinion interested in Czech politics (less than 60 percent), while less than 40 percent of people were interested in global politics and less than one third (approximately 30 percent) were interested in European politics.[13] People perceive politics as being complex and hard to understand (close to two thirds think that politics is sometimes so complex that they cannot understand it at all) and they do not believe that they can influence it. Czech political sociologist *L. Linek* describes this condition as a feeling of political alienation, and proves that it is a relatively stable feeling.[14] One quarter of a century after the fall of the communist regime, only a half of people believe that it is possible to choose better administrators in elections. There are at least two main reasons behind this distrust: first of all, people consider the system to be closed, controlled by an inertia which cannot be overcome, and secondly people's own lack of self-confidence is to blame: only one third of respondents consider themselves sufficiently competent to be involved in political events.

It is interesting that low self-confidence does not result in a feeling of satisfaction with those who, through elections, have been vested with the power to represent, but rather this turns people against those who are elected. People themselves do not believe that they can choose good representatives, which is also clearly reflected in generally low trust in other people (in all Central European post-communist countries, trust does not exceed 30 percent).[15] Low self-confidence together with considerable distrust in other people and their ability to make good rational choices, in combination with the inertia of the system,

---

13 Considering the turnout in the European Parliament elections, which was the lowest in the countries of former Czechoslovakia, it might seem that the Czech Republic is not typical. Nevertheless the results in other countries of Central and Eastern Europe are not substantially different. This is true also in terms of trust in political parties as such.

14 Linek, 2010, p. 86-114. The fact that distrust in political representatives really is a serious problem having also economic consequences is confirmed by the Global Competitiveness Report 2013–2014, produced by the World Economic Forum. Whereas in overall ranking the Czech Republic was number 46, under the item headed 'public trust in politicians' the Czech Republic ranked 146th out of 148 surveyed countries. Here is the ranking of neighbouring countries in terms of 'public trust in politicians' for comparison purposes: Poland (100), Hungary (129), Slovak Republic (139), Austria (49) and Germany (19). Schwab, Klaus: *The Global Competitiveness Report 2013–2014: Full data edition.* Geneva: World Economic Forum, 2013.

15 The countries include the Czech Republic, Slovak Republic, Hungary and Poland. EVS (2011). European Values Study 1981-2008, Longitudinal Data File. GESIS Data Archive, Cologne, Germany, ZA4804 Data File Version 2.0.0 (2011-12-30) DOI:10.4232/1.11005.

results in considerable distrust in the institutions chosen by the people. The least trusted are both chambers of the Parliament of the Czech Republic, in spite of the fact that all deputies and senators go through direct elections at four-year and six-year intervals respectively (since 1994 trust has not exceeded 30 percent).[16] There was also an interesting shift when the previously not very beloved upper chamber, the Senate, over the course of several years superseded in trustworthiness the politically and legally more important Chamber of Deputies. The reason for this may have been the majority electoral system in the Senate elections, as well as less attention being paid to the Senate by the media and by voters themselves. Less attention means less reasons for conflicts that tend to irritate the public – calm matter-of-factness is preferred.

The government of the Czech Republic, which is usually formed by the president of the strongest party in the parliament and which must rely on a vote of confidence by the Chamber of Deputies, had the support of 15 – 45 percent of respondents during the years 1998 to 2014 - on average this was approximately one third of citizens.[17] A noteworthy exception is so-called caretaker governments, which consist of experts nominated by political parties rather than members of the parties. Even though not every minister is necessarily incompetent and not every expert nominated in a caretaker cabinet is necessarily without political relations to a specific party (on contrary, it is precisely this political relation that is usually one of the reasons why the expert is trusted by the party), cabinets composed of experts are extremely popular with the public. Their popularity may reach up to 70 percent - a level that is almost unimaginable in the case of political governments. This difference indicates a certain naivety of voters as well as an overall lack of popularity among politicians and distrust in their competence and motivations.[18]

---

16 Parliaments as bodies with numerous members whose main activity consists of speaking are not usually very popular in other countries either. According to the European Values Study (EVS) only in a small number of states did reported values exceed 50 percent, or even 70 percent, of citizens who definitely, or somewhat, trust their parliaments. The average value is approximately 40 percent. If we stay in the Central European area, then, with the exception of Slovakia, whose parliament maintained the trust of more than 40 percent of citizens over the last 15 years according to EVS, the trustworthiness of national parliaments in other Central European countries has been decreasing since 1990 to the level of approximately 20 percent.

17 For an exact chart depicting the changes in popularity of Czech governments see Sedláčková, 2012, p. 193.

18 This is also why it is necessary to be vigilant in the case of caretaker governments. They disqualify ordinary politics by creating the impression that it can be done

Directly elected members of regional councils were trusted during the last decade by 40 to 50 percent of respondents, while members of local councils had the trust of around 60 percent, and permanently the greatest trust was accorded to the presidents of the republic, oscillating around 65 percent.[19] The office of the president was until 2013 filled through indirect elections (the parliament acted as the electoral college) and the first directly elected president, *Miloš Zeman*, received only about 50 percent support in regular polls. Even though it may be too early for such a conclusion, we are inclined to write that voters start to trust even the president of the republic less if they choose him themselves.[20] If this

---

technocratically, in a seemingly objective manner, i.e. without disputes regarding the "assignment" or the direction. Another risk consists in the temptation for political parties to absolve themselves of responsibility when they leave the caretakers to govern instead of them. The caretaker governments apparently involve some remnants of former authority of officials which, according to P. Rosanvallon, would have been almost completely lost otherwise (cf. Rosanvallon, 2011, p. 4). C. Skach explains in this manner the success of presidential cabinets in the late phase of Weimar Germany. Cf. Skach, Cindy: *Borrowing Constitutional Designs. Constitutional Law in Weimar Germany and the French Fifth Republic*. Princeton: Princeton University Press, 2005. Weimar also indicates a frequent union between technocratic governments and the head of state, which is similar to an attempt by Czech President M. Zeman to install a "government of experts" in 2013 against the will of the Chamber of Deputies and to maintain it in power despite a vote of no confidence. The Chamber of Deputies reacted by dissolving itself, which was followed by an election which frustrated the immediate political plans of President Zeman. If he had been successful, the parliamentary elections could have been a second-class election because it would have been far more important who the master of Prague Castle was. This caretaker government, headed by an economist, J. Rusnok, did not receive resounding popularity, as support for it was around 25 percent. This is almost ten percentage points higher than the popularity of the previous political government of P. Nečas at the end of its term, however the following coalition government of the left-wing Prime Minister B. Sobotka had at the beginning of its term in January 2014 the support of approximately 40 percent of citizens. Rusnok's caretaker government was, in comparison with other caretaker governments, exceptionally unfavoured.

19 Sedláčková, 2012, p. 193.

20 This is not only due to the fact that M. Zeman is a controversial personality. The direct election and the related campaign divides society more than the parliamentary elections. During the election, which was held at the beginning of 2013, camps of supporters and opponents were formed and have not disappeared until now. The fact that President Zeman ran for office under a specific political party whose representatives he took to his office of the president, was a violation of the nimbus of non-partisanship that is traditionally associated with the office of Czech president.

hypothesis is not confirmed by the office of the president it will certainly be confirmed by a comparison of the above percentages regarding the trustworthiness of directly elected institutions with institutions that are filled indirectly – the army, courts, and the police. Since 2008 their trustworthiness has not fallen below 45 percent, while trust in the highest courts in the long run exceeds 60 percent, and the army received in 2013 the trust of 65 percent of respondents.[21]

This confirms an insight of US political scientist *Fareed Zakaria*, who observed that people in the US trust elected institutions (Congress, in particular) much less than indirectly nominated institutions such as the Supreme Court, army or Federal Reserve.[22] Another hypothesis may lie in the degree of differentiation of a given institution from political parties, and the reluctance of respondents to distinguish between an institution and specific people and their current policy, and so on.

The above-mentioned polls also show that people find it easiest to identify with those institutions that are geographically close to them. Whereas the national parliament is trusted by less than one third of citizens, city councils are trusted by more than double the number of citizens. Even though the events taking place in Brussels are at least as important (if not more important) for the future of the state as those in the capital of the state, people monitor national politics more closely than European politics. This indicates the existence of a certain boundary, beyond which it is psychologically and practically rather difficult to perceive events in the wide context in which they take place. The solution of course is not to disregard the context. Architects and administrators of the system should be aware of the boundary and should seek ways of preventing negative consequences arising from the boundary. An important part of their job must necessarily include an effort to explain to voters in a comprehensible manner why European institutions are important, what their agenda is, and also to explain that they are interested in the opinions of citizens in individual Member States. If they underestimate the existence of this boundary, or even pretend that it does not exist, they should not be surprised by a growing feeling of alienation from the system as well as its representatives.[23]

21 CVVM SOÚ AV ČR, v.v.i., Naše společnost [Our Society], 1993-2014.

22 Zakaria, Fareed: *The Future of Freedom: Illiberal Democracy at Home and Abroad.* New York: Norton, 2003, p. 241.

23 This is one of the messages sent by voters to their representatives in European election in May 2014. In some countries (e.g. the Czech Republic and Slovakia) the turnout in elections dropped significantly (even though in Europe as a whole the turnout

It comes as no surprise that dissatisfaction with specific politicians and institutions puts a question mark over the whole democratic system as such. At the beginning of 2014 only about 45 percent of Czech citizens agreed with the Churchill-style conception of democracy as the best of all other bad systems, while 30 percent accepted that under certain conditions an authoritarian government may be better than a democratic one, and 22 percent of respondents were of the opinion that, from their point of view, it does not matter in which regime they live. The percentage of supporters of democracy remained throughout the 1990s at approximately 70 percent, however this number has been falling steadily since 2000. Development in other Central European countries is more or less similar to that in the Czech Republic, with measured figures remaining at least 20 percentage points below the figures for West Europe.[24] The foundations of democracy are far from being as strong as democracy may think. This is most probably true of every regime, as proven by the example of European communist regimes at the end of the 1980s. This was aptly expressed by the British political scientist *J. Dunn*, who wrote that "*it is very difficult, if not impossible, to state what legitimacy a certain regime enjoys, before it collapses. In practice, most regimes overestimate the degree of their legitimacy.*"[25]

I.2 Distrust in public interest

Distrust in the common (general, public) interest is a specific form of distrust. The Aristotelian idea of an individual assumes that individual "rational animals" will seek a common interest that will be beneficial to the community and therefore also to every individual. However at present there is a prevailing, considerably sceptical attitude toward that idea. Such scepticism is rooted primarily in negative experience with communist collectivism (instead of the well-functioning state that was promised, the communists built a vast and poorly

---

slightly exceeded that of 2009) and overall Eurosceptic parties became stronger (e.g. in France, Denmark and Great Britain).

24 Hungary reported approximately the same support for democracy as the Czech Republic over the course of the 1990s, however the support in Hungary did not fall significantly at the end of the 1990s, while slightly lower values were measured in Slovakia and Poland. Cf. Linek, 2010, p. 65 et seq. and survey by CVVM SOÚ AV ČR, v.v.i., Naše společnost, Postoje občanů k fungování demokracie v ČR– únor 2014 [Our Society: Attitudes of Citizens to the Functioning of Democracy in the CR – February 2014], retrieved 5.6.2014 from http://cvvm.soc.cas.cz/media/com_form2content/documents/c1/a7190/f3/pd140305.pdf.

25 Sedláčková, 2012, p. 127.

managed state)[26] and in still influential neo-liberalism, which since the 1980s - or the 1990s in Central and Eastern Europe - promoted the ideas of the free market. Instead of a shared effort to ponder what society may be like, we rather strive to create a free space in which it is up to everyone to seek his own happiness. This is why we place so much emphasis on human rights, the majority of which are purely individualistic, and why we believe that such an emphasis will result in the progress of society as a whole.

This assumption is partially justified, as expansion of the catalogue of human rights really did create an unprecedented degree of personal freedom in contemporary Europe. However it is becoming clear that this conception has its limits. "*Individualism, the substance of virtue in modern societies, starts changing colour: the proud self-reliance of free people is turning into some kind of reclusive selfishness and maximum personal freedom without a responsibility to others becomes autotelic,*" says *F. Fukuyma.*[27] Without a jointly formulated public interest, without a shared vision of society, we begin to tread water: "*Liberal democracy always relied on sound functioning of certain (shared) values.*"[28] It is a paradox that private corporations are aware of the necessity to have a common (corporate) vision and they thus formulate one. Could perhaps this be one of the reasons why many states, when compared with large (and in particular multinational) corporations, seem weak and unable, for example, to force such corporations to pay tax on the territory of their state?

This is clearly visible in fields such as the energy industry. Private players in this industry have – unlike many states – clear visions for dozens of years in advance. However, sustainable energy strategy cannot be formed by every household buying a boiler and using anything they consider fit to use as fuel, or by influential corporations dividing up mineral resources. It is necessary for society as whole, in cooperation with experts and through the representatives of citizens, to agree on an environmentally and economically appropriate strategy. An ordinary summation of individual interests will not produce a common interest and

26 The tradition of state as a poor manager survived even the fall of communism. In Czechoslovakia a specific concept of "tunnelling" was introduced to refer to extensive financial fraud in which the management of a company transferred the company's funds to other companies that were often indirectly owned by the management of the original company.

27 Fukuyama, 2006, p. 60.

28 Ibid, p. 23.

a liberal setting gives an advantage to the stronger players, who – unlike many ordinary people – will see to their interests.[29]

Liberal Europe offers a lot to its citizens (this is confirmed by the crowds of immigrants on Europe's border), however even in contemporary Europe it is not easy to live a contented life. A consumption-focused environment with highly developed marketing defended by liberal rhetoric that claims that everyone knows best what is good for him and behaves accordingly can confuse many people, not only vulnerable elderly citizens who spend exorbitant amounts on sets of pots that they do not need.[30] It is the reason why a lot of people, left to their own wits, put on weight, smoke, and fall into the trap of debt. We may consider this to be their personal failure (and clearly at least in part this is the case), but isn't it also a failure of the greater community in which we live? Traditionally, between the state and an individual, there were institutions such as the family, associations or the church which contributed to the development of human aptitudes (*M. Skovajsa* speaks about a so-called

29 Further proof of the fact that an ordinary sum of individual interests does not usually produce a common interest is a visit to the "common space" of any slightly more affluent Czech dormitory suburb. Instead of cultivated common space, a potential visitor ends up walking between high fences built around the houses. The fences might in fact look much worse if there were no limitations arising from zoning and the necessity to obtain a building permit. It is a situation remotely similar to the one we can see in Latin America: instead of an effort to improve the quality of urban planning in society in general there is separation from the society in affluent protected locations. French philosopher B.-H. Lévy describes a very specific example of this "island" mentality in the US, where there was a closed town of affluent elderly people who did not allow any younger people to live there so that they would not disturb their way of life. See Lévy, Bernard-Henri: *American Vertigo: Travelling America in the Footsteps of Tocqueville*. New York: Random House, 2006, cited from Czech translation Lévy, Bernard-Henri: *Americká závrať*. Brno: Host, 2006, p. 141 et seq. The relevant chapter is aptly titled "*Gilded apartheid for the old*."

30 Here we refer to the phenomenon of presentations of "exclusive" goods for elderly people who are offered a trip and lunch for free as well as "unrivalled" discounts, and they end up at a commercial presentation of goods. Specialised companies and their well-trained employees use psychological pressure, good marketing and often also threats and humiliation to force these people to buy usually low-quality goods, such as cooking pots, for excessive prices. Recently a Czech documentary called "Šmejdi" [Crooks] (2013, directed by Silvie Dymáková) drew the attention of the public to the practices of such traders as well as the naivety of the elderly, who repeatedly visit such events and spend their life savings.

intermediary sphere).[31] A growing degree of distrust affected also these institutions and as a result of this they are unable to sufficiently fulfil the role of a safety net that in the past used to assist people in need. It is no wonder that people expect help from the state, and when it is not provided the state loses the rest of its authority because it is unable (at least in the eyes of the public) to protect a clearly weaker party. However, should the state, in the spirit of its pastoral mission (see the introductory chapter), become involved in such matters?

R. Thaler and *C. Sunstein* are convinced that the state should not hide behind liberal rhetoric but should accept its responsibility and act, although not necessarily in a paternalistic manner, i.e. it should not use prohibitions to excessively curb the freedom of people. In particular, when dealing with matters in which the majority of society cannot reach a consensus, the state should, in their opinion, apply the policy of so-called libertarian paternalism, i.e. give people the freedom of choice but set a default in a manner that is beneficial to the people and to society. For example to stipulate that every citizen will be listed as an organ donor unless he opts out. The difference, as compared with the situation where everybody must apply to be registered as an organ donor, will be a several dozens higher percentage of registered donors. Since more donated organs means a better chance to save people who need a transplant and since the state by its decision does not deny anyone's right to opt out of the register, the state should in such cases act and enforce laws that make the society demonstrably better.[32]

II. Transferring state power to other entities within the state

The second group of internal limits on the state includes activities that were originally carried out or controlled by the state, but are currently carried out by specific groups of citizens or organisations that cannot be simply subordinated to the state. These include the activities of civil society, forms of direct democracy, the strengthening of corporativist elements of governance, and outsourcing

---

31 Skovajsa, Marek: *Občanská společnost a demokratický stát.* [Civil Society and Democratic State] In Skovajsa, Marek et al.: *Občanský sektor: organizovaná občanská společnost v České republice.* [*Civil Sector: Organised Civil Society in the Czech Republic*] Praha: Portál, 2010, pp. 74-78. The importance of intermediary institutions was also pointed out by *Ian Budge*. Budge, Ian: *Direct Democracy*. In: Binder, Sarah A., Rhodes, R. A. W., Rockman, Bert A. (eds.): *The Oxford Handbook of Political Institutions*. Oxford: Oxford University Press, 2008, p. 596 et seq.

32 These issues are convincingly described in more detail by R. Thaler and C. Sunstein in their influential publication Nudge. Thaler, Richard, Sunstein, Cass: *Nudge: Improving Decisions about Health, Wealth and Happiness.* New Haven: Yale University Press, 2008.

the most important branches of state power. Before looking at internal limits it is necessary to cover the changing nature of political parties, which immediately contribute to creating the will of state. The important questions concern who associates within political parties, and for what purpose.

II.1 Political parties

According to *B. Manin,* political parties started to become more prominent after the crisis of representation in the 19th century, which had been based on trust in individual members of parliament.[33] First they acted as *party government* or "*Parteiendemokratie.*" This conception, however, was later exhausted by a weakened trust in specific political parties as well as in political parties in general.[34] Now we live in a period when political parties often only provide services to a leader attracting the attention of the media, who communicates directly with voters, who represent a variable audience (*audience democracy*). This takes us back to personalisation, however without the original personal knowledge or personal contact. It features a greater importance of media and media consultants due to the complexity of the world in which we live, while the importance of party programme decreases.[35]

The catalogues of functions of political parties do include the role of aggregating interests as well as the role of representing, which together should contribute to defining the public interest mentioned above. However since the 18th century political parties in the form of factions were blamed for being the vehicles of partial interests. The semantics of the word "party" clearly indicates that it is not a whole, despite the fact that in the case of state party the party may tend to

33 Manin, Bernard: *The Principles of Representative Government.* Cambridge: Cambridge University Press, 1997, p. 193 et seq.

34 Sovereignty of people turned into the sovereignty of political parties. See Loewenstein, 1969, p. 397.

35 The bad state of political parties is also pointed out by P. Schmitter in his aptly-titled contribution *Parties Are Not What They Once Were.* He shows that the ability to structure the electoral process of political parties is decreasing, they provide citizens with a less stable and distinctive set of ideals and goals (symbols) that anchor their expectations about democracy (Schmitter calls it a "symbolic integration"), they participate in forming governments, and they less aggregate the interests and passions of citizens. Schmitter, Philippe: *Parties Are Not What They Once Were.* In: Diamond, Larry, Gunther, Richard (eds.): *Political Parties and Democracy.* Baltimore, USA: Johns Hopkins University Press, 2001, pp. 67-89.

become a whole and eventually to absorb the state and its apparatus.[36] Similar attitudes toward factions and partially also their related parties are found in the US Federalists, the French Jacobins, as well as German academia of the 19th century. Due to the existence of parties a member of parliament must choose between loyalty to the party and loyalty to the interests of the represented people, or at least to their interests as his conscience interprets it.

Nevertheless, for a long time political parties had a lot of adherents, including party members and loyal voters, on the basis of shared ideas or shared interests. Recent decades however have witnessed a loosening of relations where something like a column or camp political culture has operated. Within the framework of such a culture the voters inhabit a political segment which includes not only a political party but also its interest organisations, own press and so on (such a culture used to exist in the Netherlands, or to a lesser extent Austria). The number of members of political parties is falling as well as the share of large political parties in the market of votes – less voters vote for them, and it is easier for them to change their preferences.[37]

Different types of political parties are also developing. They differ not only by the fact that they possess a loose relationship to ideas and focus on a specific segment of voters defined on the basis of status or denomination, but especially because they are parties not needing members, but only voters. This is due, among other things, to a change in election campaigns which are now dominated by marketing elements and new media, which enables to attract groups of voters who otherwise would not have come into contact with any reliable party member. These contacts with numerous party members could in the past represent a very important motivation to vote for certain party; the party members also constituted the core of its electorate. Their financial contributions were also used to fund the existence of the party. If the parties have few members, everything is different, not just in terms of election campaigns – for example it must not be easy to maintain internal party democracy, and some parties or their leaders do not wish to do so anyway. Since they are political parties which – as the main channel of political participation so far – have basically a monopoly on creating lists of candidates for various elections, this has also external impacts. Citizens choose from candidates proposed by political parties. There is however a difference between the situation where candidates are chosen by hundreds

36 On this topic cf. the introductory chapters of Sartori, Giovanni: *Parties and Party Systems: A Framework for Analysis*. Cambridge: Cambridge University Press, 1976.

37 Examples include not only the Czech Republic, but also Great Britain and Austria.

of thousands of citizens, or only by individuals. The Czech political movement *Úsvit,* which in a two-hundred-member Chamber of Deputies has a faction of twelve deputies, has just nine members (!).

Without members and their contributions, parties need to seek funding elsewhere. They receive funding from the state, which has an interest in the existence of political parties in expectation of a formulation of the general interest, as well as from the financially strong personality of the founder, in relation to whom the risk that could be summarised as "he who pays, commands" is especially clear, and from business entities hoping to receive consideration, and so on. Sometimes political parties give the impression that they were formed only as a tool for doing business through other means. The business may take the form of an influence on public tenders, or specific political "business" on a small scale – a party of several members may live on contributions for the mandate of one or two senators who the party assisted to avoid the difficulties associated with the status of an impendent candidate within the elections. As a result of all of the above it comes as no surprise that political parties are not trusted by citizens,[38] which is why alternatives in the form of intensive use of the institutes of direct democracy and corporativist organisation are under consideration.[39] It

38 Distrust in political parties in the Czech Republic shows a tendency to grow. Whereas in 2008, according to the Global Corruption Barometer of Transparency International 49.8 percent of respondents considered political parties to be slightly or extremely corrupt, in the year 2013 the percentage grew to 73 percent. Transparency International: Tisková zpráva Co ukázal výzkum Globální barometr korupce? [Press Release on Global Corruption Barometer Survey Results], retrieved on 5.6.2014 from http://www.transparency.cz/gbc2013/.

39 In the Czech Republic the classical political parties, i.e. ones with a programme and organisational background, contributed to the political success of newly formed political parties, which are built around a person or a businessman (Andrej Babiš in the case of the political movement ANO, and Tomio Okamura in the case of Úsvitu přímé demokracie Tomia Okamury [The Dawn of Direct Democracy of Tomio Okamura]). They contributed by not paying attention to citizens (what and how something should be implemented, how to present it), and also by allowing citizens to perceive them in a certain way. In a stable political system it would hardly be sufficient to achieve success in politics by presenting oneself as a non-politician or hard-worker in combination with descriptions of the vices of politicians, unless various vices were truly associated with them (this was the basis of the political campaign of the ANO movement before the 2013 parliamentary elections). In 2013 in the Czech Republic the warning against ignoring the process of simple aversion to politicians turning into pure hatred became material, because in such a case there is a risk of systemic repercussions – there may be tendencies to get rid of not only specific politicians and political parties, but also

seems – schematically seen – that political parties progressed from interpreting of the interests of their members and voters to the state, through colonisation of the state for the benefit of the represented interests, to eating the state out of house and home - for example through participation in the profits from public tenders. The programme element seems no longer to play an important role in the eyes of many citizens: they do not trust the political parties to be capable of efficient governance. People should nevertheless not condemn political parties too easily, because without them everything may become more difficult, or worse. Rather, we should increase the attention that is paid to them (the constitution, funding, possible judicial control of internal matters, and so on).

The key to achieving improvement seems to be an increase in the number of members. Without this, the risk of political parties being attacked by so-called 'dead souls' is growing. Such persons are incited to join the party as completely formal members by someone who wants to make a career in the party. In some cases they are the employees of that person's company, or members of a sports association that he heads. Since even the largest political parties have district organisations of several hundred members, sometimes several dozens of votes may be sufficient to take control of that organisation. This is also supported by the fact that, since the 1990s, Czech political parties have increased the importance of district and regional organisations at the expense of central management. At first sight this may appear to be a good thing, transferring the decision-making closer to ordinary members. In practice however it has facilitated the operation of so-called godfathers, i.e. dubious entrepreneurs often on the edge of the criminal world, who control many district and regional organisations. The current clean-up is contributed to by increased activity of the police and also the weakening of specific traditional political parties, which have ceased to be attractive

---

of the regime. This is reflected for example in a survey by CVVM in February 2014 in which 33 percent of respondents agreed that the parliament could be dissolved and political parties cancelled, whereas 50 percent disagreed with this statement. The number of those who were against political parties has been growing steadily since 2004, when it was 27 percent. This reflects in part the old Czech scepticism toward political parties, which were contrasted with "apolitical politics" or "petty work." This did not relate to a reliance on the general interest as decided by the emperor, president or bureaucracy, but rather an aversion to party bickering, programme deals and parcelling out of the state. In addition to that, in 1948 political parties started to be confused with the communist (single) state party. This still has an effect in that membership of political parties is not seen as a manifestation of a natural interest in public matters, but more or less as an instrument to further one's career.

to the godfathers. The "fight against the godfathers" has helped at least three new political entities to get into the Chamber of Deputies in the course of the last two parliamentary elections. Larger political parties could return to their role as a natural connection between civil society and the state, as well as other levels of public power. These parties were traditionally the platforms for discussions on issues such as the future direction of communities.

II.2 Direct democracy and direct action

Distrust in politics is also manifested through calls for an increased involvement of elements of direct democracy (primarily referenda)[40] and for a stronger focus on the wishes of citizens who are repeatedly surveyed in various public opinion polls. It sounds logical: politicians are representatives of the people and they should fulfil the people's will. If the surveys are representative, i.e. if they include a sufficient number of respondents (usually over a thousand), they should surely reflect the will of the public. The difficulty lies in the fact that when giving their opinions in polls people are extremely unstable and respond only to what they are asked. If the person who commissioned the survey knows how to ask and asks at the right time, he is most likely to get the response he wants (and the one he has known for ages, but which now becomes more legitimate to enforce, as it has been proven to be the "the wish of the people"). Despite this, in reference to the US situation *S. M. Griffin* claims the influence of public opinion to be an informal influence of constituent power.[41]

Other forms of expression of public opinion include public meetings, petitions, strikes, letters published in newspapers, contributions on social networks, letters to legislators, and so on. We could also add direct action in the form of demonstrations, blockades, and occupation of public spaces or offices.[42] In

40 The intensive involvement of elements of direct democracy in classical parliamentary democracies may often have an anti-systemic effect and weaken parliaments that are stripped of part of their legitimacy and capacity for action by the above-mentioned transformations of political parties.

41 Griffin, Stephen M.: *Constituent Power and Constitutional Change in American Constitutionalism.* In: Loughlin, Martin, Walker, Neil (eds.): *The Paradox of Constitutionalism. Constitutional Power and Constitutional Form.* Oxford: Oxford University Press, 2007, p. 66.

42 G. Sorel, a French syndicalist influenced by vitalist philosophy was a theorist of so-called direct action at the beginning of the 20th century. He took a reserved attitude toward political parties and was more open to trade unions. He expected a systemic change to arise from general strikes.

addition, it is remotely related to the phenomenon of squatters, whose actions also include the direct occupation of real property even though this is contradictory to rules. A similar atmosphere is also typical for pirate parties, with the central requirement being a change to the copyright protection system.

A historical version of these expressions of the people would be the people on the galleries of the Convention during the French Revolution – the shouting and threatening of Parisian radicals had an immediate influence on the sessions of the Convention which aspired to be the mouthpiece of the general will of the French people. At one point they even brought cannons to the Convention, which they intended to use to demand the handing over of the Girondin deputies, and they succeeded. French historian *F. Furet* wrote the following: "*This event is of essential importance, because for the first time two crystal-clear forces stood against each other: the representatives of the nation on the one side, and proponents of direct democracy as a brute force represented by petty people and the cannons on the other side. Did democracy surrender to force, or to the people who instituted the democracy?*"[43]

In all the indicated cases there is a random however very active section of the people which claims to embody the people. These are the people who are present and who do not want to be represented: they claim that they will see to their interests themselves. This is true to a considerable extent also of referenda, which are institutionalised and therefore have clear rules and are open to everybody. Nevertheless, even in such a case it is a decision of only a part of the people, and very often a rather small part. As noted by both *J. Blondel* and *F. Zakaria*, as there is usually low turnout, organised groups with partial interests assert themselves. This results in atomisation of the political system, because bizarre answers are

---

43 Furet, Francois: *The French Revolution: 1770-1814.* Blackwell, 1996. Quoted from Furet, Francois: *Francouzská revoluce. Díl 1. Od Turgota k Napoleonovi 1770 – 1814.* [*The French Revolution. Part 1. From Turgot to Napoleon 1770 - 1814*] Praha: Argo, 2004, p. 180. As a result of these events in 1795 it was stipulated that the number of people in audience during parliamentary sessions must not exceed a half of the deputies. Cf. Hunt, Lynn: *Politics, Culture, and Class in the French Revolution.* Berkeley: University of California Press, 1984. Quoted from Huntová, Lynn: *Francouzská revoluce. Politika, kultura, třída.* [*Politics, Culture, and Class in the French Revolution*] Brno: Centrum pro demokracii a kulturu, 2007, p. 104. Robespierre on the contrary dreamt of galleries for twelve thousand people who would continuously represent the people's control over a potentially despotic parliament. Cf. Talmon, Jacob Leib: *The Origins of Totalitarian Democracy.* London: Secker & Warburg, 1952. Quoted from Talmon, Jacob Leib.: *O původu totalitní demokracie.* [*The Origins of Totalitarian Democracy*] Praha: Sociologické nakladatelství, 1998, p. 100.

given irrespective of any dependencies: for example, 'yes' to a subject-matter solution, and 'no' to funding.[44] In such a case it does not have to be completely clear that the directly expressed will of the nation should take precedence over the will of the parliament, whose role it is to formulate the general interest. This is why not all topics are commonly subject to a vote. In particular, general long-term decisions and topics that are hard to translate into a right-left division are usually excluded.[45] And this is quite apart from possible manipulations or stage-management of the plebiscite that forms only a legitimising background.[46] "*Referenda and legislative initiatives,*" says *F. Zakaria*, "*speeded up the process of taking over power from politicians and handing it to 'the people.' It is always implemented through a growing class of professional consultants, lobbyists, experts in public opinion polls and activists [...] Due to this revolution the institutions of representative democracy have lost their importance.*"[47] However, there are the institutions of representative democracy, unlike consultants and lobbyists, who has to bear the responsibility before the public.

A different question is whether referenda should be used to double the majority in the form of a veto or the positive confirmation of a decision of a state body: a resolution of the parliament is, or may be followed by, a decision of voting citizens (the vote is on the confirmation or rejection of the decision). This may be desirable particularly as an instrument to counter the alienation of the parliament and, in the case of matters of essential importance such as constitutional changes, where judicial control is restrained, if not eliminated.

The empirical people may, in the above situations, perceive the restriction to vote on an issue as its exclusion. If democracy is the government of people, in the name of what is something that is desired by 80 percent of citizens prevented from being implemented? In an exaggerated form this is included in the tool-kit of so-called constitutional populism, according to which the will of the people may take precedence over constitutional rules. The rules limit only the bodies of instituted power which do not include the people – the people act as a constantly present sovereign. However the people do not usually have the required qualities of homogeneity or focus on the general interest; the people are simply voting citizens.

44 Blondel, Jean: *Comparing Political Systems*. New York – Washington: Praeger, 1972, p. 237.

45 Cf. Budge, 2008, p. 605.

46 This is how L. Hunt perceives direct voting when she refers to Napoleon's technique of plebiscites as people's sovereignty with a single player. See Hunt, 2007, p. 247.

47 Zakaria, p. 197.

The will of the people was the main argument used by advocates for the direct election of the president in the Czech Republic, which eventually took place in 2013. The introduction of direct elections is a good example of how extremely difficult or almost impossible it is to explain to the public that it will be better if it is not the public who chooses the candidate. The difficulty was to explain the people that indirect election is better not for the politicians for whom the authority that is vested in them means a stronger hold on power (and also the benefits arising from power), but rather for the functioning of the political system. This is mentioned by *F. Zakaria*, quoted several times above, who claims that "*the more the pandering [of politicians to the public] escalates, the more negative an attitude the public takes to the politicians.*" He mentions in this context the reaction of *Winston Churchill*, who was advised by a colleague from the parliament during the Second World War to "*keep an ear to the ground.*" The British Prime Minister replied, with the irony that was so typical of him, that "*it would be very difficult for Brits to look up to a leader who was caught in such a position.*"[48]

More direct democracy generally does not result in paying more attention to the people, but rather in groups of lobbyists, consultants and activists using the open space to enforce their particular interests – which they do in the name of the people and with a rhetoric that extols the right of the people to have a say. Particular interests may be vested in a change of tax legislation, health or pension system, or a ban on the limitation of human rights. They all appear to be noble aims, however they often hide specific motivations which are far from being noble. *Zakaria's* solution is logical, however controversial: "*What we need in politics today is not more democracy but less. I do not propose that we should call for tyrants and dictators, but we should ask why some institutions within our society, such as the Federal Reserve or the Supreme Court, function so well yet others, such as legislative bodies, function so poorly.*"[49] According to *Zakaria* the main reason for this subsists in the fact that well-functioning institutions are not under the constant pressure of the public, and there are good reasons for that. Zakaria identifies such reasons using the example of the Federal Reserve: many issues are better understood by experts than the common people, policy must be applied over an extended time, and often the negative side effects are evident before the positive results. This is why the public should not decide. The difficult task of the politicians is to explain this to the public, as the English conservative politician and philosopher, *Edmund Burke*, attempted to do in his famous Bristol

48 Ibid.

49 Ibid, p. 148.

speech: "*Your representative owes you, not his industry only, but his judgment; and he betrays, instead of serving you, if he sacrifices it to your opinion. […] You choose a member indeed; but when you have chosen him, he is not member of Bristol, but he is a member of parliament.*"[50] A politician should lead society, rather than just meeting the wishes of the loudest.

II.3 Corporativism

Distrust in traditional political representation is reflected also in the strengthening of elements of corporativist organisation. This reduces the powers of the state, which is traditionally represented primarily by the legislative and executive power. Instead of major decisions being publicly discussed and adopted in parliament and then implemented by the executive power, the key discussions or decisions take place at meetings of representatives of individual groups of society, typically within a so-called tripartite framework, where government representatives meet the representatives of employees and employers, or possibly there may be other forms of social dialogue. Another form of corporativist elements is the situation where selected groups are given the opportunity to express their opinion on planned measures (for example in the form of a comment procedure or consultation), whereas another groups of citizens do not have such a possibility. Such a procedure indicates one of the main reservations toward corporativist elements, i.e. the privilege given to certain groups of citizens and their associations. This reservation is usually weakened by the argument that only organisations with mandatory membership participate in these meetings, since when membership in an organisation is not mandatory it obviously diminishes its representativeness.

Once we feel that only particular interests are involved in the political process, we fight their excessive influence through maximum openness and transparency. Then we can speak about process as a source of legitimacy of a decision, which is one of the topics of the theory of law-making. Emphasis on both of the above-mentioned aspects decreases in the case of belief in the general interest, because the typical quality of general interest is that it is capable of involving also those who do not participate. We accept the result of decision-making because it is convenient for us, or because we accept an open decision-making process which gives a chance to everyone, or possibly we perceive its conformity with values that we consider important. The first criterion is rather subjective, while the third is weak in a diversified society.

---

50 Ibid, p. 168.

Individual groups of citizens that gain advantages through more pronounced corporativist elements (such as professional associations, trade unions, or entities invited to give their comments) are influenced by state to a certain extent (state stipulates for example the legal conditions for their formation, while their internal regulations must respect the legal order adopted by parliament), but at the same time individual groups also have their independence and of course their own interests which they assert. Proponents of the general interest consider corporativist elements to be undesirable,[51] but a general distrust in political parties often results in corporativist elements being perceived as a relatively transparent safety mechanism against hidden interests within political parties.[52]

The topic of corporativist elements within a political system, for example in the Czech Republic, is on its way back unnoticed thanks to the practical activities of *President M. Zeman*. The caretaker government that he appointed, despite the resistance of political parties, in the summer of 2013 included representatives of industry. In addition, the president's advisory body includes alongside the prime minister a trade union leader as well as captains of industry to advise for example about energy policy. All this indicates that now the decision-making has shifted from garrulous and incompetent political parties to competent experts and managers. A major drawback however is the fact that the voters have no influence on them.

In addition to the tripartite framework, dominance in comment procedures, and direct entries of industry delegates in government and its decision-making bodies, corporativist practices also include creating a so-called iron triangle. This is based on gaining control over the regulation of sector policies by groups of government officers, representatives of organised interests and deputies, all related through common interests or expertise. They decide about state policy in a certain area. A variation of this was the so-called power triad in the Netherlands. It consisted of an alliance of government, bureaucracy and interest groups that tended to give the parliament the role of a mere rubber-stamper of previously

51 This was the substance of a dispute in Weimar Germany over the extent of openness of decision-making processes which could be personified as C. Schmitt against H. Heller.

52 Over the last decade trust in trade unions has ranged around 40 percent, while since 2003 it has tended to grow slowly. CVVM SOÚ AV ČR, v.v.i., Naše společnost, Důvěra některým institucím veřejného života v březnu 2014 [Our Society, Trust in Selected Institutions of Public Life in March 2014], retrieved on 5.6.2014 from http://cvvm.soc.cas.cz/media/com_form2content/documents/c1/a7205/f3/po140328.pdf.

adopted decisions. The parliament in the end activated itself, also thanks to their senators, in order to protect the primacy of politics.[53]

II.4 Civil society

The state does not consist of only authorities, laws and politicians, but rather it consists mainly of people. From time to time the state asks them about their opinion in elections or referenda, and the expressed will of the citizens within the given rules is reflected in the composition of elected bodies. However, this is not the only role of citizens in a state – especially not in a democratic state. Between individuals and the state there is the space of civil society, which may be seen as "*a space in between family, the state and market, where people associate to further their interests.*"[54] *P. Pithart* aptly describes this as "*a sum of spheres of the independence of the state,*"[55] including formal and informal associations and organisations and their activities, irrespective of whether these are purely positive activities (such as charitable organisations or environmental protection), or negative ones (such as those of skinheads or aggressive sports fans).[56] [57]

---

53 Schendelen, M. P. C. M. (Rinus) van: *The Netherlands: Parliamentary Parties Rival with Pressure Groups*. In: Norton, Philip. (ed.): *Parliaments and Pressure Groups in Western Europe*. London: Frank Cass, 1999, p. 119 et seq.

54 Definition used by CIVICUS: World Alliance for Citizen Participation. Vajdová, Tereza: *Česká občanská společnost 2004: po patnácti letech rozvoje. Zpráva z projektu CIVICUS Civil Society Index pro Českou republiku.* [*Czech Civil Society 2004: After Fifteen Years of Development. Report of CIVICUS Civil Society Index for the Czech Republic Project*] Praha: Akademické nakladatelství CERM, 2005, p. 17.

55 See his regular lectures dealing with civil society at the Law Faculty of Charles University in Prague.

56 Traditionally civil society includes primarily positive activities. We are however of the opinion that civil society may have (and actually has) also negative manifestations that we do not have to agree with (and sometimes we must not agree with), but it does not make much sense to exclude them from the sphere of civil society as they are clearly neither individual actions nor state activities. Cf. Skovajsa, 2010, pp. 62-89. The different approaches to civil society and its definitions are pointed out for example by J. Harris, who identifies four categories of definitions and offers their historical background. In: Harris, Jose: *Development of Civil Society*. In: Binder, Sarah A., Rhodes, R. A. W., Rockman, Bert A. (eds.): *The Oxford handbook of political institutions*. Oxford: Oxford University Press, 2008, pp. 131-143.

57 Civil society represents an organism with a complex internal structure that is relatively fragile. It suffered in Europe from Nazi and later communist totalitarianism. In both cases it started a gradual recovery but the process does not seem to have finished yet. Also R. Dahrendorf notes that everything requires time and that a legal system

The relation between civil society and the state - which ideally should mutually support and complement each other - in practice is not usually simple at all. *G. Almond* and *S. Verba* speak about the necessity to balance governmental power and governmental responsiveness, and consider this to be "*...one of the most important and difficult tasks of a democracy. Unless there is some control of governmental elites by non-elites, it is hard to consider a political system democratic.*"[58] Many politicians however show a tendency to perceive civil society as a sphere of latent or realised resistance against the state, which they must oppose and definitely should not easily grant concessions to. Those who are less refined escalate their rhetoric to the point of referring to representatives of civil society as self-appointed representatives who did not have enough courage to run in elections and who are now trying to gain power through means other than electoral validation.[59]

It was primarily the second Czech president, *Václav Klaus*, and his supporters in the right-wing Občanská demokratická strana [Civic Democratic Party], who became famous for repeated attacks on the civil sector in the Czech Republic.[60] It was a paradox that the biggest opponents of civil society were associated in a party called "civic."[61] The main reason for this animosity consisted primarily in

---

may be changed in six months, an economic system in six years, but that civil society takes sixty years to change. Dahrendorf, Ralf: *Reflections on the Revolution in Europe: In a letter intended to have been sent to a gentleman in Warsaw*. New York: Random House, 1990, pp. 99-100.

58 Almond, Gabriel Abraham, Sidney Verba: *The civic culture: Political attitudes and democracy in five nations*. Newbury Park, USA: SAGE, 1989, p. 341.

59 Elections nevertheless gradually lose their importance and become only one of the mechanisms of democratic society, rather than a "sacred" moment that they once perhaps were. Cf. Rosanvallon, 2011, pp. 69-71.

60 The importance and role of civil society was a repetitive and long-term source of disputes between Václav Klaus and, for example, Tomáš Halík, a catholic priest and a distinguished Czech intellectual whose merits were recently acknowledged through an award of the prestigious Templeton Prize. It was also a source of disputes with another notable Vaclav of recent Czech history: the last Czechoslovak and the first Czech president, Václav Havel. Practically the whole of Havel's work as well as the below-cited speech are proof of that controversy.

61 This is nothing new. The relation between the name of the party and its actual policy may be extremely remote. For example, Portuguese social democracy represents rather right-wing politics, but it was impossible to officially claim to be a right-wing party in post-Salazar Portugal. Even in post-war Czechoslovakia there was a significant political shift to the left and almost all parties claimed to be socialist – the divide between right and left was quite bizarre.

an unwillingness to share power with anybody else and the ability to explain this to the public in such a smart manner that the public stayed on the side of politicians rather than the representatives of civil society, who logically should have been closer to the public. Politicians as well as the representatives of civil society claim to represent the public. The former go through an official legitimising election process, while the latter derive their legitimacy from their members and supporters and further interests that official representatives often fail to notice (frequently in contradiction with their pre-election promises, government statements or the actual needs of society).

With growing feelings of alienation and a lack of belief that the representatives really represent the community, strive for the welfare of the community or are perceptive of various needs and interests, it is hard to insist on imputing the will of the people to the representatives (we are you). So, at least from the point of view of some, there may be a shift of democracy as self-government into the government of a minority over the majority. But in order to avoid the situation where every person claiming to be a representative is in fact one, there is the criterion of the public interest, in which we are partakers; providing that we believe in the public interest. A public interest that is above individual interests may be in specific situations (such as highway construction in an environmentally valuable location, or improvement of the quality of social welfare services) more aptly formulated by proponents from the civil sphere, in particular where the political representatives' attention is diverted by businessmen furthering their own business interests. There is a conflict of double legitimacy: that attributed to politicians, and that of civil society. Political legitimacy derives from general elections. It is, however, weakened by a deepening alienation of politics and people and an unwillingness or inability to deal with important topics, and it also quite logically diminishes with every day that elapses from the time of appointment to the office. Civil legitimacy derives from specific citizens (irrespective of whether they are members of an association or its supporters) and from the general interest that they defend. This does not automatically mean that civil legitimacy must take precedence over politics; for that matter, the representatives of the civil sector may try to assume power and behave in a considerably undemocratic manner, which is a risk growing hand-in-hand with a growing frustration with politics.[62]

62 The importance of (mainly active) citizens for democracy is dealt with also by P. Rosanvallon in his work Counter-Democracy. In spite of the title, he focuses his attention on the activities of citizens which enrich (and also change), rather than destroy democratic society. Rosanvallon shows that at the present time it is not sufficient

If we look at the relation between politics and civil society without prejudice, ultimately politics and the state, which is represented by politics, considerably profit from a thriving civil society. Civil society may and should be a source of personalities who will later become politicians and help to interconnect lower and higher levels of politics. It takes on many activities which can be better implemented by citizens in parallel with the state or instead of the state (social care, care for the environment, cultural development, and so on). A strong civil society pays off for the state also economically – many activities may be funded by the state to a much lesser extent than when the state must carry out these activities on its own (again, such activities may involve cultural development, social care or environmental protection), and possibly the state may delegate such activities to local government and not decide about them from the centre - which often means without a detailed knowledge of the local context, and, necessarily, at a higher cost. A strong civil society such as that in the US increases the stability of society because many matters are not derived directly from the most important constitutional bodies, and so, if these stop working or go into crisis, the entire society is not so likely to enter into a crisis too. A strong civil society creates a pluralist environment and gives people the possibility to fully realise their potential and become involved in the activities that they find most rewarding. This is in agreement with the views of *V. Havel*, who said: "*a man is not only a producer, profit maker or consumer. He is at the same time and perhaps most of all a person, who wants to be with others, who longs for various types of co-existence and co-operation, who wants to take a specific part in the life of human community, who wants to influence what is going on around him.*"[63]

Developed civil society is definitely beneficial to the state, however it is not beneficial to individual politicians whose power is actually limited by civil society. This is probably a major source of resistance against civil society – even though this may be concealed by other explanations and arguments. The more clearly and the more often the interests arising from civil society are ignored,

---

to conceive of democracy as merely electing representatives. He offers an analysis of new forms of political investment: the people as a watchdog, the people as veto players, and the people as judge. Rosanvallon, Pierre: *Counter-democracy: Politics in an Age of Distrust*. Cambridge: Cambridge University Press, 2008.

63 Havel, Václav: *Projev prezidenta republiky Václava Havla na sympóziu "Myšlenky Václava Havla a koncept občanské společnosti"* [Speech of Vaclav Havel, the President of the Czech Republic, at the Symposion 'Ideas of Václav Havel and the Concept of Civil Society'] In: Havel, Václav: *Projevy a jiné texty z let 1992-1999*. [*Speeches and Other Texts*] Spisy 7. Praha: Torst, 1999, pp. 856-7.

the more likely it is that a part of society will resign and the other part will try to come up with a new, more efficient strategy. This is one of the possible perspectives of changes in Czech civil society.

When in 2004 *T. Vajdová* published what is probably the most recent comprehensive study of the status of Czech civil society, she reached the conclusion that Czech civil society had attained a relatively good status, as approximately a half of all citizens are involved primarily in the fields of the environment and social services.[64] According to the study, civil society should in the future focus primarily on its structure: to increase the number of active members, donors and volunteers, to improve co-ordination and co-operation with small companies, to gain more financial certainty, to become more professional, and in particular to learn to explain better to the public what civil society does and why it is important.[65] Civil society has been at least to a limited extent successful in achieving that. The most distinct Czech example is a project called "Rekonstrukce státu" [Reconstruction of the State], under which almost twenty non-governmental organisations dealing with good governance, transparency and the accountability of public administration joined forces. Under the leadership of the three largest involved organisations ("Transparency International," "Oživení" [Recovery], and "Frank Bold") the project has been monitoring Czech politics for several years and is trying to push through nine basic laws or amendments that are missing in the Czech Republic (for example more transparent funding of political parties, the abolition of bearer shares, the online publishing of contracts made by public bodies, and passing the civil service act).[66] Many politicians have committed to support their demands and the government of *B. Sobotka*, which commenced its work at the beginning of 2014, included many of the laws in its coalition statement. It is clear that by far not all the demands will be pushed through, however the Reconstruction of the State project demonstrates the capacity of current Czech civil society to put in place coordinated, long-term, professionally managed campaigns that are successful in the media.[67]

---

64 Similar conclusions were also reached by Pospíšilová, Tereza: *Česká občanská společnost – data, fakta a měření.* [Czech Civil Society – Data, Facts and Measurements] In: Skovajsa, 2010, pp. 113-143.

65 Vajdová, 2005, in particular pp. 10-13, 74-6.

66 See Rekonstrukce státu [Reconstruction of the State], retrieved on 5.6.2014 from http://www.rekonstrukcestatu.cz/.

67 The difference becomes clear in particular in comparison with previous appeals (Impuls 99, Děkujeme, odejděte or Holešovská výzva), which were limited to statements regarding poor conditions, but however did not create structures for long-term

The activities of civil society have, from the point of view of our topic, one additional important impact: active citizens do not only limit the real power of the state by taking over a part of the activities that used to be performed by a great and caring state, but they also diminish citizens' expectations of the state. If citizens do not wish to or cannot rely on the state in various areas and they voluntarily or out of necessity take the initiative, logically they rely less on the state in other areas too. This is not however a linear process and often the state, which in many respects is not trusted, is criticised for injustices that have been experienced irrespective of whether these are the fault of the state or not. This again raises the question of to what extent the state should take a pastoral approach, and where it should trust the maturity of the judgement of its citizens and allow them to be responsible for their own decisions.

II.5 Outsourcing

The last field that we would like to mention, at least briefly, deals with delegating part of the tasks of the state to external organisations (so-called *outsourcing*). This manner of procuring various activities comes from the private sector and in particular from IT services. It is gradually expanding to other activities and is penetrating also the performance of tasks of state administration.

The main motivation for the delegation of selected tasks is supposed to be the reduction of costs, since in particular activities not related to the core business of the organisation or requiring the one-off involvement of highly specialised expertise are not worth being performed by the organisation's own employees. At the same time this enables the organisation to focus more precisely on its core business. *J. Donahue* and *R. Zeckhauser* identify four basic motivations of the state to delegate some of its tasks to external entities: resources (i.e. the ability to accumulate additional resources), productivity (i.e. efficiency), information (knowledge of important information without which performance of the given activities becomes difficult, if not impossible), and legitimacy (according to the authors it is better if the state does not perform certain tasks directly, such as in the case of corrupt states where delegation to a private entity may increase the legitimacy of the activity).[68]

pressure on politicians. After temporary interest on the part of the public, the appeals, as well as their demands, were forgotten and politics remained unchanged.

68 Donahue, John D., Zeckhauser, Richard J.: *Public-Private Collaboration*. In: Goodin, Robert E., Moran, Michael, Rein, Martin: *The Oxford Handbook of Public Policy*. Oxford: Oxford University Press, 2006.

There is traditional outsourcing relating to IT services, data management, facility management, security, or the operation of canteens. In addition to these simply support activities, there are now also number of other activities of public administration representing the substance of performance of activities of the state being delegated to external entities. They include important and a growing number of activities: from various legal services (producing expert opinions), the collection of receivables (the institute of private law enforcement agents) and contracts relating to the environment, to the operation of state technical inspections of vehicles.[69]

The delegation of tasks of the state to private entities, of course, involves certain risks. *J. Donahue* and *R. Zeckhauser* identify four basic risks. Firstly there is the risk of diluted control, because the state is losing immediate control over the performed activity even in cases where the power is delegated on the basis of a well-drafted contract. Secondly, delegation does not have to prove to be efficient in the end because the costs as a result of incorrect calculations, transaction costs or abuse on the part of an external entity may turn out to be higher than if the state performed the activity itself using its own resources. The third risk is reputational vulnerability, because the poor reputation of those entities performing the activities is transferred also to the party who commissioned it, i.e. the state (some of the violence committed in Abu Ghraib prison against Iraqi prisoners was not perpetrated by the US government, but by external entities whose responsibility is, in the eyes of many – at least in the Muslim world – automatically transferred to the US). Fourthly, the excessive use of external services also involves the risk that the state will gradually lose the ability to carry out the activities itself (diminished capacity).[70] We may add one more risk which is clearly visible from a Central European perspective: delegating the tasks of the state facilitates the abuse of public money which may be spent on overpriced contracts with companies personally related to the officers who decide on the delegation of the tasks. Delegation also involves the question of responsibility for decisions and especially for bad decisions, as well as the question of attributability of the act of performance of state administration. Is it performed by the delegator, or the organisation to which it was delegated? In the case of delegation to law firms, potential mistakes are covered by obligatory liability insurance, while for other delegations of tasks the entity performing an outsourced activity does not necessarily have to be insured.

69 On the basis of administrative decision of the relevant regional authority of the Czech Republic, periodic inspection of vehicles may be carried out by private entities.

70 Donahue, Zeckhauser, 2006, pp. 507-8.

In any case, outsourcing is a manifestation of a trend that is opposite to the trend of the past, which still takes place in the field of human rights (social rights in particular): while the state, under pressure from the public, keeps taking on new tasks, it delegates through outsourcing the performance of some of these to non-state bodies.[71] The scope of delegated activities has a tendency to grow, which leads critics to warn against the excessive privatisation of state administration.

Conclusion

At the end of this chapter we would primarily like to indicate a possible answer to the dilemma described in the above text. We described the negative consequences of direct democracy in terms of supporting populism, strengthening lobby groups, enabling politicians to get rid themselves of responsibility, and making the implementation of long-term visions more difficult. At the same time we pointed out the relative weakness of civil society especially in post-communist countries. Both phenomena however bring the serious considerations of intellectuals and activists to a difficult decision. Should they fight for more democracy and a stronger voice of civil society, which both diminishes the power of politicians in power and enables the enforcement of certain reforms or prevents regulations and decisions by politicians motivated by mercenary intentions? If they attempt to do that they may have to face the risks described by *F. Zakaria* concerning the US experience, which made the politics there dependant on lobbyists and well-organised activists who are capable of furthering their interests with the support of media, at the expense of public interest.

A satisfactory solution, at least to a certain extent, may be to balance both tendencies. Currently Czech society, similarly to the majority of post-communist countries in Central and Eastern Europe, is struggling with seemingly omnipotent politicians who, in the absence of a strong civil society, are capable of abusing public offices for their own enrichment. Therefore there is no solution other than to strengthen the civil sector and at the same time make sure that its pressure does not begin to empty politics of content. This will, however, take quite a long time.[72]

---

71 This, among other things, blurs the difference between private and public corporations. If a private corporation lives primarily on public contracts it becomes somehow less private than if the majority of its business comes from private entities.

72 To achieve a relative harmony between the power of politicians and influence of civil society is not particularly easy in any society. Cf. Almond, Verba, 1989, pp. 342-344.

Jan Kysela

Conclusions

I. Summary

Contemporary states – European in particular – are great in terms of the scope of tasks of their governments, but weak in terms of their ability to carry out these tasks efficiently. This was our initial thesis. We attempted to formulate a number of hypotheses explaining why this is the case. Very significant are the expectations that are attached to a modern state which would have earlier been distributed among the church, community, different gilds, and the family. Expectations, often not very realistic, motivate the growth of the state; however various factors, or forces, act against it. We divided these into external and internal, giving a special position to human rights, which operate across the board.

As external limits on the power of the state we identified the deepening of relations within the international community, international law, European integration and the law connected with it, and also slightly less personal processes such as globalisation.

The international community is becoming more interlocked, i.e. more limiting for individual states. One manifestation of the intertwining of states within the international system is the expansion of international law in terms of the number of international treaties, as well as the issues thus affected. International judicial bodies with a compulsory jurisdiction are being created. Along with states and international inter-governmental organisations, other actors have been appearing in the international system, such as supra-national corporations, global movements (like *Greenpeace*), international (supranational) crime and international terrorist networks, and also individuals (both billionaires and refugees). Their power and influence may compete with many states, yet they are not thoroughly regulated by international law or the law of states. State borders do not mean much for supra-national corporations, who are capable of influencing the elites of states in order to create ideal conditions for their businesses. In principle, states have no protection against such pressures other than mutual co-operation and co-ordination. Co-operation and co-ordination increase their chances of achieving an intended result, but also limit the states by new considerations for their partners.

A special chapter was devoted to the legitimacy of international law, where traditional emphasis on the will of states conflicts with a more recent emphasis on human rights. International law was explored both as an assessed and an assessing system. An example of the first type was the regime of international sanctions relating to the safeguarding of due process. An example of the second type was the imposition of the death sentence on foreigners in violation of obligations regarding consular protection in the US. The US response to the decision of the International Court of Justice proved the veracity of *U. Haltern's* observation that national governments do not accept international judgments completely submissively; in this context he mentions the Republic of South Africa, Iceland, Iran and Nicaragua.[1] Some international organisations have emancipated from individual states through a transition to majority, rather than unanimous, voting. In this way a part of the powers of states is conferred to international organisations. If there is no unanimous vote, the decisions of international organisations may conflict with the will of states. International law has become a noteworthy title for both individuals and legal entities to bring cases against states before international bodies (arbitrations, courts) - not only against foreign states, but also their own. Thus international law has become a test of the conduct of the state toward its own persons. On top of this, it influences the national legal environment by adjusting national legal rules to international law regulations, or through the direct impact of various incorporating clauses. Such clauses are adopted by states in order to reduce the risk of breaching international obligations merely through legislative inaction, which was not such a problem when there were no enforcement mechanisms, or when international "public opinion" was different. In the current world, states must pay more attention to what is considered to be a standard of civilisation. This is formulated and supervised not only by government agencies, but also to a large extent by the mass-media, non-governmental organisations, activists, and so on. An obliging approach to international law is perceived to be a part of this standard. However, it is important to note that various international obligations do not fit together in harmony: for example, unlimited business activities in the interest of free trade may conflict with standards of human rights and environmental protection. So we cannot say that international law, through its restriction of the discretion of states, represents always and under all circumstances the desirable "good" for everyone.

The clearest limitation on states is currently represented by the European Union as an area of conferred powers. The European Union is a hybrid entity in which we find both federative and confederative elements built on the "chassis" of an international organisation. It is thus rather complicated to assess how

1 Haltern, Ulrich: *Was bedeutet Souveränität?* Tübingen: Mohr Siebeck, 2007, p. 6.

it fulfils certain standards: should these be standards of a state, or those of an international organisation? The debate about democratic deficit derives its importance from this. Nonetheless, the power of individual states does not act in areas of the complete conferral of powers, while in other cases Member States are bound to transfer European obligations to national law and it is forbidden to cause conflicts with European law in general. Different types of interaction between states and the European Union have been described in detail. Special attention was given to the clause providing for the protection of the constitutional identity of the Member States, and implementation of the principle of subsidiarity. These both represent instruments used by states against "European power" which the states find too intrusive.

Human rights appear to be a limit on all public power and, when they act horizontally, also a mutual limit on individuals. With regard to their international basis, they can be considered external limits (including justified humanitarian intervention). At the same time they belong among internal limits, as they are regularly codified in catalogues of a constitutional nature which restrict legislative as well as other activities of states. They restrict them in two ways: in the form of a negative obligation as a prohibition, and in the form of a positive obligation as an order to ensure the implementation of a certain right. Both are directed against free legislative discretion.

The emphasis placed on human rights means a strengthening of judicial power at the expense of classic political powers. From the point of view of the functioning of the state, this means a change in the division and balancing of powers, which becomes even more obvious as judges depart further from the wording of constitutional and general laws. If human rights have the value of a trump which "overtrumps" other arguments, the ultimate interpreter of human rights becomes, potentially, almighty: they reveal what is forbidden, or what must be. An interpreter of this kind need not be just a national court, but also an international court, whose decisions are not hampered by a constitution.

From the point of view of a democratic state, the significance of political processes which create a majority will has weakened in favour of individual perception of subjective rights. Consequently, the nature of political participation has changed and a new phenomenon of achieving interests through litigation has emerged. Activists and their organisations provide support to parties to cases regarding the language and form of law. Indeed, what is of primary importance here is not to persuade the majority, but rather the court. It is not necessary to pass an act, because the desired result can be achieved by reference to general values, such as human dignity.

The last set of factors impacting on the power of the state issues from society. The ability of a state to enforce its objectives is connected with the extent to which the state and its objectives are considered to be legitimate. Legitimacy may depend on harmony with values, the current wishes of citizens, or due process (compliance with rules, openness of decision-making, and so on). Legitimacy may be placed at the input, or at the output of the decision-making process. Regardless, it fluctuates around trust as the category symbolising the foundation of social capital. And it is trust in the state and its institutions which has in recent decades markedly dropped, not only in post-communist Eastern and Central Europe. It is noticeable also in the distance exercised toward political parties, which acted as the main channel for political participation throughout the 20th century.

In the Czech Republic, the attitude to political parties is the combination of a number of resentments stemming from the 19th century and aversion to the communist state party after 1948, a reaction to attempts by political parties to monopolise the public space in the 1990s, and their shift to simple rent seeking, scandals, and so on. If political parties represent a kind of circulation of blood in the state, it can hardly be expected that they will not manifest defects. Whose interests are served by the will of the state as formulated by them? As a result of such doubts we can see in the Czech Republic a response in the form of emerging protest political movements, calls for direct democracy as a panacea to resolve all problems, or attempts to establish a power block interconnecting the newly directly elected president of the republic with various politicians and large economic players.

An increase in transparency has had an impact on the manoeuvring space of the state as well. It is possible to find information on practically anything and some decision-making processes are under continuous surveillance in almost real time. This may prove beneficial in combating cabinet politics, yet it may also reinforce the influence of organised interests. No incident is distant enough not to shake public opinion. Frequent elections and even more frequent monitoring of public support for political parties and politicians has made public opinion a factor in home and foreign policy that cannot be ignored. Indeed, this may have been anticipated since the development of newspapers in the 19th century. The question of who controls the media is thus made even more important. The media is an example of social power that is comparable with the power of the state in terms of its ability to shape public matters. But state power is divided, balanced and checked, while the various types of manifestation of social power are not in the limelight as a potential danger to freedom. Moreover, state and social power sometimes merge when so-called privatisation of the state occurs, i.e. a transfer of the exercise of state power to private entities. The erasure of the distinction between the public and private sphere is noticeable in the other direction, too, when the state shows an interest in the use of public funds provided to private persons. Such persons become subject to checks, which would otherwise be unjustified in the case of private persons.

II. What is left of sovereignty?

We stated in the introduction that we would return to the topic of sovereignty, which crosses individual thematic areas. It is a concept rooted in the Middle Ages, combining the claims of popes (*suprematio*) with those of emperors and French kings (*souverain*). Its modern shape was moulded by *J. Bodin*, while later sovereignty experienced a marked depersonalisation, which was to the advantage of the state, or to the somewhat abstract people. Consequently, we may speak of the sovereignty of the state, the monarch, the people, the parliament, the constitution, a rule, or the legal order as a whole. It is possible to distinguish at least external (negative) sovereignty, understood as independence from external forces, and internal (positive) sovereignty, which is exclusive power in the given territory. There is also material sovereignty (deciding on what sovereignty consists of) and formal sovereignty (a residual and final power to decide on an exception to the rules). If there is a trend toward a more intertwined world, to which concepts such as sovereignty relate, what then is left of sovereignty if it was in the early modern period consolidated in opposition to the idea of suprastates or empire?

We fear the answer is ambiguous and of course it depends on definitions which may be applied to both the international and national environment. Certainly, we should not arrive at the conclusion that in principle everything is sovereignty, because then sovereignty does not mean anything.

As regards the first relationship, it applies that, if sovereignty is to mean the complete mutual independence of states, then it does not exist and may have never existed. If sovereignty is limited to sovereign equality among states, nothing has changed with it, since even states facing humanitarian intervention are considered to be equal. In reality, however, the international community tends not to consider as tenable all manners of exercising state powers through mere reference to sovereignty (see below).

As regards the European Union, different variations exist: the sovereignty of states only, sovereignty of the Union and the states, or the sovereignty of no one, because it is a post-sovereign model. *U. Beck* considers Europe to be a laboratory testing inclusive sovereignty, which consists in a concession of sovereign rights in exchange for gaining political regulatory power on the basis of international co-operation.[2] The question obviously is whether it is necessary to describe political regulatory power as sovereignty. Equally important is the fact that the Member States not only participate in creating the will of the European Union, but are also prepared to wrench themselves from the constraints of primary law (see reactions to the financial crisis), or to invoke residual power in the case of the excessive exercise of conferred powers (compare the case law of many constitutional courts). Evidently, they (reasonably) consider themselves to be the ultimate power, which does not exclude far-reaching submission in common situations. Sovereignty becomes active (revives) in exceptional situations – primarily, secession from the Union. Even this shows the ambivalent nature of sovereignty as a legal and political as well as normative concept, burdened by empirical recourses. It is one thing for the state to have the inalienable right to leave the Union, but the actual (im)possibility to lead the state and its economy out of the millions of relationships that have been created is quite another thing altogether.

Moreover, the European Union raises a question regarding the construction of legitimacy: is it derived from states or from a specific European people? What extent of input legitimacy do we really demand? Is relative satisfaction with output performance not enough for us? This type of reasoning is problematic, because it represents a resignation to influencing the output which we may like, but if we cease to like it there is not much left to be done, because the decision-makers are beyond our reach. One of the key issues therefore regards what impact the existence of the European Union has on the sovereignty of the people as the legitimate source of public power. The less it is an international organisation, the greater the demand for a clearer chain of legitimacy.

Even more difficult is the question of sovereignty within the state. It appears that, ultimately, we will always conclude that the ultimate power, i.e. the sovereign, is the people, since no one can rule for long without the support of the people or against their will. From the beginning of the 19th century the people have been promoted as the only legitimate source of rulership, so even those governments who do not feel the urge to be controlled or freely confirmed by empiric, real people refer to it. But "the people" is abstract, and may finally only represent a significant part of the public, which certainly can be exposed to the influence of disgruntled minorities. A change in countenance of that important part of the

2 Beck, 2007, p. 158.

public would mean the collapse of the power arrangement. Thus, *Marsilius of Padua's "pars valentior"* plays an important role.

The question of limitation is complicated, too. If sovereignty is to be legitimate justified power, not only as regards its origin but also as regards its content, it may not be limitless, because it will be measured against the standard of legitimation. If it is found excessive when compared to such a standard it would not be sovereignty any more, but merely a power. In such a case there must be someone who will assess whether such sovereignty is justified. But if someone assesses a sovereign, he himself becomes a sovereign – which was already realised by *T. Hobbes*. Such a person cannot therefore be individual people as they are punishable – they do not comply with the requirement of ultimate authority. So, the people again? But if the people are to assess the legitimacy of acts, whose acts will these be? If they are acts of established bodies, they were not sovereign and are limited by definition. If they are acts of the people, will the people assess itself and limit itself according to such assessment? The sovereign may, of course, limit himself, however the question is what will happen if he does not wish to limit himself. He may certainly yield to international pressure to adopt a constitution conforming to established standards, however he may decide to suffer applicable sanctions – the freedom of choice lies with him.[3] And, what is important, from the point of view of sovereignty all decisions will be legitimate.

The American political scientist *C. H. McIlwain* concludes his book on the history of constitutionalism with two lessons: (1) no practical limits may ultimately be imposed on the political power of the people; (2) yet we must resolve the sensitive problem of a possible conflict between the law and the will, which means that we must make it possible to appeal from drunken people to sober people, i.e. to protect individuals and minorities, particularly in times of hysteria.[4] This has the nature of self-correction of an enlightened society, which is how *S. Holmes* answers the question of how a democratic constitution can limit people in a legitimate way.[5]

It appears reasonable to consider sovereignty to be limitless which, of course, does not mean that its manifestations may not be considered illegitimate, immoral, or trampling on human rights according to external standards. The

3 And it would be no novelty. In the 19th century, Great Britain coerced weak states such as Brazil into the abolition of slavery by means of so-called gunboat diplomacy. Compare Krasner, 1999, p. 38.

4 McIlwain, 2007, pp. 129-130 and 135-136.

5 Holmes, Stephen: Foreword. In: Sajó, András: *Limiting Government. An Introduction to Constitutionalism*. Budapest: CEU Press, 1999, p. XI.

external standard of assessment may be subjective. In this case, sovereignty is manifested by breaching the rules of an established order, possibly by its destruction. It is not clear, however, what we may attain by incorporating content legitimacy as its defining mark - unless we claim that the destruction of the order by the people who do not respect for example human rights is not a manifestation of sovereignty, but of naked power, because if it were real sovereignty it would respect human rights. And while the phrase "sovereignty of the people" creates the impression that such sovereignty should be respected, "naked power of the masses" actually does not create such an impression. However, for this purpose it would be necessary to rely on a clear value base which is independent of the will of the concrete community, i.e. a transcendent base - as used to be the case with God, natural law and natural rights.

However it appears equally possible to arrive at the conclusion that sovereignty has disappeared from this world because the twilight of the modern state, with which it was connected, has begun. What we have in mind is not so much the impact of globalisation on the mutual dependence of states - because in history complete independence was to be seen only exceptionally. More significant are changes toward network structures, heterarchy and the decisive paradigm of human rights, all of these being the limits to limitlessness and fixed finality. *D. Held* mentions in this sense the loss of sovereignty of states, or its survival in the form of divided power, as a consequence of the development of international law, the internationalisation of many problems, and the growth of security dependence.[6]

The disappearance of sovereignty may be the result of the loss of belief in sovereignty, as it is an idea, not reality.[7] As an idea, it helps to create the human world by interpreting it and encouraging us to engage in certain conduct: what to take into account, what to submit to. If the idea of human rights were to be its alternative, then its sustainer could be the international community, but even then it would rather be *pars valentior*, meaning that not all would be concerned, but only those who set the trend. They would be the final power if they wished to use it; they would be legitimated by human rights, regardless of the fact that experience teaches us that human rights are given effective attention mainly when they merge with power interests.

We may also take the view that no power is final or limitless. And even from this perspective we would deem as legitimate only such power that respects

6 Beck, 2007, pp. 51-52.

7 Haltern, 2007, p. VII.

human rights. Everything else is mere naked power which, of course, exists, but can be shattered by another naked power.

And how can power applied to dissenting individuals be legitimated without fictively including them in the general will or general reason of the sovereign? A pragmatic solution can be found in reference to the legitimacy of the system in the form of "the best of possible worlds": since there is no better system which would generally guarantee the rights of individuals, the individual is bound to respect even such act with which he disagrees. No matter what, he is ruled by someone different from himself; the general will is still a fiction. In a democratic state, however, he may exert some influence on the ruler and is protected from him. The key factor in this way of thinking is that the individual is deemed to be the ultimate goal of existence of the political arrangement (equal respect for everyone), which need not necessarily apply everywhere. Without that, the basic argument for the conferral of only a part of one's natural rights to the whole, which then does not have the entitlement to interfere within the sphere of elementary freedom of each individual, is not very persuasive.

III. In conclusion

We have not written a normative work but have rather described generally what is occurring and how this impacts on the strength and freedom of states. A normative view might perhaps embrace the proposition that prudence is sensible. Surely no one volunteers to sacrifice him or herself on the altar of the state and its omnipotence today. Yet it is sensible to distinguish between the interconnection of states through bonds of co-operation and co-ordination, and their dissolution to the level of provinces of a world community. States have been tested and have proved themselves in many ways, irrespective of the many different reforms they require. However, they are quite conceivable, comprehensible and their legitimacy is derived from a known source. Ultimately what matters is what the alternatives are, and whether these are surely better.

Bibliography

Agamben, G., 2012: Homo sacer. Praha: Oikoymenh.

Alexy, R., 2002: A Theory of Constitutional Rights. Oxford: Oxford University Press.

Alexy, R., 2004: Menschenrechte ohne Metaphysik? Deutsche Zeitschrift für Philosophie 52 (1).

Alexy, R., 2005: Balancing, constitutional review, and representation. International Journal of Constitutional Law 3 (4).

Alexy, R., 2009: On Constitutional Right to Protection. Legisprudence 3 (1).

Allan, J., 1996: Bill of Rights and Judicial Power – A Liberal's Quandary. Oxford Journal of Legal Studies 16 (2).

Almond, G. A., Verba, S., 1989: The civic culture: political attitudes and democracy in five nations. Newbury Park (USA): SAGE.

Alston, P., Goodman, R., 2013: International Human Rights. Oxford: Oxford University Press.

Anderson, B., 2008: Představy společenství. Úvahy o původu a šíření nacionalismu. Praha: Karolinum.

Arendt, H., 2011: O revoluci. Praha: Oikoymenh.

Armstrong, K. A., 2013: The new governance of EU fiscal discipline European Law Review 38 (5).

Arnaiz, S. A., Llivina A. C., 2013: National Constitutional Identity and European Integration. Intersentia, Cambridge.

Ashiagbor, D., 2013: Unravelling the Embedded Liberal Bargain: Labour and Social Welfare Law in the Context of EU Market Integration. European Law Journal 19 (3).

Avbelj, M., Komárek, J. (eds.), 2012: Constitutional Pluralism in the European Union and Beyond. Oxford and Portland, Oregon: Hart Publishing.

Balthasar, A., 2011: Nichtdiskriminierung und Unionsbürgerschaft in einem Staatenverbund. Zugleich eine Auseinandersetzung mit (vornehmlich) dem

Urteil des EuGH vom 13.04.2010, C-73/08 (Bressol). Zeitschrift für Öffentliches Recht 66 (1).

Bankowicz, M., 2013: Kritikové marxismu. Brno: Barrister & Principal.

Barak, A., 2001: Constitutional Human Rights and Private Law. In: Friedman, D., Barak-Erez, D. (eds.): Human Rights in Private Law. Oxford, Portland: Hart Publishing.

Bárány, E., 2007: Pojmy dobrého práva. Bratislava: Eurokodex.

Barber, B., 1983: The logic and limits of trust. New Brunswick: Rutgers University Press.

Barnard, C., Odudu, O., 2009: The outer limits of European Union law. Oxford: Hart.

Barša, P., 1999: Politická teorie multikulturalismu. Brno: Centrum pro demokracii a kulturu.

Barša, P., 2007: Síla a rozum. Spor realismu s idealismem v moderním politickém myšlení. Praha: Filosofia.

Bauman, Z., 1999: Globalizace. Důsledky pro člověka. Praha: Mladá fronta.

Beck, U., 2007: Co je to globalizace? Omyly a odpovědi. Brno: Centrum pro demokracii a kulturu.

Bedi, S., 2009: Rejecting Rights. Cambridge (UK): Cambridge University Press.

Beitz, Ch. R., 2009: The Idea of Human Rights. Oxford: Oxford University Press.

Bellamy, R., 2007: Political Constitutionalism. Republican Defence of the Constitutionality of Democracy. Cambridge: Cambridge University Press.

Belling, V., 2009: Legitimita moci v postmoderní době. Proč potřebuje Evropská unie členské státy? Brno: Masarykova univerzita.

Berman, P. S., 2004-2005: From International Law to Law and Globalization. Columbia Journal of Transnational Law (43).

Besselink, L. F. M., 2012: Respecting Constitutional Identity in the EU (comments on case C-208/09, Ilonka Sayn-Wittgenstein – note of the author). Common Market Law Review (49).

Besselink, L. F. M., 2010: National and constitutional identity before and after Lisbon. Utrecht Law Review (3).

Bickerton, Ch. J., 2012: European Integration: From Nation-States to Member States. Oxford: Oxford University Press.

Binder, S. A., Rhodes, R. A. W., Rockman, B. A. (eds.), 2008: The Oxford handbook of political institutions. Oxford: Oxford University Press.

Blanke, H.-J., 2006: Protection of Fundamental Rights afforded by the European Court of Justice in Luxembourg. In: Blanke, H.-J., Mangiameli, S. (eds.): Governing Europe under a Constitution. The Hard Road from the European Treaties to a European Constitutional Treaty. Berlin and Heidelberg: Springer.

Bleckmann, A., 1997: Staatsrecht. Köln: Carl Heymanns Verlag.

Blondel, J., 1972: Comparing Political Systems. New York, Washington: Praeger.

Bobbio, N., 1996: The Age of Rights. Cambridge (UK): Polity Press.

Böckenförde, E.-W. 1991: Grundrechtstheorie und Grundrechtsinterpretation. In: Böckenförde, E.-W: Staat, Verfassung, Demokratie. Studien zur Verfassungstheorie und Verfassungsrecht. Frankfurt am Main: Suhrkamp.

Bogdandy, A. von, 2008: Pluralism, direct effect, and the ultimate say: On the relationship between international and domestic constitutional law. International Journal of Constitutional Law 6 (3&4).

Bogdandy, A. von, Schill, S., 2011: Overcoming absolute primacy: respect for national identity under the Lisbon Treaty. Common Market Law Review (48).

Bourgorgue-Larsen, L. (ed.), 2011: L'identité constitutionelle saisie par les juges en Europe. Paris: Editions A. Pedone.

Bross, S., 2008: Überlegungen zur europäischen Staatswerdung. Juristenzeitung.

Bruun, N., Bücker, A., Dorssemont, F., 2012: Balancing Fundamental Social Rights and Economic Freedoms: Can the Monti II Initiative Solve the EU Dilemma? The International Journal of Comparative Labour Law and Industrial Relations 28 (3).

Buchanan, A., 2004: Justice, Legitimacy, and Self-Determination. Moral Foundations of International Law. Oxford: Oxford University Press.

Buchanan, A., 2010: Legitimacy of International Law. In: Besson, S., Tasioulas, J. (eds.): The Philosophy of International Law. Oxford: Oxford University Press.

Burke, P., 2007: Společnost a vědění. Od Gutenberga k Diderotovi. Praha: Karolinum.

Carrozza, P., 2007: Constitutionalism´s Post-Modern Opening. In: Loughlin, M., Walker, N. (eds.): The Paradox of Constitutionalism. Constitutional Power and Constitutional Form. Oxford: Oxford University Press.

Chalmers, D., 2013: Democratic Self-Government in Europe. Domestic Solutions to the EU Legitimacy Crisis. Policy Network Paper.

Cohen-Eliya, M., Porat, I., 2012: Proportionality and Constitutional Culture. Cambridge: Cambridge University Press.

Craig, P., 1999: Unreasonableness and Proportionality in UK Law. In: Ellis, E. (ed.): The Principle of Proportionality in the Laws of Europe. Oxford: Hart Publishing.

Dahrendorf, R., 1990: Reflections on the Revolution in Europe: In a letter intended to have been sent to a gentleman in Warsaw. New York: Random House.

Dashwood, A., 1996: The Limits of European Community Powers. European Law Review.

Dawson, M., de Witte, F., 2013: Constitutional Balance in the EU after the Euro-crisis. Modern Law Review 76 (5).

De Wet, E., 2006: The Emergence of International and Regional Value System. Leiden Journal of International Law (19).

Dehousse, R., 2003: Beyond representative democracy: constitutionalism in a polycentric polity. In: Weiler, J. H. H., Wind, M. (eds.): European Constitutionalism Beyond the State. Cambridge: Cambridge University Press.

Den Otter, R., 2009: Judicial Review in an Age of Moral Pluralism. New York: Cambridge University Press.

Dinan, D., 2012: Governance and Institutions: Impact of the Escalating Crisis. Journal of Common Market Studies 50 (Supplement s2).

Dobner, P., Loughlin, M., 2010: The twilight of constitutionalism? Oxford: Oxford University Press.

Donahue, J. D., Zeckhauser, R. J., 2006: Public-Private Collaboration. In Goodin, R. E., Moran, M., Rein, M.: The Oxford Handbook of Public Policy. Oxford: Oxford University Press.

Dreier, H., 1993: Dimensionen der Grundrechte. Von der Wertordnungsjudikatur zu den objektiv-rechtlichen Grundrechtsgehalten. Hannover: Hennies und Zinkeisen.

Duina, F., Oliver, M. J., 2005: National Parliaments in the European Union: Are There Any Benefits to Integration? European Law Journal 11 (2).

Dworkin, R., 1978: Taking Rights Seriously. Cambridge (MA): Harvard University Press.

Ehrenzeller, B., 1993: Legislative Gewalt und Aussenpolitik. Basel, Frankfurt am Main: Helbing & Lichtenhahn.

Eliade, M., 2009: Mýtus o věčném návratu. Praha: Oikoymenh.

Elster, J., 1989: The Cement of Society: A study of social order. Cambridge: Cambridge University Press.

Farrall, J. M., 2007: United Nations Sanctions and the Rule of Law. Cambridge: Cambridge University Press.

Filip, J., 2009: Biojurisprudence – nový pohled na právo nebo jen nový směr právní vědy? Časopis pro právní vědu a praxi (2).

Filip, J., Svatoň, J., 2011: Státověda. Praha: Wolters Kluwer.

Fisahn, A., 2009: Europäische Union in der Legitimationskrise. Kritische Justiz 42 (2).

Fischer-Lescano, A., 2014: Troika in der Austerität. Rechtsbindungen der Unionsorgane beim Abschluss von Memoranda of Understanding. Kritische Justiz 47 (1).

Foucault, M., 2009: Zrození biopolitiky. Brno: Centrum pro demokracii a kulturu.

Fredman, S., 2008: Human Rights Transformed. Positive Rights and Positive Duties. Oxford: Oxford University Press.

Freeman, M., 1996: The Philosophical Foundations of Human Rights. Human Rights Quarterly 16 (3).

Friedman, T. L., 2007: Svět je plochý. Stručné dějiny jednadvacátého století. Praha: Academia.

Fukuyama, F., 2006: Velký rozvrat. Lidská přirozenost a rekonstrukce společenského řádu. Praha: Academia.

Fuller, L. L., 1978: The Forms and Limits of Adjudication. Harvard Law Review 92 (2).

Furet, F., 2004: Francouzská revoluce. Díl 1. Od Turgota k Napoleonovi 1770 – 1814. Praha: Argo.

Furet, F., 2007: Francouzská revoluce. Díl 2. Ukončit revoluci. Od Ludvíka XVIII. po Julese Ferryho (1815 – 1880). Praha: Argo.

Gardbaum, S., 2003-2004: The 'Horizontal Effect' of Constitutional Rights. Michigan Law Review (102).

Georgiev, J., 2009: Doslov. In: Belling, V.: Legitimita moci v postmoderní době. Proč potřebuje Evropská unie členské státy? Brno: Masarykova univerzita.

Gerloch, A., 2013: Teorie práva. Plzeň: Aleš Čeněk.

Glendon, M. A., 1991: Rights Talk. The Impoverishment of Political Discourse. New York: The Free Press.

Goldoni, M., 2012: Constitutional Pluralism and the Question of the European Common Good. European Law Journal 18 (3).

Gregárek, M., 2012: Justifikace státu: legitimita, ospravedlnění a neradikální rámec filosofického anarchismu. In: Kosek, J., Gregárek M.: Stát, právo a (ne) spravedlnost. Dvě studie z právní filozofie. Praha: Právnická fakulta Univerzity Karlovy.

Griffin, S. M., 2007: Constituent Power and Constitutional Change in American Constitutionalism. In: Loughlin, M., Walker, N. (eds.): The Paradox of Constitutionalism. Constitutional Power and Constitutional Form. Oxford: Oxford University Press.

Grimm, D., 2009: Souveränität. Herkunft und Zukunft eines Schlüsselbegriffs. Berlin University Press.

Grimm, D., 2012: Die Zukunft der Verfassung II: Auswirkungen von Europäisierung und Globalisierung. Berlin: Suhrkamp.

Grimm, D., 2012: The Achievement of Constitutionalism and its Prospects in a Changed World. In: Dobner, P., Loughlin, M. (eds.): The Twilight of Constitutionalism? Oxford: Oxford University Press.

Guastaferro, B., 2012: Beyond the Exceptionalism of Constitutional Conflicts: The Ordinary Functions of the Identity Clause. Yearbook of European Law (1).

Häde, U., 2012: Rechtliche Bewertung der Maßnahmen im Hinblick auf eine 'Fiskalunion'. Berliner Online-Beiträge zum Europarecht (77).

Halberstam, D., 2008: Constitutional Heterarchy: the Centrality of Conflict in the European Union and the United States. University of Michigan Law School. Public Law and Legal Theory Working Paper Series, Working Paper (111).

Haltern, U., 2007: Was bedeutet Souveränität? Tübingen: Mohr Siebeck.

Hamran, L., Szabová, E., 2013: European Public Prosecutor's Office – cui bono? New Journal of European Criminal Law 4 (1-2).

Hamuľák, O., 2013: Integrující se Evropa a suverenita České republiky. Olomouc: Acta Iuridica Olomoucensia.

Harel, A., 2003: Rights-Based Judicial Review: A Democratic Justification. Law and Philosophy (22).

Harlow, C., 2002: Accountability in the European Union. New York: Oxford University Press.

Hart, H. L. A., 1994: The Concept of Law. Oxford: Clarendon Press.

Havel, V. et al, 1985: The power of the powerless: citizens against the state in Central - Eastern Europe. London: Hutchinson.

Havel, V., 1999: Projevy a jiné texty z let 1992-1999. Praha: Torst.

Hilf, M., 1993: Die Richtlinie der EG – ohne Richtung, ohne Linie? Europarecht 28 (1).

Hinarejos, A., 2013: Fiscal federalism in the European Union: Evolution and future choices for EMU. Common Market Law Review 50 (6).

Hirschl, R., 2006: The New Constitutionalism and the Judicialization of Pure Politics Worldwide. Fordham Law Review.

Hix, S., 2005: The Political System of the European Union. Basingstoke: Palgrave.

Holländer, P., 2012: Filosofie práva. Plzeň: Aleš Čeněk.

Holländer, P., 2012: Základy všeobecné státovědy. Plzeň: Aleš Čeněk.

Holmes, S., 1999: Foreword. In: Sajó, A.: Limiting Government. An Introduction to Constitutionalism. Budapest: CEU Press.

Hunt, L., 1984: Politics, Culture, and Class in the French Revolution. Berkeley: University of California Press.

Huntová, L., 2007: Francouzská revoluce. Politika, kultura, třída. Brno: Centrum pro demokracii a kulturu.

Isensee, J., 2013: Die heikle Weltherrschaft der Menschenrechte. In: Breuer, M. et al. (eds.): Der Staat im Recht. Festschrift für Eckart Klein zum 70. Geburtstag. Berlin: Duncker und Humblot.

Ishay, M. R., 2007: The Human Rights Reader: Major Political Essays, Speeches, and Documents from Ancient Times to the Present. London: Routledge.

Jackson, R., 1999. Sovereignty in World Politics: a Glance at the Conceptual and Historical Landscape. Political Studies 47 (3).

Jacobsohn, G. J., 2010: Constitutional identity. Cambridge (MA): Harvard University Press.

Jellinek, G., 1906: Všeobecná státověda. Praha: Jan Laichter.

Kantorowicz, E. H., 1997: The King's two bodies. Princeton: Princeton University Press, 1997.

Kelsen, H., 1926: Základy obecné teorie státní. Brno: Barvič a Novotný.

Kelsen, H., 1933: O podstatě a hodnotě demokracie. Praha: Orbis.

Kelsen, H., 1933: Ryzí nauka právní. Brno, Praha: Orbis.

Keohane, R. O., 2002: Ironies of Sovereignty: The European Union and the United States. Journal of Common Market Studies 40 (4).

Kinsbury, B., 1998-1999: Foreword: Is the Proliferation of International Courts and Tribunals a Systemic Problem? New York University Journal of International Law and Policy (31).

Klabbers, J., Peters, A., Ulfstein, G., 2009: The Constitutionalization of International Law. Oxford: Oxford University Press.

Kmec, J., Kosař, D., Kratochvíl, J., Bobek, M., 2012: Evropská úmluva o lidských právech. Komentář. Praha: C. H. Beck.

Koh, H. H., 1996: Transnational Legal Process. Nebraska Law Review (75).

Kokott, J., 2010: The Basic Law at 60 – From 1949 to 2009: The Basic Law and Supranational Integration. German Law Journal 11 (1).

Komárek, J., 2011: Judicial Lawmaking and Precedent in Supreme Courts. LSE Legal Studies Working Paper (4).

Komárek, J., 2014: Waiting for the Existential Revolution in Europe. Jean Monnet Working Paper (04).

Král, R., 2013: Questioning the Recent Challenge of the Czech Constitutional Court to the ECJ. European Public Law (2).

Krasner, S., 1999: Sovereignty. Organized Hypocrisy. Princeton: Princeton University Press.

Krisch, N., 2010: Beyond Constitutionalism. The Pluralist Structure of Postnational Law. Oxford: Oxford University Press.

Kuhnert, K., 2006: Bosphorus – Double standards in European human rights protection? Utrecht Law Review 2 (2).

Kumm, M., Comella, F. V., 2005: The primacy clause of the constitutional treaty and the future of the constitutional conflict in the European Union. International Journal of Comparative Law (2-3).

Kysela, J., 2014: Ústava mezi právem a politikou – Úvod do ústavní teorie. Praha: Leges.

Kysela, J., Hůlka, Š., 2005: Mezinárodní smlouvy – jejich klasifikace, sjednávání, ratifikace a právní účinky. Právní rozhledy (6).

Ladrech, R., 2007: National Political Parties and European Governance: The Consequences of 'Missing in Action'. West European Politics 30 (5).

Laffan, B., 1996: The Politics of Identity and Political Order in Europe. Journal of Common Market Studies 34 (1).

Lenaerts, K., 1990: Constitutionalism and the Many Faces of Federalism. American Journal of Comparative Law.

Lévy, B.-H., 2006: Americká závrať. Brno: Host.

Lindseth, P. L., 2010: Power and Legitimacy. Reconciling Europe and the Nation-State. Oxford and New York: Oxford University Press.

Linek, L., 2010: Zrazení snu? Struktura a dynamika postojů k politickému režimu a jeho institucím a jejich důsledky. Praha: Sociologické nakladatelství.

Loewenstein, K., 1969: Verfassungslehre. Tübingen: Mohr.

Loughlin, M., 2000: Sword and Scales. An Examination of the Relationship between Law and Politics. Oxford and Portland, Oregon: Hart Publishing.

Loughlin, M., 2004: The Idea of Public Law. Oxford: Oxford University Press.

MacCormick, N., 1999: Questioning Sovereignty: Law, State, and Nation in the European Commonwealth. Oxford: Oxford University Press.

Maduro, M., 2005: The importance of being called a constitution: Constitutional authority and the authority of constitutionalism. International Journal of Comparative Law (3).

Maduro, P. M., 2003: Europe and the constitution: what if this is as good as it gets? In: Weiler, J. H. H., Wind, M. (eds.): European Constitutionalism Beyond the State. Cambridge: Cambridge University Press.

Maduro, P. M., 2013: A New governance for the European Union and the Europe: democracy and justice In: European Parliament: Challenges of multi-tier governance in the European Union. Effectiveness, efficiency and legitimacy. Compendium of Notes. Brussels.

Mahlmann, M., 2008: Elemente einer ethischen Grundrechtstheorie. Nomos Verlagsgesellschaft: Baden-Baden.

Mair, P., 2006: Popular Democracy and the European Union Polity. In: Curtin, D, Wille, A. (eds.): Meaning and Practice of Accountability in the EU Multi-Level Context. Connex Report Series (7), Mannheim.

Malíř, J., 2013: Judicialization of international relations: Do international courts matter? The Lawyer Quaterly 3 (3).

Manin, B., 1997: The Principles of Representative Government. Cambridge: Cambridge University Press.

Maršálek, P., 2008: Právo a společnost. Praha: Auditorium.

Mattson, D. J., Clark, S. G., 2011: Human dignity in concept and practice. Policy Sciences 44 (4).

Maurer, A., Wessels, W. (eds.), 2001: National Parliaments on their Ways to Europe: Losers or Latecomers? Nomos: Baden Baden.

Mayer, F. C., 2011: Rashomon in Karlsruhe: A reflection on democracy and identity in the European Union. I-CON (3-4).

McCrudden, Ch., 2008: Human Dignity and Judicial Interpretation of Human Rights. European Journal of International Law 19 (4).

McGuinness, M., 2007-2008: Three Narratives of Medellín v. Texas. Suffolk Transnational Law Review (31).

McGuinness, M., 2008: Medellín v. Texas, 128 S.Ct. 1436 (2008). Case Comment. American Journal of International Law (102).

McIlwain, Ch. H., 2007: Constitutionalism: Ancient and Modern. Indianopolis: Liberty Fund.

Michelman, F., J., Ferrara, A., 2006: Polemika o ústavě. Praha: Filosofia.

Micklitz, Hans-W., de Witte, B., 2012: The European Court of Justice and the autonomy of the member states. Cambridge (UK): Intersentia.

Möllers, Ch., 2008: Der vermisste Leviathan. Staatstheorie in der Bundesrepublik. Frankfurt am Main: Suhrkamp Verlag.

Moran, M., 2006: Inimical to constitutional values: complex migrations of constitutional rights. In: Choudhry, S. (ed.): Migration of Constitutional Ideas. Cambridge: Cambridge University Press.

Nussbaum, M. C., 2012: Personal Laws and Equality: The Case of India. In: Ginsburg, T. (ed.): Comparative Constitutional Design. Cambridge: Cambridge University Press.

Ondřejek, P., 2012: Princip proporcionality a jeho role při interpretaci základních práv a svobod. Praha: Leges.

Ondřejková, J., 2010: Smíšená forma vlády a Evropská unie. Právník (7).

Pavlíček, V., 1999: Suverenita v procesu integrace (retrospektiva a perspektiva). In: Pavlíček, V. (ed.): Suverenita a evropská integrace. Praha: Karlova Univerzita v Praze.

Petrusek, M., 2006: Společnost pozdní doby. Praha: Sociologické nakladatelství.

Polanyi, M., 1951: The Logic of Liberty. Chicago: University of Chicago Press.

Prechal, S., 2005: Directives in EC Law. Oxford: Oxford University Press.

Přibáň, J., 2009: The Self-Referential European Polity, its Legal Context and Systemic Differentiation: Theoretical Reflections on the Emergence of the EU's Political and Legal Autopoiesis. European Law Journal 15 (4).

Přibáň, J., 2010: Multiple Sovereignty: On Europe's Self-Constitutionalization and Legal Self-Reference. Ratio Juris 23 (1).

Přibáň, J., 2011: Lesk a bída právního pozitivismu. In: Přibáň, J., Holländer, P. et al.: Právo a dobro v ústavní demokracii. Praha: Sociologické nakladatelství.

Přibáň, J., 2013: Ranní červánky globálního konstitucionalismu: O „radostné" právní vědě v postnacionální společnosti. Právník (2).

Puetter, U., 2012: Europe's Deliberative Intergovernmentalism: The new role of the Council and European Council in EU Economic Governance. Journal of European Public Policy 19 (2).

Raz, J., 1986: The Morality of Freedom. Oxford: Clarendon.

Raz, J., 2010: Human Rights Without Foundations. In: Besson, S., Tasioulas, J. (eds.): The Philosophy of International Law. Oxford: Oxford University Press.

Reich, N., 2012: How proportionate is the proportionality principle? Some critical remarks on the use and methodology of the proportionality principle in the internal market case law of the ECJ. In: Micklitz, H.-W., de Witte, B.: The European Court of Justice and the autonomy of the member states. Cambridge (UK): Intersentia.

Reinhard, W., 2007: Geschichte des modernen Staates. München: C. H. Beck.

Rivers, J., 2006: Proportionality and Variable Intensity of Review. Cambridge Law Journal 65 (1).

Romano, C., 1998-1999: The Proliferation of International Judicial Bodies: the Pieces of the Puzzle. New York University Journal of International Law and Politics (31).

Rorty, R., 1998: Human Rights, Rationality, and Sentimentality. In: id.: Truth and Progress: Philosophical Papers (3). Cambridge (UK): Cambridge University Press.

Rosanvallon, P., 2008: Counter-democracy: politics in an age of distrust. Cambridge: Cambridge University Press.

Rosanvallon, P., 2011: Democratic Legitimacy: Impartiality, Reflexivity, Proximity. Princeton: Princeton University Press.

Rosenfeld, M., Sajó, A., 2006: Spreading Liberal Constitutionalism: an Inquiry into the Fate of Free Speech Rights in New Democracies. In: Choudhry, S. (ed.): Migration of Constitutional Ideas. Cambridge: Cambridge University Press.

Rosenne, S., 2007: Three Central Elements in Modern International Law. In: Rosenne, S.: Essays on International Law and Practice. Martinus Nijhoff Publishers: Leiden, Boston 2007.

Sadurski, W., 2014: Reason of State and Public Reason. Ratio Juris (1).

Sarat, A. (ed.), 2010: Sovereignty, Emergency, Legality. Cambridge: Cambridge University Press.

Sartori, G., 1976: Parties and Party Systems: A Framework for Analysis. Cambridge: Cambridge University Press.

Sartori, G., 1993: Teória demokracie. Bratislava: Archa.

Scalia, A., 2009: Mullahs of the West. Judges as Moral Arbiters. Warsaw: Rzecznik Praw Obywatelskich.

Schäfer, A., 2006: Die demokratische Grenze output-orientierter Legitimation. Integration.

Scharpf, F. W., 2010: Legitimacy in the Multi-level European Polity. In: Dobner, P., Loughlin, M.: The twilight of constitutionalism? Oxford: Oxford University Press.

Schendelen, M. P. C. M. van, 1999: The Netherlands: Parliamentary Parties Rival with Pressure Groups. In: Norton, P. (ed.): Parliaments and Pressure Groups in Western Europe. London: Frank Cass.

Schiemann, G., 2006: Grundrechte im Privetrecht der Bundesrepublik Deutschland. In: Tichý, L. (ed.): Základní lidská práva v jednotlivých právních odvětvích. Grundrechte und Einzelne Rechtsgebiete. Praha: Eva Rozkotová – IFEC.

Schmidt, S. K., 2000: Only an Agenda Setter? The European Commission's Power over the Council of Ministers. European Union Politics 1 (1).

Schmitt, C., 2008: The Leviathan in the state theory of Thomas Hobbes: meaning and failure of a political symbol. Chicago: Chicago University Press.

Schmitter, P., 2001: Parties Are Not What They Once Were. In: Diamond, L., Gunther, R. (eds.): Political parties and democracy. Baltimore (USA): Johns Hopkins University Press.

Schütze, R., 2013: From Dual to Cooperative Federalism. The Changing Structure of European Law. Oxford: Oxford University Press.

Schwartzberg, M., 2009: Democracy and Legal Change. Cambridge, New York: Cambridge University Press.

Scicluna, N., 2012: EU Constitutionalism in Flux: Is the Eurozone Crisis Precipitating Centralisation or Diffusion? European Law Journal 18 (4).

Sedláčková, M., 2012: Důvěra a demokracie: přehled sociologických teorií důvěry od Tocquevilla po transformaci v postkomunistických zemích. Praha: Sociologické nakladatelství.

Šejvl, M., 2013: Stát jako nositel sekularizace? Právník (10).

Shapiro, M, 2008: Courts in Authoritarian Regimes. In: Ginsburg, T., Moustafa, T. (eds.): Rule by Law. The Politics of Courts in Authoritarian Regimes. Cambridge, New York: Cambridge University Press.

Shapiro, M., 2002: The Success of Judicial Review and Democracy. In: Shapiro, M., Stone Sweet, A.: On Law, Politics and Judicialization. Oxford: Oxford University Press.

Shaw, M. N., 2008: International Law. Cambridge: Cambridge University Press.

Sieber, U., 2010: Rechtliche Ordnung in einer globalen Welt. Die Entwicklung zu einem fragmentierten System von nationalen, internationalen und privaten Normen. Rechtstheorie 41 (2).

Skach, C., 2005: Borrowing Constitutional Designs. Constitutional Law in Weimar Germany and the French Fifth Republic. Princeton University Press.

Skinner, Q., 2012: O státě. Praha: Oikoymenh.

Skovajsa, M., 2010: Občanská společnost a demokratický stát. In Skovajsa, M. et al.: Občanský sektor: organizovaná občanská společnost v České republice. Praha: Portál.

Snyder, F., 2003: The unfinished constitution of the European Union: principles, processes and culture. In: Weiler, J. H. H., Wind, M. (eds.): European Constitutionalism Beyond the State. Cambridge: Cambridge University Press.

Sörensen, G., 2005: Stát a mezinárodní vztahy. Praha: Portál.

Soto, H. de, 2000: The Mystery of Capital: Why Capitalism Triumphs in the West and Fails Everywhere Else. New York: Basic Books.

Starck, Ch., 2001: Human Rights and Private Law in German Constitutional Development and in the Jurisprudence of the Federal Constitutional Court. In: Friedman, D., Barek-Erez D. (eds.): Human Rights in Private Law. Oxford, Portland: Hart Publishing.

Stern, K., 1988: Staatsrecht der Bundesrepublik Deutschland. Bd. III/1. Allgemeine Lehren der Grundrechte. Munich: C. H. Beck.

Stern, K., 2000: Idee der Menschenrechte und Positivität der Grundrechte. In: Isensee, J., Kirchhof, P. (eds.): Handbuch des Staatsrechts der Bundesrepublik Deutschland. Bd. V. Allgemeine Grundrechtslehren. Heidelberg: C. F. Müller.

Sunstein, C. R., 2000: Constitutional Agreement without Constitutional Theorie. Ratio Juris 13 (1).

Sztompka, P., 1999: Trust. A Sociological Theory. Cambridge University Press: Cambridge.

Talmon, J. L., 1952: The Origins of Totalitarian Democracy. London: Secker & Warburg.

Talmon, J. L., 1998: O původu totalitní demokracie. Praha: Sociologické nakladatelství.

Tamanaha, B., 2004: On the Rule of Law: History, Politics, Theory. Cambridge: Cambridge University Press.

Tasioulas, J., 2013: Human Rights, Legitimacy, and International Law. The American Journal of Jurisprudence 28 (1).

Thaler, R., Sunstein, C., 2008: Nudge: Improving decisions about health, wealth and happiness. New Haven: Yale University Press.

Thiele, A., 2010: Das Rechtschutzsystem nach dem Vertrag von Lissabon – (K) ein Schritt nach vorn? Europarecht 45 (1).

Tichý, L., 2014: Obecná část občanského práva. Praha: C. H. Beck.

Tocqueville, A. de, 2003: Starý režim a revoluce. Praha: Academia.

Tushnet, M., 2008: Weak Courts, Strong Rights: Judicial Review and Social Welfare Rights in Comparative Constitutional Law. Oxford: Oxford University Press.

Vajdova, T., 2005. Česká občanská společnost 2004: po patnácti letech rozvoje. Zpráva z projektu CIVICUS Civil Society Index pro Českou republiku. Praha: Akademické nakladatelství CERM.

Velký sociologický slovník 1, 1996, A-O. Praha: Karolinum.

Wagnerová, E. et al., 2012: Listina základních práv a svobod. Komentář. Praha: Wolters Kluwer.

Waldron, J., 1993: A Rights-Based Critique of Constitutional Rights. Oxford Journal of Legal Studies 13 (1).

Waldron, J., 1999: Law and Disagreement. Oxford: Clarendon.

Waldron, J., 2005-2006: The Core of The Case Against Judicial Review. The Yale Law Journal (115).

Waldron, J., 2009: Judges as moral reasoners. International Journal of Constitutional Law 7 (1).

Walker, N. (ed.), 2006: Sovereignty in Transition. Oxford, Portland: Hart Publishing.

Weatherill, S., 2011: The Limits of Legislative Harmonization Ten Years after Tobacco Advertising: How the Court's Case Law has become a 'Drafting Guide'. German Law Journal 12 (3).

Weiler, J. H. H., 1990-1991: The Transformation of Europe. Yale Law Journal.

Weiler, J. H. H., 2011: The political and legal culture of European integration: An exploratory essay. International Journal of Constitutional Law 9 (3-4).

Weiler, J. H. H., 2013: Epilogue: Judging the Judges – Apology and Critique. Adams, Maurice, de Waele, Henri et al. (eds.): Judging Europe's judges: the legitimacy of the case law of the European Court of Justice. Oxford: Hart.

Weinrib, L. E., 2006: Postwar Paradigm and American Exceptionalism. In: Choudhry, Sujit (ed.): The Migration of Constitutional Ideas. Cambridge: Cambridge University Press.

Wendel, M., 2011: Lisbon Before the Courts: Comparative Perspectives. European Constitutional Law Review (1).

Weyr, F., 1937: Československé ústavní právo. Praha: Melantrich.

Wincott, D., 1998: Does the European Union Pervert Democracy? Questions of Democracy in New Constitutionalist Thought on the Future of Europe. European Law Journal 4 (4).

Wintr, J., 2013: Principy českého ústavního práva. Plzeň: Aleš Čeněk.

Wolfrum, R., 2008: Legitimacy and International Law from a Legal Perspective: Some Introductory Considerations. In: Wolfrum, R., Röben, V.: Legitimacy and International Law. Beiträge zum auslandischen öffentlichen Recht und Völkerrecht (194). Berlin, Heidelberg, New York Springer.

Zakaria, F., 2003: The future of freedom: illiberal democracy at home and abroad. New York: Norton.

Zbíral, R., 2008: Teorie a praxe vyjednávání v Radě Evropské unie. Brno: Mezinárodní politologický ústav Masarykovy univerzity.

Zbíral, R., 2011: Analýza míry vlivu EU na vnitrostátní legislativu: Srovnání situace v ČR s jinými členskými státy. Právník 150 (11).

Index